Enter Jerry Baker's World of Broad Leaf Ferns,
Frilly Dillies, Huza, Inch Plants,
Begonias, Dumb Cane, English Ivy, and Mings!

Jerry Baker, America's Master Gardener, shares his expert advice, practical shortcuts, inspiration, canny strategies, and time-tested tips with house plant lovers everywhere. He even reveals the recipe for his Grandma Putts' Homemade Plant Food! Here's everything the house planter needs to know—and every house plant wishes he did know—including:

- 10 fool-proof tips on growing seeds and young plantings
- 14 drinks plants prefer to tap water
- The perfect light to grow by
- Savvy advice on container, herb, and organic gardening
- Sure-fire cures for bugs and blotches

All of this and much more in Jerry Baker's inimitable, fun-loving, motivating spirit. With his help, your plants will become a beautiful source of pride and pleasure.

Jerry Baker's HAPPY, HEALTHY HOUSE PLANTS

JERRY BAKER, America's Master Gardener, is known to millions as the gardening spokesperson for K-Mart and for his daily show on Cable Health Network. The best-selling author of PLANTS ARE LIKE PEOPLE, TALK TO YOUR PLANTS, THE IMPATIENT GARDENER, and JERRY BAKER'S FAST, EASY VEGETABLE GARDEN (available in a Plume edition), he has educated and entertained millions with his enjoyable, down-to-earth, step-by-step approach to gardening.

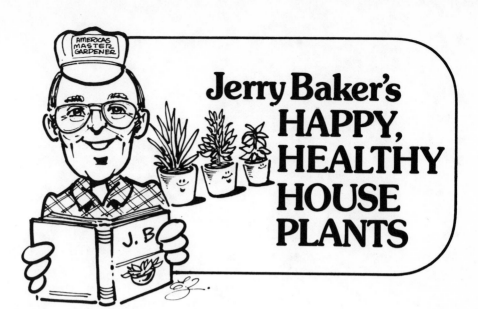

Jerry Baker's HAPPY, HEALTHY HOUSE PLANTS

Jerry Baker's HAPPY, HEALTHY HOUSE PLANTS

ILLUSTRATIONS BY ERV ZACHMANN

A PLUME BOOK

NEW AMERICAN LIBRARY

NEW YORK AND SCARBOROUGH, ONTARIO

PLUME TRADEMARK REG. U.S. PAT. OFF. AND FOREIGN COUNTRIES
REG. TRADEMARK—MARCA REGISTRADA
HECHO EN HARRISONBURG, VA., U.S.A.

SIGNET, SIGNET CLASSIC, MENTOR, PLUME, MERIDIAN and NAL BOOKS
are published in the United States by New American Library,
1633 Broadway, New York, New York 10019,
in Canada by
The New American Library of Canada Limited,
81 Mack Avenue,
Scarborough, Ontario M1L 1M8

Library of Congress Cataloging in Publication Data

Baker, Jerry.
  Jerry Baker's happy, healthy house plants.

  1. House plants.   2. Indoor gardening.   I. Title.
II. Title: Happy, healthy house plants.
SB419.B123   1985   635.9′65   85-10651
ISBN 0-452-25734-4

Designed by Barbara Huntley
First Printing, September, 1985
  2 3 4 5 6 7 8 9
PRINTED IN THE UNITED STATES OF AMERICA

To my wife Ilene,
the sunshine of my life

Acknowledgments

As much as I like to write, talk, and perform for you, the truth of the matter is that I don't do all of these things alone.

I go to a group of guys and gals who bend over backwards for me, and they deserve a great deal of credit:

Carole Compton, my manuscript typist, who makes out my terrible handwriting (all of my books are handwritten). My hand and pen may chase my brain across the page, but she always makes me look like a champ.

Fruit Basket, Flowerland of Grand Rapids, who always have tons of information at their fingertips for me to use.

K-Mart Corporation, with which I am proud to be associated as their garden spokesman.

Robert Vincent Sims, who spent the most part of a couple of days matching plants and furniture up for you. Vince Sims is an honest to gosh horticultural explorer searching out more and more varieties of plants around the world for you to enjoy.

Jim Greene, my best friend and boss, who is always encouraging me to go for it.

Grace Smith, who makes my tangled days appear routine, plus keeps Baker, Greene and Ball running like a clock. She also edits one of the largest church newspapers at

Shrine of the Little Flower in Royal Oak, Michigan, and takes loving care of my compost specialist Arnold (Smitty) Smith and never complains.

Bob Render and Hyponex, a longtime friend and sponsor.

Brad Nichols, of Wilt Pruf Corporation, a plant's best friend and mine.

Ted Lakomowski and the student body of Hardrock Horticulture Center, who test products, tools, my Grandma Putt's formulas, new ways to grow, as well as old ones, keep their grade point averages way above average, win hundreds of ribbons at fairs, score higher on state certifications than other competitive colleges, and never complain. Oh, I am sorry I neglected to tell you, Hardrock Horticultural Center is a landscape, nursery, and greenhouse management associate degree program of Jackson Community College, inside the walls of Southern Michigan State Prison at Jackson, Michigan.

Dale Foltz, the warden, who is something pretty special.

Tom MacCubbin, Urban Horticulturist and garden TV star of Orange County, Florida.

Contents

Introduction

This book, like the dozens of others I have written on home gardening indoors and out, deals head on with each phase of house plant care and culture, in a fun, fast, easy, and economical way so you can get the most out of each house plant you currently have and any new ones you may be contemplating adding at home or at work.

As many of you know, my knowledge has come from experience, not just from books. I have been gardening since I was six years old, living with my Grandma Putt. By the time I was eleven I was professionally working as a landscaper and greenhouseman; granted, the 19 panes of glass I broke in the greenhouse, with rocks as the movers were busy unpacking at our new home in Kansas City, Missouri, in 1941, gave the owner an incentive to hire me just to pay off the damage.

There are few chores that I have not been assigned in the greenhouse, nursery, or in landscaping over the years. My techniques, remedies, and recommendations have been criticized from time to time by those who have never had to use what was at hand for either effectiveness or economics.

My suggestions may make you laugh and at times question my sanity; just do it! It's the results we are both concerned with, not the method of application.

In writing this guide, I have avoided the use of any more botanical names than are necessary; in most cases I have used common names.

There have been so many changes in building techniques, heating, lighting, and air circulation that we now have literally thousands of selections of plant species; over 25,000 orchids alone. There is no excuse for not having happy, healthy plants—from the most indestructible Sansevieria to the petite African violets—with no more effort than it takes to make a bed, wash dishes, pump gas, or make a cup of instant coffee.

I try to give you as many alternatives in variety as I can, and do the same in chemical and organic forms of plant foods and insect and disease controls.

As you read through these pages, you will notice that all of the plants are not necessarily exotic. Fruit, nuts, and vegetables make super house plants, even ordinary grass grown in pots can be a super house plant.

I will touch on the Glasshouse Gang, growing plants, and handling problems in your own greenhouse. Hydroponics (growing plants without soil) can make your green thumb throb, so let's find out which plants can swim and which can't.

There will be something of interest to every one of you, from starting seeds indoors for your spring vegetable and flower gardens, to the collection and propagating of exotic varieties of special plants.

I attempt to help you laugh as you learn how to improve your personal *green scene* in the fun, fast, and easy way my Grandma Putt and other wise old green thumbs taught me.

As you begin to read through this book, don't be afraid to skip around wherever your interest carries you. That's what you should follow—your interest. This book is between you, me, and our plants.

JERRY BAKER

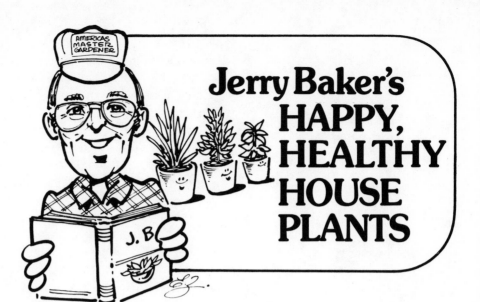

1

What Am I Looking For?

SELECTION

A plant is more than just a pretty flower or handsome foliage —it's a friend!

The sizes and varieties of plants to choose from today are almost limitless. Containers, hangers, and plant accessories run the full range of colors, shapes, and materials. The shapes and colors of foliage and flowers are nearly endless. It is no wonder that apartment and home dwellers are spending nearly 7 billion dollars a year worldwide on plants, pots, lights, food, insecticides, and plant parenthood gadgets.

A reasonable, well-selected number of plants in your home will improve and maintain your health, both mental and physical, enhance a decor, physically brighten the atmosphere and biologically filter the environment, and supply the needed oxygen for your existence.

You folks who think a plant is just a plant, green leaves and bright flowers, may be wondering: What's with this psychological, physiological, and esthetics hocus-pocus? Well, just think for a minute about the last plant you bought. Were you simply drawn to its physical attractiveness? Did you give any consideration to its care and needs? Did you totally ignore the possibility that the plant wouldn't match the style of furniture or color scheme of the room? Did the poor plant end up sticking out like a sore thumb, destined to become a true wallflower? Instead of admitting you made a mistake in your selection, and finding a good and compatible home and friend for your misfortune, did you blame it on the "stupid plant," which you claim just wouldn't grow for you (which might just be true if the poor plant could have its own way!). If so, you're not alone. I have also found that most professional and semiprofessional interior designers are guilty of selecting and placing plant varieties in rooms with nothing in mind but the temporary esthetic result its presence creates until they have collected their fee. When the plant expires, they blame its death on the client's neglect or the grower's quality, never once admitting even to themselves that it might have been a poor selection for the comfort-zone conditions that were available.

Most retail florists can be faulted on their recommendations of house plants to their customers. They have two things in mind: the sale and the profit, not once feeling the pangs of guilt for sending a poor plant to its death.

From a 7-year study that I conducted with the help of Barbara M. Arnold, a psychologist from the New School for Social Research, I have come up with suggestions that will allow me to recommend plants that will allow both you and the plant the opportunity of enjoying each other's company.

LET'S GET PERSONAL
Sex

Whether you are male or female makes a great deal of difference in type of plant selection: foliage, flowering, or special foliage.

Men, as a rule, are partial to flowering and colorful foliage plants because of the challenge in growing and maintenance technique. Orchids, violets, miniature roses, Gloxinias, Bromeliads, mums and geraniums are the flowering plants men are most frequently attracted to, while Croton, rex begonias, and Coleus round out the foliage interests. Seldom will a male plant person select a particular flowering plant for its esthetics.

TO LOVE AND TO CHERISH

Women, on the other hand, fall in love with darn near any plant that bears a flower or berry for just the opposite reason, because it is esthetically appealing. Yet, when it comes right down to purchasing, women will shy away from this group after having experienced a difficult time with a violet or two in past tries, and select the corn plant, ferns, ivies, and vines, and almost any of the other foliage plants available because of their reputation for simple care and longevity.

Marital Status

Marital status has a great deal to do with how you view selecting plants.

Married Males who display an interest in plants are generally interested in propagation, competition, and production propagation (cutting and breeding) competition (growing bigger, better and more flowers). They're interested in producing vegetables from seed to save money and demonstrate the offensive platitude that is expected of the provider. Bromeliads and orchids will fill the bill nicely.

Married Females, as a rule, are more conservative in their selection of plants, and tend to look for pleasing and practical plant materials that will look out for themselves and require very little extra care or money. They also do not engage much beyond sticking a broken stem or leaf in a glass of water to root, or drop orange, grapefruit, or lemon seeds in a pot that already has another plant in it, because they are sure it won't grow. Very few married women take a serious interest in plant propagation or seeding production because of the lack of surplus leisure time. Their best bets are Hoya, artillery plant, asparagus fern, inch plants (wandering Jews), wax begonias, pothos, spider plants, prayer plants, and Sansevieria.

Single Males do not begin to take a serious interest in their personal environment until they have accepted the responsibility of self-maintenance, and therefore we are consulted by single males around the age of 24 to 25 years and up when they have an apartment or share one. They are generally interested in large, hardy foliage plants, such

as Dracaena, Pandanus, schefflera, Veitchii, and the invincible Philodendron Selloum and Sansevieria. Even plastic is not out of the question for this group.

Single Females, when they are younger and do not yet have the responsibility of a family, are excellent and ardent personal environmentalists. They experiment with almost any type of plant material, and are not afraid to fail. They learn from these mistakes and can begin to practice the formula for future success in their own life. Plants can assist in this training through the necessary steps that ensure bright happy plants, people, and pets, and that is *pride, patience*, and *persistence*. Unless there are other factors such as life styles and living conditions, I will not restrict my recommendations to any specific list of plants.

Divorced Males in their first 18 months to 2 years are generally a hopeless case when it comes to plant interest and care. I highly recommend floral paintings and artificial plants rather than torture the poor live plants. The exception is that many show an interest in the cactus family and I concur.

Divorced Females, on the other hand, seem to regrasp the personal environmental interest that is exhibited in younger single females. Even if the divorce has been an unhappy experience, the plant interest seems to be a therapeutic relief. Strawberry begonias, wax begonias, prayer plants, violets, and other blooming plants that need special care are recommended, along with any and all foliage plants that will be comfortable in the existing comfort zone of your dwelling.

The Widowed Male generally gains the responsibility of tending his deceased wife's prized and loved plants and is at a loss as to where to begin. In most cases, he can't bear to give them away as a result of a guilty feeling, but in most cases he would be extending the loved feeling by passing on healthy and attractive blooming plants to children, relatives, and close friends and only retaining those foliage plants that do not require more special attention than he is capable of administering. It may seem cruel to most of you that I make this recommendation, but I have witnessed too often the deepened depressed state that a widower can fall into by being surrounded by slowly dying plants that his wife took such great pride in, a feeling of total helplessness. On the other hand, he recognizes the smiling face of a favorite plant of his wife's at a child's, grandchild's, or friend's home and he feels great satisfaction and fond memories of past sweet times.

Widowed Females tend to give more attention to the plants in their environment and expand their interest range. They will show more interest in propagation and cuttings and, if their husbands had a plant hobby, they will generally dive in right where he left off and carry on—often times with better results—even though she used to complain about all the time and money he spent on plants, pots, and gadgets.

Age

Age has a great deal to do with your involvement and interest in the plant world and is taken into consideration when recommending plant varieties.

18–25-year-old females can add any plant they can afford, if the living conditions are compatible to the plant's needs. Males are best advised to admire the female's plant collection and green thumb ability.

Those between the ages of *25 and 35* display a turn-around, with the lack of time available as the result of children; the female now fits the profile of the married female, while the formerly uninterested male finds a challenging and rewarding hobby that he can afford and enjoy. Most small greenhouses and homemade kits are being purchased by males of this age bracket.

35–50 find an environmental harmony developing between the male and female in which the male tends to consider the female's taste when propagating plant materials, though he will now begin to lean toward a specialization for his own pride of accomplishment. Cross-pollinating and special breeding techniques are this age group's challenge. The female is now broadening her selections to include plants that require a little more time and attention, such as the flowering house plants, and attractive multifoliage group, and will demand her share of space in the greenhouse as well.

YOU MUST HAVE I.D. TO BUY THIS PLANT

Over 50 These are the topnotchers. Both females and males have by this time learned the secret of green thumb success: *pride, patience,* and *persistence.* They can tackle any plant variety they so choose, since they will not take a foolish chance with a plant's life by acquiring one that they know they don't have the growing conditions to nurture.

Dependents

HELP!

For those of you who have not already recognized the significance between the number of dependents, type, and ages, here is your enlightenment:

Children, especially very young and dependent (birth to school age), are, as a rule, the reason why most women restrict their plant selections to those that are safe, hardy, and mostly self-sufficient, e.g., pothos, Philodendron, piggyback plant, Peperomia, Dracaena, schefflera, Sansevieria, Hoya, wandering Jew, and asparagus fern. Once the children remain in school for most of the day, women's interest and time for expanding their selections will improve.

Parents will be both a help and a concern. On occasions they will offer the same degree and quality of green thumb advice as they do with child rearing; it won't hurt to listen to both from time to time. You will also be pleased to see how the quantity, quality, and assortment improves when a senior citizen is permitted to share in the green thumb experience.

Pets are dependents and must be considered when selecting plants. Cats are attracted to hanging vines and soft moving foliage such as Aralia, Norfolk Island pines, and palms. It is important that you do not place plants in a pet's favorite lounging spots. A large pot planted with ordinary rye grass seed and placed near their feeding area will generally do the trick.

Occupation

Remember, these recommendations are for your place of work only.

I NEED A VACATION

Professional People who do not use plants to enhance an office decor or create an image are making a great mistake. Those who haphazardly use plant materials without some thought given to their image are also making a mistake. Surgeons, attorneys, presidents, chairmen of the board, and other executive officers should display tall, strong, no-nonsense plant materials with very little drooping foliage; never small leaves or frail foliage, no dish gardens or terrariums. Hanging plants are a no-no. A single potted flowering plant or fresh floral arrangement is suggested for the desk of the receptionist or secretary only. Keep in mind now, I am talking about their place of business, not their homes.

Physicians, dentists, and other professional people who come in close contact with the general public, middle management, and labor, and who need a more relaxed atmosphere and the confidence of their clientele should decorate with medium-sized foliage plants. Softer-look hanging baskets are recommended here, but not too many small flowering plants, nor ferns: one exception, asparagus plumosa (fern) in a hanging basket, as well as Hoya, inch plant, pothos, and variegated strawberry begonias can be hung. Angel wing begonia and rex begonias will also do. Again, fresh, bright flowering plants should be used only in a reception area.

Career Persons will use the same formula as professional recommendations, depending on their management position and the degree of command they wish to control.

There is a *sad* situation that exists even today in the business world. Men who have more than one or two plants in their offices are thought to be somewhat strange, almost like playing with dolls; however, at home a large plant collection is considered to be a true masculine accomplishment. Several large and famous companies go so far as to restrict the number of plants that a male employee can have in his office, while allowing the female employees as much greenery as they please. What nonsense!

Here are my suggestions for *male-occupied offices:* tiger aloe, rex begonias, Dracaena, fiddle-leaf fig, Japanese fatsia, Monstera, Yucca palm, schefflera, and any of the do-it-yourself plants (avocado, lemon, lime or orange).

Even though the *female employees* are unrestricted, they are judged on the appearance of their working area. Spindly, pale, and sickly foliage can be held against them, so they should pick hardy, full-bodied foliage plants that can look out for themselves to some extent. The above list has a lot going for it, and then add Chinese evergreen, Norfolk Island pine, cast iron, inch plant, pothos, Hawaiian ti, sago palm, Canary Island ivy, indoor oak, Peperomia, Burgundy Philodendron, and Sansevieria.

Income

As you no doubt have already discovered, house plants are no longer cheap. With the increased interest in plants, the prices increased also. Your income will have a great deal to do with the sizes and varieties you are able to afford. My first and most sincere suggestion is to join a local garden club or start one of your own; this will give you an opportunity to learn and trade among other members, and will help keep your costs down and your collection and varieties up.

If you are on a **low or fixed income**, my suggestion is that you mix economy, practicability, and imagination to improve and increase your plant assortment:

1. Grow vegetables as house plants, e.g., peppers, tomatoes, and cucumbers for a start.
2. Avocado pits, orange, lemon, and lime seeds.
3. Evergreen cuttings from any of the junipers make super plants, and you look like a super green thumb.
4. Stick with the big ten in house plants:

African violets	Philodendron ivy	Sansevieria
grape ivy	piggyback plant	wandering Jew
Maranta fern	pothos	wax begonias

Don't let your income confuse your ability to develop a successful green thumb. In 9 out of 10 cases, on a one-to-one basis, a fixed- or low-income green thumber will outperform their more affluent counterpart, primarily because they appreciate the plant and the investment. Any and all of the above plants can become part of your plant family,

SEE? MONEY DOES GROW ON TREES

and even though they are suggested for those with limited means, they are by no means stigmatized as pauper plants.

With more spare cash to invest, the **medium-income** person can afford almost any of the nearly 5,000 colors, shapes, and varieties of plants available from the mass growers. When you have spare cash, try the following.

Cacti
Aloe, bunny ears, duck wings, golden lace, jade plant, Mexican giant, panda plant and spider.

Succulents
Aloe vera, burro's tail, necklace vine, rosary vine, and wax flower (Hoya).

Color Foliage
Arrowroot, Burgundy Philodendron, Caladium, Coleus, copper leaf, Croton, Hawaiian ti, Merry Christmas begonia, peacock plant, Peperomia, purple heart, rex begonia, seersucker plant, Soffron pepper panamiga, treeline begonia, and velvet plant.

When *money is no object*, the selection is unlimited. Wealth, however, does not ensure longevity. In the one-to-one situation, you must take into consideration all of the other factors we have discussed. Odds are you have more space and you will be prone to purchasing larger, more mature plants. Just make sure that you continue the same care program that the plants were formerly accustomed to. Make sure that the plant foliage, color, and size complement the decor. Here are a few plants that will be conversation pieces: calico-hearts, Chinese pod, dragon plant, elephant's-foot, foxtail fern, Ming Aralia, moonstones, old man cactus, olive indoor oak, orchids, panamiga, pretty pebbles, rattail cactus, rice paper plant, sea shells, spider brake fern, staghorn fern, and Streptocarpus.

Location

In the majority of cases, plants are selected on a hit or miss basis, and the person selecting and the person recommending are usually expecting the plants to die sooner or later—

hopefully later. What a hell of a way to start a relationship with a plant! Most pets fare only a bit better, but they have one advantage—they can run away if neglected or mistreated. Plants are stuck. The type of building has a great deal to do with the longevity or mortality rates of plants, so try to give your plants and yourself an even break by selecting a plant that has a better than even chance at survival.

There are very few plants that cannot be successfully grown in most of the **newer designed apartment complexes** with larger glass areas, better ventilation systems, and all-season climate control, i.e., 70° F steady temperature year round. The only hang ups that cause your plants some aggravation are the lack of proper humidity and heavy western exposures. If this is your situation, try succulents, e.g., Pittosporum, Lantana, Kalanchoe, Hoya, Hibiscus, cactus, Amaryllis, aloe, Sansevieria, Fatshedera. Apartments built in the 1950s and 1960s were not, as a rule, designed with anything but profits in mind, and in most cases heat, light, and humidity all leave a great deal to be desired for most plants, and will keep you hopping to ensure proper comfort for your plant friends. As a result, you won't have a great deal of luck with the plants listed above, unless you can recreate normal living conditions with plant lights, additional humidity, and a controlled heat area, which can be done with soil heating cables available at most outlets that sell plants.

If you live in a **single-owned occupied dwelling** (house), your only restriction in successful plant growing will be your own imagination, lack of persistence, or lack of patience. There are a few homes that don't have some degree of good light in one room or the other. Older and more modern homes have a great deal in common when it comes to light. Older homes have long windows, while their new counterparts have large picture windows. The older homes with tall ceilings, steam heat, and no air-conditioning give your plants a better than even chance for survival with little effort on your part. The homes with low ceilings, air-conditioning, forced air, or electric heat make it touch and go for most of the more exotic house plants (refer to the suggestions for apartment dwellers).

If you are one of the multitude of **retail and service**

stores using live plants for display and decoration, do your pocketbook and plants a favor and select plants that can take the everyday grind of the business world, e.g., severe lighting, unbalanced or changing temperatures, lack of or limited humidity, unbearable pollution from smokers, dust, and friction. The conditions that most publicly exposed plants must contend with are pinching fingers and pulling hands to see whether they are real, trash, coffee, coke, cigarette and cigar butts dumped on the soil, not to mention unattended children, pampered pets, and clumsily placed shoes and *derrières* (rumps). These conditions sure as hell limit your selections. Yucca, Dracaena, spider plant, grape ivy, and pothos are your best bet if you need something to hang around. Honduras rubber tree (if you will not over water) is good. Bromeliads, rex begonias, Philodendron Selloum, and Ming Aralia round out your possibilities for business plants, while Sansevieria is a good last bet.

Doctors, lawyers, and other professional people must keep in mind the living conditions that they have to offer the plants, the personal image and decor involved, as well as the budget of available time and money.

Restaurants, lounges, and snack bars are prime candidates for the new and popular green scene, but in most cases, what results is a hanging, potted disaster. All any designer or new owner need do is go directly to a growing greenhouse for expert and money-saving advice. Subdued lighting for mood, high temperatures, high humidity, oily smoke and steam from tobacco, tableside cooking, and heavy traffic take their toll on most any plant that is asked to live the night life of the beautiful people scene, unless they are constantly bathed and lighted in the off-hours. Plants in places of professional entertainment must be fed very small amounts of plant food every time they are watered to help them survive. You must also take into consideration the ability of the plant to hold its foliage even when it is ill so it will not drop into the customer's soup, soufflé or hairdo.

Also keep in mind plants that are not insect attracters since an aphid, red spider, or mealy bug doing the back stroke in the beef broth doesn't bring back too many customers. When consulted in this area, I do not recommend any hanging plants, but if you insist, I'd suggest kangaroo ivy, pothos, and grape ivy, only because they are tough and when the leaves fall on the table you can say they are table decorations. Dracaena Warneckii, Yucca Dracaena Margarratti, Sansevieria, and Bromeliads are a start. If you desire flowering plants, then I suggest that they be only what is in season and sprayed for insects before they are placed for the short time they are attractive. Some of the finest decorative effects with plants in food establishments are attained with potted plants placed at different levels, out of traffic areas and with mirrors as backdrops rather than with hanging baskets.

Entertainment

"BYE... HAVE FUN TONIGHT"

GET THE CARDS

Your entertainment habits and practices have a great deal to do with your personal environmental green thumb success, since time is the most important factor necessary for the proper care and condition of your own green scene.

If you are a person or family who is **constantly on the go,** I suggest that you select any of the plants on the retail and service establishment list. These are plants that can look out for themselves with little more than a "Howdy, how are you?" and an occasional drink with some food added as you move from party to party or trip to trip. A friend with a key to stop by from time to time will help.

If you are one of those who has found comfort in your own home with friends, and **entertain at home** with large or small groups, but relatively often, then I suggest that you make your selections based on your time to care, comfort conditions, decor compatibility, and plant budget. I do, however, hope that you will select plants of medium sizes and shapes, since they will be exposed to a great deal of movement and possible accidents. Cut flowers should always be part of your table decorations, and can be prolonged by adding a capful of Prolong Cut Flower Extender or 1 tablespoon of clear corn syrup per quart of room temperature water.

When I ask if a person "neithers," I am referring to a person or family who has a **mixed bag social and travel schedule** (which without too much imagination covers

I LOVE CROWDS

about 60% of the population). This means that if all grow factors are go, they can have the pick of the plant litter.

Group-Size Preference

The size of the groups that you entertain will only influence the plant size and will not have any bearing on variety, though some varieties will be ruled out simply because of their natural growth habit and size.

If you indicate **large groups**, you will follow the same suggestions as were made to the restaurant and lounge crowds. Select plants that stand up and don't drop foliage.

If you have **medium-size groups**, which are the holiday family groups, you are restricted only by the everyday space you have available and the comfort conditions you can provide.

Small groups or very little entertaining leaves you open to shoot the works on your selections, as long as you pay attention to all other normal considerations.

Room Sizes

The sizes of rooms will influence your selection and success factor the same as dwelling suggestions, so refer to those plant varieties as well as to my suggestions for the size of plant appropriate for the frequency and size of entertainment you conduct.

Large rooms and high ceilings will permit you to go for the tree-type plants if all other conditions are normal. Avocado, bamboo palm, false Aralia, Norfolk Island pine, schefflera, and weeping fig are my suggestions. Don't forget the rubber tree.

Medium- or average-size rooms present a problem of plant selection, when a room becomes overcrowded with furniture. When you are decorating the interior of your home, office, or apartment, balance the quality of furniture, plants, and wall decorations so that the room is inviting to enter and occupy. Do not let any of the three categories become overbearing.

The rule for **small rooms** and plant selections is common

YOU AND YOUR COLDWATER FLATS

sense and imagination. Always remember priority prevails—necessities first, then accessories and decorations.

If I'm not mistaken, **9-foot ceilings** are normal throughout the world, and the only problem this presents to most plants and the people who like plants is that their eyes and hopes are usually higher than their ceilings. Stay away from the tree types or you may have to raise the roof.

Low ceilings, though cozy, cause a problem or two when it comes to decorating, furnishing, and walking. Clusters of plants that all like the same comfort zone make low-ceiling rooms attractive. Here is where the ferns, wandering Jews, piggyback, Chinese evergreens, and Peperomia all come in nice. If you want large but not too tall plants, Ming Aralia or the palms are the ones.

Your Health

Let's not fool ourselves, our own health and mental attitude have a great deal to do with the success or failure of any undertaking. How we feel physically and/or mentally has a super deal to do with plant performance and results.

When you indicate that your health is **good** and mental attitude positive, I see no reason why you can't expect excellent luck in your green scene.

If you indicate that your health is merely **fair,** you have good days and bad. Your plants have a great deal more patience and understanding than you do, so on those days when you feel under the weather, don't push your green thumb chores. Relax—your plant friends will understand.

If you are **not as chipper as you would like** to be, it should be obvious to you that you may have to limit the number of plant friends that you keep for company. So, why don't you refer to the list of plants recommended for general business conditions, since they can help you out and look out for themselves with very little burden placed upon you?

Physical Structure

The question of physical structure and its relationship to successful plant care raises a questionable eyebrow or two

GREAT POSE!

until I explain. The reaction then usually changes to, "That makes a lot of sense." Can't you just picture an ant taking an elephant for a walk on the end of a leash? Or, how many times have you seen a very small statured person being dragged around by a Great Dane, Saint Bernard, or other strong, large dog and thought how ridiculous it looked, not to mention the strain on the person being pulled. Plant selection and plant care depend a great deal on your ability to maintain them both physically and psychologically. Esthetic compatability with both room decor and your physical structure, health, and dexterity play a large part in both your plants' success and yours.

If you are built with rather **large bone structure,** there will be nothing to prevent you from having a plant family containing any size, color, or shape plant you want, provided that all of the cultural practices (food, water, and cleanliness) and the comfort zone are maintained (heat, light, and humidity), but—and this is a big but—you will look, feel, and be better able to handle comfortable, stronger stemmed, and taller plant varieties with larger foliage. Yucca, Ming Aralia, split-leaf Philodendron, Dracaena

Warneckii (and most all other Dracaenas), Sellarum palms, dumb cane, rubber tree, and schefflera are a few to consider.

If you are what might be considered of **medium or average bone structure,** your only restriction will be cultural practices, comfort zone, good decorative taste, and common sense as to the height and size of plant you can handle.

Some of the greatest green thumbs come attached to **small-structured and -statured people,** and the same rule applies to this group as to their large-boned soil brothers and sisters. If you've got the time, money, proper conditions, patience, and intestinal fortitude, you can tackle any plant on the green scene, even a giant redwood, if you have the space. As a rule, you will find that the nearly 1,800 to 1,900 other plant varieties, sizes, and shapes available will satisfy your decorative taste and fit your growing year.

Height

Your height will follow the same direction in plant selections as bone and body structure. Tall folks can maintain the taller tree-type plants without the danger of falling from a ladder or chair, while you folks who are not nicknamed "Stretch" will be able to tend lower plants without a sore back—so, it all works out. Again, let me remind you that how and with what you design your own personal green scene is all up to you, your plants, and the prevailing growing conditions. Our one-to-one conversation is merely a guide to help you better enjoy your plant friends' company.

Weight

I do not know of any man or woman who is not weight conscious one way or the other, and as funny as it may seem, folks feed their plants in the same habit pattern as they themselves eat. What I am referring to in your plant selections and care ability as it pertains to your own physical stature is your ability to safely handle your plants. Again, use the same common sense and good taste factors we have discussed in the previous three areas: health, physical structure, and height.

Your Complexion

No! I'm not kidding about your complexion being a deciding factor in your selection and placement of plant materials. When we are discussing your personality, personal image, and representation where clothes, cars, and home decor are concerned, your personal appearance is a big deciding factor. Color and depth of color have a great deal to do with pleasing, compatible results, i.e., your complexion.

Your personal environment is the areas of space that you work, live, and play in and should always be designed, decorated, and climatically controlled to make you feel, look, and behave in a manner that will allow you maximum relaxation and enjoyment. Feeling good has a great deal to do with how you think and look. When you are selecting permanent-type plants to fit into your green theme, make sure that you stand near a mirror where you can see how the depth of color of the foliage affects the contrast. If you

I BELIEVE IN THE NATURAL LOOK

THE REAL YOU. . .

Your Disposition

are *light or pale complected,* do not select foliage or flowering plants that are lighter than your complexion. Your undertones pink, yellow, olive, or tan will have a great deal to do with your complexion and selections of clothes, decor, and plant materials.

If you indicate that you are of *medium complexion* in your race, your considerations need only be compatibility between theme and decor; however, you too must watch for undertone subversion. You will notice that I referred to race. The dark-skinned races have the same degree of depth as well as undertones; notice sometime and you will be very surprised at how easy it is to see the pink, yellow, tan, olive, or browns.

Dark complexion is something that a great number of light-skinned folks attempt to secure, while those with naturally dark complexions try to lighten theirs. In your personal environment simply avoid colors of plant materials or furniture coverings that are darker than your complexion. It is an accepted fact that dark-complected folks fit esthetically into the green theme much easier than their lighter brothers and sisters.

None of us are the same person day to day, month to month, or even minute to minute. Stress and experiences cause short- and long-term changes in our actions and attitudes. Therefore, as our stress sources increase, decrease, or change and we hopefully mature with age and experience, our disposition becomes stabilized—often referred to as permanent personality projection, which then guides our predictable actions. If you are to have truly enjoyable green thumb success, you must be aware of who and what you really are.

If you are really a *patient* person, you should have the greenest scene in your neighborhood, and be able not only to give your own plants the utmost 'tender loving care,'' but be a great guide and inspiration to those who lack your patience.

It may not be necessary to caution you, but I will just to be on the safe side. There are two types of patient personalities: the persistent type, who is the action person; and then the person who is procrastinatingly patient, the wait-and-see type who takes little action. We need action for results.

If you can admit that you are **impatient,** you aren't too bad off, but you can cause your green scene to be constantly in disarray and your green theme always in question. A little sign of immaturity is that you are consistently stuck with the larger, more mature plants that take little time and effort: Yucca, rubber trees, most Dracaenas, Aralias, dumb cane, Philodendron, Selloum, Sansevieria, and cacti. Impatient gardeners cost themselves a great deal of money, effort, and aggravation. Try to remember that some of the best growing plants take a great deal of time.

If you are really **complacent** ("Let John do it"), you are a great friend for the patient green thumber. You will enjoy his or her results and appreciate their efforts and by the same token be inspired to try some of the simpler, more successful growing projects yourself. Most of us have certain degrees of complacency in us, so you are one of a very large crowd. Try being a player more often and not always a spectator. You will find that you will enjoy the game more.

Attitude

You may think that disposition and attitude are really the same wolf in different clothing. On the contrary, they both play the same degree of importance in plant growing success, but are at different ends of the action ladder and play a different part in selection, breeding, and care of the plants in your green scene.

As a **positive thinker,** you will try new varieties that fit into your theme and growing conditions with the total confidence of success. Any plant welcomes your friendship.

If you really believe that you have a "black thumb," I highly suggest that you head for the plastic plant counter. If you are in doubt about your ability to keep your plant fam-

ily healthy and happy, you and your plants are in for a rough road. Begin to change your attitude by "growing slow" with hardy, easy to care for plants and build your confidence: Sansevieria, arrowhead, prayer plant, grape ivy, wandering Jew, Peperomia, Dracaena, Yucca, and pothos.

If I were a plant and you stopped, picked me up, and looked me over, I would let my leaves droop and look like hell so you wouldn't select me. Folks with **complacent attitudes** tend to buy on impulse with little or no concern shown for decor, comfort, or care for the plants we have discussed so far, and when the poor plant expires, shrug and say, "That's plant life!" Have a heart, folks! Make sure you have what it takes to keep plants healthy and happy on your green scene.

Your Ambition

Ambitious gardeners are a godsend to the plant world, if they are not **overly** so. That's to say that they bite off more than they can chew or plant more than they can pamper. If you really want to keep your green scene bright and healthy, it is absolutely necessary that you take firm and complete charge and be totally aware of the needs, wants, and habits of all your plant family members.

If you are a **persistent** cuss, just make sure that your patience and personal pride are in the same proportions and you will have no growing problems.

You can't afford to remain **meek** if you want healthy and attractive plants around you. If a plant is growing out of its space, you must take firm action and prune, pinch, or cut back severely for the plant's own good and others around it. If you continue to be meek, the insects will literally eat up your green scene in front of your eyes. So, spray, dip, douse, and cut when and where necessary.

With a **take it or leave it ambiguous attitude** or an "I'll do it tomorrow" motto, you might as well hang pictures of flowers on the wall and place plastic palms here and there, and then all you have to contend with is dust. Plants will be happier too.

Your Taste in Furniture and Decor

When we begin to develop our personal environment, we must have a theme in mind, what some refer to as atmosphere. Colors, shapes, sizes, lighting, and sound all go into its makeup and final result (which is referred to as setting the scene to complement your choice in furniture, fixtures, decorations, and various coverings so that you end up with an enjoyable, attractive, functional, healthy environment where you can relax, enjoy, be creative; not have a hodgepodge, or mixed bag of chairs, couches, curtains, and pots). Now, let's get a couple of things straight. Your financial position has nothing to do with this. I have over the years seen some of the best results created by people who didn't have the proverbial pot nor window to throw it out of. While, on the other hand, I have witnessed a million-dollar mess or two. Here is the not-so-secret secret to green scene success as it pertains to furniture and decor: "Use your eyes and common sense."

If *modern* is your choice, great! No, it doesn't make any difference what country you have selected as your theme. To begin, you will use very few plants in this clean-lined styling. Make sure that they are seldom taller or shorter than half the height of the object they are closest to. As a rule, plants that are used on this green scene are specimen plants that take the place of a piece of furniture. I have rarely seen a flowering plant properly used in the modern motif. These will do: Sansevieria, Ming and false Aralia, Dracaena, jade plant, broad-leaved ferns (not the small-leaved Boston or frilly dilly), dumb cane, fig, lemon, orange, and bamboo. Hoya, inch plant, spider plant, and wandering Jew round out the hanging plants.

If *traditional* is your choice, you tend to get away from the large spike and wide-leaved plants used in modern and come more to the smaller-leaved ferns, Bromeliads, such flowering plants as African violets, mums, and some Begonias. Screw pine, pothos, common Philodendron ivy, Pittosporum, Hastatum Philodendron, Azaleas, Gardenias, Gloxinia, and Fuchsia set off the traditional scene. Aspara-

IT'S MIX AND MATCH, NOT MISMATCH

gus fern, Fittonia, strawberry begonia, and English ivy will do for hangers.

Spanish motif lets you use a little imagination but not too many plants. Jade, most any of the succulents and cacti, Bromeliads, chenille, citrus plants and trees, ornamental peppers, Jerusalem cherry, Croton, crown of thorns, fiddle-leaf fig, Kalanchoe, and lipstick plant are ones I'd consider.

A *colonial* decor can be set off in a most pleasant way if you will use a few less plants than you would like to since we want harmony not hilarity , which is what you feel when you enter a room that is cluttered with too many plants and too much furniture. African violets, geraniums, some of the begonias, cyclamen, English ivy, grape ivy, large- and small-leaved ferns, Peperomia, piggyback plant, prayer plant, velvet plant, and asparagus fern are suggestions for colonial decor.

Color Preference

What you see is what you get when it comes to a personal preference in colors. Your likes and dislikes of particular colors are a dead giveaway to your total personality, physical condition, and mental attitude. I can look over a collection of garden or house plants, furniture coverings, and clothing collection and pretty well tell what chance the person to whom they belong will have for success in dealing with a job, marriage, sports, plant and pet care. Color psychology is not just a bunch of mumbo-jumbo, it is a sound scientific evaluation of the normal reactions that man has toward colors in his or her everyday environment. Pittsburg Plate Glass Company did extensive research on color use and reaction. Also, Faber Birren (renowned color expert and author), Dr. Max Luscher, R. Orshak, Sister Kenny, and hundreds of other psychologists all agree that color preference is both a conscious and subconscious key to our psychological and physical health conditions. Here is what you can expect of persons whose green theme and green scene are backed or accented by the following color selections. This is also a means of checking to see whether they are completely honest in their disposition, attitude, ambition, and evaluation.

GOT THE BLUES?

Gray as a favorite color indicates that you are a loner and do not care to get too involved in any one area. If you dislike gray, you are a go-getter.

Blue indicates that you can handle just about any situation that comes up without becoming too emotionally upset. If you dislike blue, you have a short fuse.

Aqua as your number one color choice tells us that you have an above-average ability for selection and design and will dress and decorate with superb taste. Rejection of aqua means that you are one who objects easily and without any specific reason.

Green as your favorite color lets the world know that you don't have too much to hide and are proud as peaches of yourself and your actions. Reject green and you let it be known that you don't think you are being given an even break from people around you.

Red for a number-one choice tells the world that you like everything about it and the people in it. You like to try new things just for the hell of it. Put red down and you let it be known that you are lacking in self-confidence and you tend to let people walk all over you.

Yellow as a first preference as a rule lets me know that you are always on the move looking for something, but aren't quite sure what. You will darn near always be the first one to offer a helping hand to anyone you know. Turn your back on yellow and you let folks know that they always have to keep proving their love, devotion, and honesty to you.

Pink is a sure sign that you are more than just a little spoiled, self-centered, selfish, and afraid to grow old. You might also tend to appear conceited on many occasions. If you are turned off by the color pink, it is a sign that you can look out for yourself, don't like to waste time, effort, or money, and, as a rule, say what you think at the time (you don't mean any harm but you do hurt feelings easily).

Lavender at the top of your color list says that you are warm, gentle, outgoing, unrealistic, a follower but seldom a leader, and that you do not like to hear things the way they really are. When lavender is a disliked color, you can bet the person can see the forest for the trees, gets the most out of life because he or she knows what is beyond their reach and why, and does not waste time or energy worrying about it but moves on to realistic goals and achievements.

Orange as your favorite color tells us that you like a good time as much as the next person, but you must have a reason for doing it, i.e., income, health, or improved position in job or life. Thumbs down to orange simply means you don't have time to waste on phoney folks, ideas, or actions.

Brown lets it be known that you can be a great friend, good provider, and excellent lover; however, if anyone deceives you, even a little bit, you never forgive and never forget. You are not vindictive without cause, but you are hard and stubborn. Say no to brown and we can count on you to show up for work or play without fail. It will take a lot to make you say uncle because you have a physical drive factor par excellence.

Black as a first choice lets people know that they don't ever want to cross you, because your temper tantrum could be physically or financially disastrous. You are tough to reason with. If black is your last choice, you can be considered as one of the crowd.

Don't let any of this information go to your head, but if you find that you are bearing down on one color too much in the design of your green scene, stop and see if something is bugging you that you weren't aware of. This is just one more little service from *flower power.*

Your Light Preference

The first book I wrote was called *Plants Are Like People,* and I am firmly convinced of that to this day. I could even write a sequel to that book called *People Are Like Plants.* No, not because they are both occasionally potted, but more because of the fact that their enjoyable comfort zones and cultural practices are so similar, and when any part of either is neglected, they both suffer nearly identical results. And lack of proper light is one of the biggest problems that both you and your plants suffer.

People can move to a location where they can secure the benefit of light. Plants are stuck and can't do much more than attempt to grow toward any light available; this movement is called *phototropism.* You and your plants need proper light if both of you are to have healthy and attractive complexions and not always appear pale and sickly. The best book I have ever read on the proper use of lighting in plant growing is written by Sandra Erikson for Duro Lite Lamps, Inc., 1710 Willow Street, Fair Lawn, NJ 07410. Two dollars should cover the cost and improve you, your plants, and your whole green scene, making it brighter and happier.

In time, the rays of sunlight cause the fading of colors in fabrics and bleaches wood and wall coverings, not to mention the uncomfortable heat of the afternoon sun; therefore, we may keep our shades drawn for a good part of the day. Second, certain decorative themes look more appealing in subdued light, *but* (another big one) not enough of the right kind of light (full spectrum red, yellow, blue, and violet) will give your plants one hell of a headache. I use Duro Lites to supplement or replace the furniture-damaging heat of the sun with super results and spectacular effects. Following are plant suggestions for your taste in lighting:

Bright light, which is plenty of sunlight or the use of larger Duro Lites: jade, cacti, succulents, purple passion, crown of thorns, African violets, Dracaena, dumb cane, gardenia, zebra plant, wandering Jew, Norfolk Island pine, Chinese evergreens, Maranatha, piggyback plants, Peperomia, all palms, citrus, and other flowering plants.

Subdued light, which means a sheer curtain placed over windows for privacy: asparagus fern, avocado, weeping fig, Boston fern, and most all other ferns. Philodendrons, rubber trees, schefflera, Hoya, Sansevieria, grape and kangaroo ivy, English ivy, Swedish ivy, and most all of the plants recommended for bright rooms as well. Blooming plants and colored foliage will need the closer positions to the light in subdued conditions.

If you are a recluse or romantic and **dimly lit locations** are your bag, take pity on your plants from time to time and let a little sunshine in. Even though I am offering you some green suggestions for your theme, these plants will need an occasional dose of the bright lights. Most of the Dracaenas, grape and kangaroo ivy, Sansevieria, fiddle-leaf fig, rubber trees, and ferns round out the basic list for you to choose from.

2

Who's Who in House Plants

BRIEF PROFILES OF THEIR LIKES AND NEEDS

Growing house plants takes a little bit more knowledge and effort than simply plunking a plant or two on a window sill. For your plants' and your pocketbook's sake, take a few minutes to learn what makes plants tick and how. Yes, you can call this a short course in biology and botany.

Anatomy of a Plant

Plants have four important parts:

Flowers These house the plant's reproductive machinery. The colors, smells, and shapes of the flowers help to attract the birds and bees to carry the pollen; indoors that will be *you* and a fine bristle brush.

Leaves These are the built-in food factories of plants as well as the cooling system. The surface of the leaf absorbs the maximum amount of light to manufacture food; this is called *photosynthesis*. The underside of the leaf is its cooling system, which contains large numbers of stomata that let out gases and water vapors—it's the same as humans perspiring.

Stems It appears to most of us that the stem is merely a support for the leaves, flowers, and birds, and it's true, but the stem is also the way food, water, and minerals are transported up from the roots to all parts of the plant itself. A small injury to any part of the stem can destroy a large portion of a plant.

Roots These snarled, wiry, hair masses hidden below the ground get very little attention from most house planters. They're taken for granted to look out for themselves and are not considered too important. If this description fits your attitude, your plants and your green thumb are doomed. Roots are the most important part of any house plant for you to be concerned with. Keep a plant's feet (roots) comfortable and the rest of the plant will respond.

The primary function of this or any other house plant book is to help you understand the needs, uses, and protection of your plant selections, and that's exactly what we are about to do.

WHO'S WHO

To add to your understanding of what it means to cohabit with a plant or two, I have made some comments about the most popular house plants available to you and done a brief

profile of their likes and needs. You will notice that the botanical name as well as the common appears because many reference texts do not list common names. Why? Well, one plant can have as many as 9 to 10 or even more common names, depending on what part of the country you come from or what country you come from.

I'm tempted to go into great detail on plants and varieties, but the whole idea of this book is to keep things fast and easy. So, without further ado, here is who's who:

African Violet *(Saintpaulia eonantha)*

The Afridan violet is by far the most popular indoor blooming house plant, with its thick, hairy, little leaves of varying shapes acting as a green collar for the blue, purple, white, and pink flowers. The African violet likes a good, rich, light soil, so I use the Hyponex Professional Mix. Keep them damp, but never wet. Feed and water with room temperature water, never cold, and don't get any on the leaves. The African violet likes warm, humid air when it is in bloom and prefers a medium light. These little beauties are worth a try.

Aluminum Plant, Watermelon Plant
(Pilea cadierei)

I prefer the common name of watermelon plant instead of aluminum because the leaves look like flattened out watermelons—oval-shaped green leaves with gray-white stripes. This plant grows fast in regular potting soil that is kept damp, well drained. Good air circulation, dry in winter, humid in summer, and medium light is best. Keep it pinched back to make it full, but don't let it get tall and fall over.

Areca or Butterfly Palm *(Chrysalidocarpus lutescens)*

This palm is a soft palm with dozens of stems per pot. Plant in half-and-half media mix. Keep evenly damp in medium light. This plant is a good house plant.

Arrowhead Nephthytis
(Syngonium Podophyllum)

This plant is like a child—as it grows up it changes, and small wings grow behind the older leaves. Good-looking plant too. If you keep it in medium light, regular soil, growing on a totem pole and damp, it'll do well.

Artillery Plant *(Pilea microphylla)*

It does not look like you would think a plant with this name should look. It looks like an overgrown stem of parsley. The reason for the artillery name is that when you touch the plant, it shoots its pollen off in all directions. Medium light, half-and-half media mix, well drained and constantly damp, and fresh moving air will keep its gun loaded. I'm not big on this plant. *HANDS OFF!*

Asparagus Fern *(Plume, Plumosa, Spencer)*

As you can see, there are several different kinds of asparagus ferns that all resemble each other and will be advertised that way. They are all nice-looking and are, as a rule, used as hanging plants, except at my house. I prefer them on a table. They drop their needles like crazy up high. The asparagus ferns use regular potting soil and wish to be damp at all times. Cool nights are right up their alley and they have a real preference for well-circulated air (no-smoking rooms are best for these guys).

Baby's Tears (Irish Moss) *(Helxine soleirolii)*

It is hard to believe that this quite simple little plant has some other common names and is often sent to people not as a gift, but as a message. It is commonly referred to in some circles as "mind-your-own-business" or the "Corsican curse." Its origin, by the way, is Corsica. Whatever you call it, keep it damp, in professional mix and well-circulated,

PALM

humid air with cool evenings, and good middle-of-the-road medium light.

Balfour Aralia *(Polyscias balfouriana)*

This is a tall plant as a rule with pretty round leaves. The greenhouse, as a rule, plants several in one pot. This plant does not like to be moved and loses its leaves, but they will return. Keep old Balfour in bright-to-medium light. Use regular potting soil kept regularly damp. Keep the air moist and well circulating.

Bella Palm *(Chamaedorea elegans 'bella')*

This gentle, thin-stemmed, leathery, dark-leaved palm is another prayer answered for folks with a low light problem. It will grow in most average room conditions and only asks that you keep its roots damp. Use the half-and-half soil blend.

Bird's-Nest Fern *(Asplenium nidus)*

There are folks who argue that this tall, wide-leaved fern is not a fern at all (it is). Bird's-nest and its almost look-alike mother fern grow in a funnel-shaped rosette. Plant this fern, like most of the other ferns, in Hyponex Professional Planter Mix. Keep it in a shady place, room temperature, but not too humid. Mist spray often, but do not let water collect inside the rosette.

Bloodleaf Achyranthus *(Iresine lindenii)*

Here is a plant to brighten a room with its green top and blood-red bottom leaves and stems. To keep it bright, put it in a bright light, and make sure that you keep its regular potting soil evenly damp. Temperature should run a little to the cool side.

Bromeliads
(Ananas cryptanthus, Guzmania, Tellandsia, Vriesea)

All of the Bromeliads agree that they prefer bright lights and rich organic-based soil, so use the half-and-half mix, so that you ensure really good drainage. These plants love warm, humid rooms and a regular shower. There are a lot of different varieties to pick from, and if you ever get hit by this plant as a hobby, you will need to double your house size.

Buddhist Pine, Japanese Yew
(Podocarpus macrophylla)

This is an evergreen, with narrow dark-green, needlelike leaves. It also has cones. This plant grows big, big, big. It needs light (medium-to-bright) and regular soil, kept damp. The air must be cool and well circulated. It's good for large, cool vestibules and entry halls.

Burro's Tail *(Sedum organianum)*

Here is another hanging plant that is sure to attract attention with its thick fleshy blue-green leaves and pink flowers trailing below. They need bright light, regular soil, well soaked, and then let run dry. Here is another plant that loves cool nights with good air circulation.

Caladium *(Coladium hortulanum)*

This group of plants is grown outdoors more than in. They like it in medium light where it is warm and humid. Keep them evenly moist and let them rest pretty dry when they lose their leaves. Use the professional planter mix. Caladium, like the begonia, are best displayed en masse as a backup or accent plant because of the big, arrow-shaped and colored leaves.

Calathea (*Ornata sanderiana*)

Here we go again with a plant that wants to show off. The oval-shaped leaves are green on top to a purple on the bottom, with pink tints in between. Another backup or accent plant. Needs warm, humid air. Use half-and-half media mix. Keep close to wet. They look better when there are several in a crowd.

Cape Primrose, False African Violet
(*Streptocorpus saxorum*)

You have a plant here that is not an everyday house plant. This plant is something you want after you have time to fuss. A big leaf with lavender blue. Bright light and regular potting soil kept damp with regular, well-circulated air make this plant content.

Century Plant, American Aloe
(*Agave americana miradorensis*)

This big fat gray-green plant, with its sharp needle spines, flowers once in its life after 20 years and then dies. Keep Fat Albert in regular potting soil, soaking it once in a while when the soil runs dry. Keep in bright light.

Chenille Plant (*Acalypha hispida*)

This is a pretty plant, but not too practical. Its long, fussy, red tails will get the kids and cats in dutch. The chenille plant likes regular potting soil, to be kept evenly damp, bright-to-medium light, and good air circulation.

Chinese Evergreen (*Aglaonema species*)

This house plant is the best green-leaf investment you can buy. Chinese evergreens are tall, large, oval pointed, dark-green leather-leaved plants that love a low-light room, dry air, and room temperature. Use the half-soil, half-planter mix. This plant should live 25 to 30 years without repotting.

Chinese Holly Grape
(Mahonia lomarifolia)

This guy has rather wide fern-type leaves and is not the most attractive thing I have seen, but you folks buy quite a few. Keep him in bright light, evenly damp, half-and-half media mix, with temperatures to the cool side.

Citrus Trees (Grapefruit, Lemon, Lime, Orange)
(Citrus mites)

When I wrote this plant's profile (that's what these brief descriptions are), I was in Orlando, Florida, appearing at the Lue Botanical Gardens, at a home lawn and garden show. There were over 7,000 people in two days asking questions. Guess what the big house plant questions were? You got it. How do I keep my young citrus trees alive indoors?

They must have bright surroundings and well-circulated air. Regular potting soil, watered well and then let dry out.

ORANGE TREE

Climbing Fig *(Ficus Pumila)*

Here you go! A vine-type plant to grow indoors on a trellis or wall if it is really a humid room . . . if not, forget the dude. He will quit the job and tell you to go bag it. He has real small leaves, less than an inch. Now here is what this plant with a chip on his shoulder wants! (No ifs, ands, or buts about it.) Medium light (not too medium, yet not too bright). The air must be in the mid-to-upper 70s and extremely well circulated. Keep the soil (half-and-half) evenly moist (not too wet and not too dry). I know what you are thinking . . . tell it to go bag it!

Coffee Plant *(Coffea arabica)*

Here is a plant that many a house plant collector shows off. If you do it right, they look super. If not, they look terrible.

The coffee tree is a close cousin to the citrus trees. They like medium light. The air must be circulating and the room in the normal humidity range. Use the half-and-half media mix. This slender, shiny-leaved, red- and green-berried plant looks super in any decor, if you keep it healthy.

Coleus *(Coleus blumei)*

This is an inexpensive house plant with many colors and combinations of colors. Coleus can be easily grown from seed or cuttings in regular potting soil, kept damp in a bright-to-easy-medium-light location and where the air is circulating.

Copperleaf Plant
(Acalypha wilkesiana macafiana)

This is the brother to the chenille plant. It has marbled red and brownish foliage, which you have to keep bright and damp with half-and-half media mix.

Coral Berry *(Ardisia erispa)*

This plant is a small shrub, with shiny, green, thick leaves with pink flowers, which end up looking like holly berries, if you play bumble bee and brush the flower about the time they flower. The coral berry likes medium light, cool, dry, well-circulated air (try using a small fan up high). Keep moist, not wet, and use regular potting soil.

Corn Plant (a Dracaena)
(Dracaena Fragrans Massangeana)

Here is a special Dracaena, in that it is a real tree-looking plant, and is easy to grow. The ends of the leaves turn brown if it gets too much light. Plant the Dracaena in a half-and-half Hyponex potting soil and planter mix. Likes fresh, warm, dry air. Water well and then let run almost dry before watering again.

Croton *(Codiaeum variegatum)*

This is one of the more colorful house plants, but a real troublemaker when it is brought indoors. Totally demanding and not worth the bother unless you have the time and patience for this Croton. Bright, bright lights to hold its colors, regular potting soil kept constantly damp. High humidity is absolutely needed with warm temperature. Let's face it, folks, this is really meant to be one of the Glasshouse Gang. I bring these out to show off just for company and then back they go.

Crown of Thorns *(Euphorbia splendens prostrata)*

Granma Putt said that a crown of thorns should only be grown near a copy of the New Testament. This plant is never bothered by the children or pets in the house. This gray-stemmed, needle-covered plant, with sparce green leaves and red flowers that look like Impatiens needs bright light. Regular potting soil is needed with good drainage. House temperatures will do well, but water real well and then let dry out. Crown of thorns will drop its leaves from time to time, but don't worry.

Date Palm *(Phoenix voebelenii)*

There are two good date palms—the standard (phoenix dactylifera) and the miniature date palm (phoenix roebelenii), and if properly taken care of with normal room temperatures, medium light, good air circulation, half-and-half soil, kept damp, not wet, and sprayed twice a year with Wilt-Pruf to conserve moisture in the foliage, they will prosper. The foliage is stiff and spiney. This palm can really take it.

Dracaena (Gold Dust, Janet Craig, Warnecki)

Here are plants that can be described as streetfighters. The Dracaena family will grow in almost any kind of light, from

DRACAENA

low to direct. But they prefer mild. Water well and let water run through. Take off excess and pour through again. Let set 15 minutes and remove surplus. Use half-and-half soil. Likes dry, well-ventilated rooms and can handle cool nights. They are space fillers and can be used as great one-onlys, in groups, or combined with other plants.

Dragon Tree (a Dracaena)

You can see from these plant profiles that the Dracaena family is one of the most popular. The dragon tree has thick, fleshy, sword-shaped leaves of a blue-green color. It likes regular potting soil, and good drainage is necessary. It will tolerate dry rooms at normal temperatures and wants to be wet but not soggy.

Dumb Cane (Giant, Spotted), Golden Dieffenbachia (Pecta)

These big white-spotted leaves are a real space filler and are easily grown. They need a bright medium light, with a half-and-half media mix, watered well, and then let run a little to the dry side. These plants, as a rule, are not very expensive.

Elephant's-Foot Tree, Ponytail, Bottle Palm
(Beaucarnea recurvata)

I like the elephant's foot description best, because the trunk really does look like that. The top looks like a lot of thin green straplike leaves. When you have this plant, you have a conversation piece, one that is easy to care for. It must have bright light, regular potting soil, with very good drainage. Water real good once and let it run through. Don't water again until it's dry. It prefers a cool evening's sleep.

Emerald Ripple Peperomia (Peperomia caperata)

All of the Peperomia are plants with character. Emerald ripple is by far the prettiest, with its wrinkled heart-shaped

IVY

leaves in heavy clusters marked by brown spots in the bottom of the wrinkles and gray-white on top. The ripple has greenish flowers on top of long, stemlike spires. Medium light is required, and regular potting soil, kept damp, does the trick. It will do well in a normal comfort zone if the air is on the move.

English Ivy *(Hedra helix)*

English ivy is an attractive tangled mess when it's happy. Its shiny green leaves in a variety of different shapes cascade down, shoot up, and pile one on top of the other. To be happy, they must have the bright lights, damp regular potting soil, cool fresh air (almost cold) with good fresh showers often.

Euonymus

This is a shrub that can be grown indoors and out, and is a great addition to a commercial planter. It can be pruned and shaped. There are many different leaf color combinations. (All green to yellow green to gray green.) It takes any light except deep shade, needs half-and-half media mix, and should be kept damp.

False Aralia, Mock Cannabis
(Dizygotheca elegantissima)

A great many of you folks know that I was an undercover narcotics police officer for a number of years. On several occasions, we had officers from the precinct arrest and bring folks in for possession of and growing cannabis/marijuana. The evidence was, in fact, a false Aralia. It looks just like it, folks, and one of the best-looking house plants you could ask for. The thin, green, bronze leaves on a thin stem grow well in medium light, warm temperature, and good air circulation. Use the professional mix for media and run a little dry.

Fan Palm *(Chamaerops numilis)*

This stiff-leaved, bushy palm is great for the front window of a bank because it looks like it means business. Bright light, but cool air is needed. Use half Hyponex Professional mix, one quarter planter mix, and one quarter sharp sand (builders' sand, not beach sand).

Fiddle-Leaf Fig *(Ficus lyrata)*

Here is another plant that can hold its own with half a chance. I think of this as a professional plant and highly recommend it for use in offices and retail outlets, especially restaurants, if you will wash its foliage at least twice a week with the warm tea and soap solution. It would prefer the no smoking section. The fiddle-leaf fig with its big, crinkly leaves and shag bark stem looks terrific with most of the robust decors. It, like its brother the rubber tree (surprised?), wants bright light, but will go down to medium reluctantly. It is happiest if you water it from mildly damp to close to dry. Use regular potting soil, with one-half professional mix. The air can be dry if well circulated. It is a good plant friend to have around.

Fishtail Palm *(Caryota mites)*

I recommend this palm to many professional men for their reception rooms. Its dull, dark, ragged fishtail foliage gives the impression of no nonsense. It likes low light in a dry room with cool temperatures. Regular potting soil should be used and kept damp but not wet or it will begin to rot.

Flame Violet *(Episcia cupreata)*

The flame violet is a great high-humidity hanging plant, with its metallic copper-colored, hairy leaves and red tube flowers. It prefers medium light, Professional Planter Mix. This is a plant that will make you the talk of the plant crowd.

Fluffy-Ruffle Fern *(Nephrolepis exaltata)*

FERN

Here you go. A real thick dwarf fern that looks good on tables. Fluffy only wants better than average humidity, medium light, regular potting soil and damp at that—fluffy must drain well. This is a great plant to use in a group as a collar for a larger blooming plant (azalea, gardenia, mum, or poinsettia).

Gardenia *(Gardenia jasminoides)*

This is the gracious lady of the windowsill, with her shiny green leaves and gorgeous white fragrant flowers. Since she is a star, she must have bright lights, half-and-half potting soil and Professional Planter Mix. Plenty of humidity is required, and mist spray often. Night temperatures cannot go below 65°. Keep out of all drafts.

Geranium *(Pelargonium hortorum)*

This and the fern were the mainstay for most of the pioneer wives to brighten up the windowsill and windowboxes in those early days. As a matter of fact, they were considered a weed, much like the dandelion. Today, the geranium is the second most popular potted plant. There are over 400 different kinds, grown for flowers, foliage, and fragrance. The geranium is easily propagated and can grow both indoors and out. This house plant demands very little, and several should be in your collection. Keep the geranium in bright light, half-and-half potting soil, and Professional Planter Mix, kept damp. Circulate the air.

German Ivy or Parlor Ivy *(Senecio mikanioides)*

This plant is a great space filler in between plants. It has bright green ivy-shaped leaves on climbing limbs and branches. German ivy prefers bright light, fresh dry air, regular potting soil, and it wants a good stiff drink (then not to be watered again until it is nearly dry). Cool temperatures do not cause it discomfort.

Giant White Inch Plant *(Tradescantia albiflora)*

My Grandma Putt called this the "gift ribbon ivy." Green pointed leaves with plenty of white stripes, real pale lavender flowers. Regular potting soil should be used for this plant, and it should be kept damp in bright light. This is an easy hanging basket to grow.

Gold Dust Ivy *(Hedra helix Goldust)*

Same category with another collar—speckled ivy. Remember it needs bright light, and cool, damp air and regular potting soil.

Gold Dust Tree *(Aucuba japonica variegata)*

A tall spindly tree-form plant that never impressed me, but you always see it in plant displays, usually with leaves fallen off. Regular potting soil, kept damp, medium light. Nothing special.

Golden Bird's-Nest Sansevieria
(Sansevieria trifasciata Hahnii)

The Bird's-Nest Sansevieria is a family of three brothers; dark green, gold, and silver. Try them all. You can hardly do them in, no matter how bad a green thumb you think you have.

These plants grow in a thick circle of thick pointed, spike-shaped leaves. They prefer bright light, but do fine in medium to shady. Use regular potting soil, drench and let run dry. They pretty much look out for themselves.

Golden Pothos, Devil's Ivy
(Scindopsus aureus)

While the florists and scientists argue over how to classify it, we will think of it as pothos. Its big, heart-shaped, variegated leaves climb up or hang down over everybody's soup in most every restaurant in the country. It's a super hardy, attractive plant that the growers can't grow enough of to keep up with the demand. To keep it on the move in whichever direction you choose, keep it in bright light, regular potting soil, and don't over water. Dry circulating air will help nicely.

Golden Trumpet *(Allamonds catharteca)*

Looks like the old over-the-fence trumpet vine. Dark green skinny leaves, wooden stems, yellow flowers. Needs plenty of humidity, well-circulated air, half-and-half media mix. Keep it damp.

Gold Vein Bloodleaf *(Iresine lindenii formosa)*

This dandy is different from his brother only in that his leaves have yellow veins running through them. Care is the same as Achyranthus, his brother.

Grape Ivy *(Cissus rhombifolia)*

Grape ivy is a first cousin to the kangaroo vine. It is used in restaurants like crazy and that's a shame because it sure wrecks a lot of soup. They often do not take care of it, and the leaves drop off into my soup or the red spider (its favorite bug) crawls all over. Grape ivy needs lots of medium light, 16 hours a day. Let soil run a little to the dry side, then water (I unhang and dunk the pot). Use regular potting soil. Keep the air circulating. It likes a cool evening.

Hagenburger's Ivy
(Hedra canariensis variegata)

Like all the other ivies, you must keep this one cool, damp, bright, and happy. It has a variegated (marble) foliage.

Hahn's Self-Branching Ivy
(Hedra helix Hahn's self-branching)

This is a cousin to English ivy, but is brighter green and thicker than English ivy, growing everywhere at once. It also has bright light, damp regular potting soil, and cool, fresh air requirements. It also likes a shower regularly.

Hastatum Philodendron *(Philodendron hastatum)*

This is a good-looking plant with arrow-shaped leaves, with cream streaks. Climbs like the dickens. It's not too finicky on the light; sun to shade will do. Regular potting soil is fine, but must be kept damp. Needs some humidity and circulating air. Give it a shower twice a week.

Hawaiian Ti *(Cordyline terminalis)*

Here, again, is a great plant to keep to accent a lamp, figurine, special vase, or other table item. Its tall, reddish, spiked foliage creates a good accent. It likes high humidity and good air circulation. Use half-and-half soil and mix. Keep damp and well-drained.

Heart-Leaf *(Philodendron oxycardium)*

This is the old standby for most of us who want a hanging vine that looks like it. With its big heart-shaped leaves, thick and cascading down from above—What more can you ask for?

You can't, but the phily can. He would like a favor in return. Plant him in regular potting soil and keep it damp and not soggy wet. Keep him away from the window in the winter because he freezes easy. Dry, well-circulated air will help.

Holly Fern *(Mahonia lomarifolia)*

Once you set up a routine for this guy, you must stick to it. He does not like surprises. His hairy, brownish, dark-green leaflets are tough and will be satisfied with the same comfort zone you like if you keep his half-and-half soil mix evenly damp.

Iron-Cross Begonia *(Begonia Masoniana)*

These plants are known for the super color, shape, and texture of their foliage. Many have designs on them. They are, as a rule, better grown and displayed in groups of three or more, with another plant as the center of attraction. They need medium light in a room temperature area with good moving air and humidity. Plant in the half-and-half media mix.

Jade Plant, Chinese Rubber Plant
(Crassula argentea)

The jade plant's worst enemy is man. This big burly bucko can live to be an old man 4′ to 5′ tall with a big old trunk if you will just keep him in medium bright light, in regular potting soil with a half dozen pieces of broken crock mixed in so that he drains well. Really water well and let the water run through. The jade plant likes cool night temperatures and normal dry house temperatures will be OK if you keep the air circulating.

Japanese Aralia *(Fatsia Japonica)*

This, my friends, is one good, fast-growing house plant, with its dark-green heart-shaped leaves. This plant is a show-off all by itself, if you give it its own way. Place it in medium light, keep it evenly moist, and use regular potting soil. Keep the air circulating and make sure that you let it sleep at night in a real cool room. If the temperature is too warm, the leaves will turn yellow and drop off.

Japanese Littleleaf Boxwood
(Beyus microphylla japonica)

This shrublike little bush is great if your place is not dry, as plenty of humidity is needed. It also likes medium light and regular soil, kept damp.

Joseph's Coat *(Alternanthera versicolor)*

Light little plant with roundish leaves looking like corregated cardboard of purple and pink. Bright light will fill the bill with regular soil, kept damp.

Jungle Geranium *(Ixora species)*

If you have a jungle geranium growing on your tabletop, you had better know all the answers about it because you are going to get all the questions about it. It is available in red, pink, yellow, rose, and orange. It has thick leathery, glossy green leaves. Bright to medium bright light will hold both the flower and foliage color. Regular potting soil, room temperatures, and humidity keep it on the grow. Keep the soil evenly damp.

Kangaroo Ivy *(Cissus antarica)*

This is a thick, bushy plant that climbs up anything it can get its tendrils on. Pretty, green leaves with red-brown veins and stems distinguish it from other ivies. It needs medium light, regular potting soil, good drainage, dry air, and cool nights. This plant is super for you kids with small apartments, because you get lots of plant for your buck. Buy or make a trellis for it to grow on and you've got a whale of a room divider.

Lipstick Plant *(Aeschynanthus lobbianus)*

This plant, like the chenille plant, tempts pets, people, and kids to play with its long red flowers, that have yellow throats on waxy green leaves. It is, I think, a little more sturdy-looking and is a little more practical than the chenille. Bright to medium light will please this lady. Use Professional Planter Mix and keep damp. Fifty percent humidity is a necessary condition, as is good air circulation.

Maidenhair Fern *(Adiantum)*

This fern is not a forgiving plant friend if your place is dry or overly warm. Maidenhair fern is a dark-stemmed, dark-green wedge-shaped leaf that want to be kept constantly damp, cool, and shady. Use half-and-half media mix. She will change after she's been married a year or so and has a couple of kids!

Marble Queen Pothos *(Scindapus aureus)*

This is another one of the hardest working indoor plants you can find. They fight to stay alive no matter how hard the elements around them are against them. Their green leaves have marbled marks on them which makes them a standout, good climbing vine. They like medium light and the soil should be half-and-half, drenched, and then let it dry out.

Medicine Plant, True Aloe *(Aloe vera)*

Every home should have a couple of these around for cooking burns and sunburns. Aloe juice is used in cosmetics, soaps, shampoos, and drinks for hangovers and health. In the north it is great for chapped hands and cheeks. Gray-green spiked leaves identify this plant. It prefers bright light, half-and-half media mix, kept a little to the dry side. Water well, then let dry out.

Ming Aralia, Parsley Tree

I like this one for a man's office because it looks like it can take care of itself. The parsley-type foliage is at the ends of the branches. It loses leaves when you first bring it home, but it will be OK. It needs bright light, regular soil, plenty of humidity, and good air circulation.

Moon Valley, Friendship Plant *(Pilea involucrata)*

Copper-red quilted foliage makes this an attractive plant, though the flowers don't show much. Easy to care for. They need medium light, regular potting soil, and to be kept damp and have air circulation.

Moses-in-the-Bullrushes, in-the-Cradle, on-a-Raft *(Rhoeo spathacea)*

Take your pick on the name you prefer, but we do know it's "Moses." This plant is another that Grandma Putt kept growing near the Old Testament. The big protective, sharp green spiked leaves with purple undersides cradle the dainty white flowers in the cradle. A good choice for any room. Plant this in regular potting soil, keep damp not wet, circulate the air, dry will do, and make sure the light is medium.

Narrow-Leaved Pleomele Song of India

Here is a thick-leaved (spiked) plant that is great for when you are sort of, but not obviously, developing a space. It looks like a Dracaena, but it is not. It likes room temperatures and dry air. Keep the foliage dry, but the roots wet. Use regular Hyponex potting soil with just a little Professional Mix added.

Natal Plum *(Carissa grandiflora)*

Here we go, an instant bonsai tree. Just remove a few of the branches. The Natal plum, when in bloom, smells terrific and the white flowers become red plum-looking fruit, but I don't eat them. This plum likes the bright light and cool air. Plenty of showers also keep the regular potting soil damp.

Needlepoint Ivy *(Hedra helix)*

Same clan as all the hedra helix, the ivies. This one is lighter green than most, with more space between leaves. Like all the rest, it needs bright light, cool air, damp soil, and regular potting soil.

Norfolk Island Pine *(Araucaria excelsa)*

NORFOLK PINE

Here is a plant that when properly tended is the envy of most house plant owners. If not, it looks terrible! The Norfolk Island pine, also known as the Miami pine, with its spruce tree look is a great indoor Christmas tree. It needs mild to bright light. Use Hyponex Professional Mix soil. Provide good drainage. It likes cold nights and dry air. You must constantly turn this plant.

The brother to this plant is a mean-looking guy named Bill (araucaria bidivilii) known as the monkey puzzle tree. This is the same plant with sharp, dark leaves. (No one messes with Bill!)

Peace Lily *(Spathiphyllum clevelandii)*

Here is a pleasant surprise for a low-light location. This spathiphyllum, like most of the others in the same family, has dark green, leatherlike foliage, with a lilylike flower that is really a sheath around the stem. Along with shade, keep wet, in low humidity, and plant in half Hyponex Regular Potting Soil and half Hyponex Professional Planter Mix.

Piggyback Plant *(Tolmiea menziesii)*

The piggyback plant always looks great to you folks in pictures and at the plant department, and you just can't resist, so home it comes and up it goes into a hanging basket in front of a bright sunny window in a warm, dry room. The next thing you know, the leaves have a white to tan scar on them and it dries up. What happened? The piggyback plant was born in Alaska. Does that tell you anything?

These green, hairy-leaved plants that carry their young on their back like a papoose, want medium light, cool, well-circulated air (68°). Regular potting soil, well drained. "I can't stand warm humid air," is what they'd like to tell you.

Pineapple *(Ananas comosus)*

Waste not, want not. And I don't when it comes to pineapple tops. I simply place the twisted off top into a clay pot filled with Hyponex Professional Planter Mix. If you intend to plant the top, you cannot cut it—you must twist it off. Set in a very bright location and keep warm and evenly moist. You must also have good, well-circulated humid air. Yes, you can end up with a fruit, but it won't be too tasty. First, however, you will have an attractive cluster of violet flowers.

Polynesia, Satin Pellionia *(Pellionia pulchra)*

This plant has gray-green leaves with brown veins and is used when you want a full hanging basket. Most light will do with half-and-half media, which must be kept damp.

Polypody Fern *(Aureum glaucom polypodium)*

This is a big fern. At least the leaves are bigger than most fern-type leaves. The foliage looks more like tropical foliage and has a base (fur covered rootstalk). This one needs bright to medium light and half-and-half media mix. It should be kept damp and have fresh circulating air.

Prayer Plant, Rabbit Tracks
(Maranta leuconeura kerchoveana)

With a monicker like that, you would expect a plant the size of an oak tree, but the prayer plant (sometimes called rabbit tracks) is a gentle little lady with light- and dark-green leaves trimmed in red with 5 spots. At night she bows her head and closes her leaves as if praying.

My Grandma Putt, who I lived with as a youngster and who I write about as my garden teacher, always kept Maranta, the prayer plant, growing near a copy of the New Testament, where it grew beautifully, but when it was moved, it *withered* and *went*. The crown of thorns was also grown by an open Old Testament.

Maranta prays that you will: keep her in a medium light; keep her evenly damp in regular potting soil in humid, well-circulated air with the temperature over 75°. Bless you.

Purple Heart *(Setcreasea purpurea)*

Here is a plant that looks like it is totally confused. Its big leaves are purple with lavender flowers. It needs bright light, regular potting soil, soaked, and then dried out. Good air circulation is also necessary for purple hearts.

Purple Waffle Plant *(Hemigraphis "Exotica")*

REX BEGONIA

This is a great trailing plant to use if color is desired, but you don't want the hassle of flowers. It's thick, waffle leaves need a good supply of the red light range, so keep it in a well-lit area. This plant needs a light soil mix (Hyponex Professional Planter Mix). Mist from time to time with a tea and soap spray, but no ammonia. The purple waffle is a heavy drinker, so be alert.

Rex Begonia *(Begonia rex)*

This begonia is taken care of in the same manner as the iron cross. Since I am on the begonias, the flowering wax begonias make pretty good house plants if you keep the half-and-half soil damp (not wet), have medium light, and plenty of humidity. If you give them a little more light than medium, but not bright, they will stay low and fat.

Ribbon Plant (a Dracaena) *(Chlorophytum comosum)*

The ribbon plant is a twin sister to the spider plant (Chlorophytum comosum).

Rosary Vine, String-of-Hearts, Chinese-Lantern, The Worry Bead Plant *(Ceropegia woodii)*

Here is a plant that knows what to expect when it comes to live with you. It brings a lunch bag. The small beads are filled with stored food. The rosary vine, with its heart-shaped leaves and red lanterned flowers, is a hearty soul. If you water it once and let it dry pretty much, plant it in the Professional Mix, and set it in a medium spot, she will smile with long chains and pretty flowers.

Rose of Jericho, Resurrection Plant *(Seleginella lepidophylla)*

Here is a plant that travels by mail by the thousands. It is a mail-order bonanza. Rose of Jericho is a dry-looking plant that grows best in Professional Planter Mix. Keep evenly damp. You must keep a good, humid condition if this plant is to survive.

Rubber Plant *(Ficus elastica)*

RUBBER PLANT

This is one tough cookie, if you give it half a chance. It is usually sold as a single-stemmed plant, at a ridiculously low price, to bring people into a store (buy it!). The rubber plant can raise the roof if you keep it in a bright to medium light area. Dry, well-circulated air will put it on your side. It must have a regular potting soil with one-third of the Hyponex Professional Mix added. Watering seems to be the most ticklish area. Water it well, let it run all the way through. Now pour the excess back through the soil, let set for 10 minutes, and take the excess away. Do not water again until the soil is better than two-thirds dry. If you overwater, the bottom leaves will turn yellow and drop. This plant can be cut back to encourage branching.

Schefflera, Umbrella Tree or Shopping Center Palm
(Schefflera actinaphylla)

You want a tree for the living room? You got it with this guy! If he likes your home and you treat him right, he'll raise the roof. No matter how well you treat him, as he gets older, he loses his lower leaves. You must keep him in bright light. The soil should be regular potting soil, really soaked and then let run to the dry side. You must keep the air on the move, and give him a good soap-and-water shower twice a month.

Screw Pine *(Pandanus Veitchii)*

The screw pine looks like the top of a pineapple that didn't make it. Tall, saw-toothed spiked leaves have brought out the worst in many a lady who snagged a pair of hose just walking by. Here is a great plant for traffic control and room dividers (no one will cross this line). Grows well in most homes with little care. It needs regular potting soil, deep damp, and medium light.

Sensitive Plant *(Mimosa pudica)*

SCHEFFLERA

You can easily hurt this plant's feelings if you reach out and try to touch it (it is heat sensitive). This shy little character is the smallest of the mimosa family, and the biggest is a full blown tree (it grew in Brooklyn). Though very few of you will ever see the flowers in your homes, this plant has a puffy lavender pink flower. The foliage is in the form of a finely divided fern leaf that droops in fear when touched. Too much plant petting ends up killing this poor thing. HANDS OFF!

Give this pretty little thing its medium light spot, with good circulation, humid air in an average 72°–75° room. Use the Professional Mix and keep it evenly damp.

Shrimp Plant *(Beloperone guttata)*

I like this lady, even though some people refer to her as scrawny. Don't you believe it! Dark-green leaves with pretty red-pink shrimptail-like things at the end of the stems. Bright lights, regular potting soil, water well, and then let run dry. Good air circulation is a must.

Silver Lace or Table Fern

Here is a good selection for the bedroom or den, where it is usually cool and dimly lit. The fronds on this fern are deep cut, almost wing-like, with a silver stripe on them. They want heavy organic soil (half Professional Mix and half potting soil). Keep damp, well drained, cool, and in medium to low light.

Silver Tree Panamiga *(Pilea)*

Like its cousins, it has deep burgandy-colored leaves with a silver stripe and, with one exception, prefers the same care as moon valley—it needs more light.

Snake Plant, Mother-in-Law's Tongue, Barber Shop Begonia (All Sansevieria) *(Sansevieria trifasciata)*

An old standby and one of the first and most popular house plants brought to the Americas from Europe. This plant is nearly indestructible. Use regular planting soil, water well each time you water, and then let it go to dry before watering again.

Spider Plant *(Chlorophytum capense, comosum)*

This is one of my favorites because I get my money's worth. She throws off long stems, off which leafy plantlets appear with roots attached, ready to grow. I do and so should you. It grows in medium light and gets upset if the light is too

SPIDER PLANT

bright (tips of leaves turn brown). Cool nights and warm days suit it best. Good air movement is necessary and regular potting soil should be used.

Split-Leaf Philodendron, Swiss Cheese Plant or Hurricane Plant *(Monstera deliciosa* or *pertusum)*

This is another one of those plants that looks as if it might be saying "You want to fight, buster!" Good-looking plants that deserve waiting rooms and shopping centers. They grow to 3 or 4 feet with big split leaves with holes in them to let rain through. They grow well in regular potting soil kept evenly damp. Good air circulation of most any temperature except freezing.

Staghorn Fern *(Platycerium bifurcatum)*

A trophy for the wall of any plant grower, with its big thick wide antler-shaped foliage, growing out of a professional planter mix, covered with sphagnum moss, and supported with a nylon or plastic screen. Mount this on a piece of bark and keep evenly damp, in medium light, and in a breezy location. Too much light will yellow the leaves and turn the tips brown.

Strawberry Begonia *(Saxifraga sarmentosa)*

This dainty little lady, with her dozens of children out on little lines, has round leaves with silver-gray tops and purple-spot bottoms. The strawberry begonia needs regular soil, well soaked and then dried out, cool night temperatures, and well-circulated humid air in the daytime.

Striped Inch Plant *(Callisa elegans)*

This plant also is called wandering Jew. This plant will make almost anyone a green thumb. Used in hanging baskets and table planters, it only asks that you keep it damp and use a regular potting soil. It will do well in medium to bright light, but not direct.

Swedish Ivy *(Plectranthus australis)*

Swedish ivy is a thick, fat, green-leaved fooler. When you have forgotten to water it and it goes bone dry, you panic because it is just hanging there on death's bed. You run for the water can and douse it good, just knowing its a goner. And what to your wondering eyes should appear a few minutes later? A fat and sassy, bright-eyed, bushy-tailed Swedish ivy that looks and acts like nothing happened. It's tough, and asks very little. Regular potting soil, keep damp (but don't panic if you forget), well drained, medium light, dry morning air.

Sweetheart Ivy *(Hedra helix)*

This hedra helix differs only in the leaf shape, which is like a heart instead of a star. To take care of it, treat it like the rest. It needs bright light, cool air, and regular potting soil kept damp.

Tahitian Bridal Veil *(Gibasis geniculata)*

Dense little leaves in a great mass and then covered with tiny white flowers make this a most attractive plant to hang around the house in a bright light with good air circulation. Use the Hyponex Professional Planter Mix, water it well, and then let it run dry. You will like the Tahitian bridal veil plant. I do.

Tree Ivy, Aralia Ivy, or Fat Lizzie *(Fatshedera Lizei)*

Fat Lizzie was a poor choice for a nickname, since one of these in a pot looks like a skinny scarecrow waiting for the birds. As a rule, four of these plants are planted in a large pot with regular potting soil. A trellis or other support is needed, as they grow 3' to 5' tall. Crowded in a pot in a bright location, kept evenly damp, in half-and-half media mix, with plenty of fresh air, mostly to the 65° to 68° side, they look terrific.

Umbrella Plant *(Cyperus alternifolius)*

This plant's name tends to confuse a lot of you because the schefflera is sometimes called the umbrella plant or tree. This plant has 2- to 3-foot-tall stems with foliage that resembles wide-blade grass and appears like an open umbrella. The umbrella plant likes dry, medium, room conditions. It likes the half-and-half soil blend, and likes to sit in water (a must).

Variegated Balfour Aralia
(Polyscias balfouriana marginata)

This one is the brother to the regular Balfour with one exception—its leaves have light spots or flashes on them. Care is the same.

Variegated Mock Orange
(Pittosporum tobira variegatum)

This is a nice thick gray-green-foliage plant with nice-smelling flowers. Foliage is low and flat. Provide medium light and regular potting soil, kept damp. Keep the air moving around this growing lady.

Variegated Peperomia *(Peperomia obtusifolia variegata)*

Most folks overwater and overfeed the "peps"; four to five dozen different varieties to pick from. If you are to get the most out of these plants, you should keep them in bright light, use a half-and-half media mix, water well, then let run some to the dry side. This pep has green and white leaves.

Variegated Swedish Ivy *(Pelclranthus oertendahlii)*

Here is the other Swedish ivy (australis), the blond brother with light streaks through the fat, thick leaves that turn purple underneath as they grow older. Its care is the same as its brother.

Variegated Wandering Jew
(Tradescantia fluminensis variegata)

When you have met one of these wanderers, you have met them all. Easy to grow if you keep them damp and in medium light, but turn them often.

Variegated Wax Ivy *(Hoya carnosa variegata)*

I like this plant family because it is always so clean and neat looking. The leaves always look wax coated, are firm, rich, and thick. It makes a super hanging plant, if you can provide good air circulation. Cool nights and bright days are good for this ivy. Plant it in regular potting soil, water heavily, then let run dry. Keep this family's feet pinched in a tight pot.

Velvet Leaf Kalanchoe *(Kalanchoe)*

This plant is part of the pomp and ceremony for Christmas because it blooms yellow or orange at that season. It needs medium to bright light, cool temperatures, and regular soil. It also needs to be kept damp. Good humidity helps.

WANDERING JEW

Velvet Plant, Purple Passion Plant
(Gynura aurantiaca)

Once you see this pretty lady you won't forget her velvet purple fur and veined leaves. When she flowers, it looks like orange bushes. Bright light with damp, regular potting soil is what she needs. Air has got to keep moving. You can pinch this one often without fear. Repot the foliage you pinch off.

Watermelon Peperomia *(Peperomia sandersir)*

If you have grown one Peperomia, you have grown them all. This is the watermelon pep.

Wax Plant *(Hoya carnosa tricolor)*

Here is a pretty plant with shiny green leaves and white, waxy flowers with pink centers that smell good. Home for Hoya is regular Hyponex Potting Soil. Water well and let run dry. Cool nights and well-circulating air will keep this sweet smeller hanging around for a long time.

Weeping Fig *(Ficus benjamina)*

You want a tree in your living room? This is it. Thick drooping branches with lots of dark-green, shiny pointed leaves. Here's the catch . . . You must spoil it. It has to have bright to medium light. The more light, the more leaves and vice versa. Keep the soil moist at all times. Use regular Hyponex Potting Soil. It will tolerate dry room air if the air is kept moving, which means keeping a fan going for most of the day. This tree, even when it is a small plant, does not like being moved. Every time it is moved, it drops its leaves, and you panic. Don't! It will always lose leaves when it first comes home from the plant store. Be quick to prune off dry tips to force more branching.

White-Nerved Fittonia, Silver Nerved and Red Nerved *(Fittonia argyroneura)*

These Fittonia plants are described between trailing, creeping, and climbing, so take your pick. They have oval leaves and the veins are so stated for each. Their needs are simple for your home to provide; they need humid, well-circulated, room temperature air. Use regular potting soil and keep it evenly damp. They favor a medium light to the bright side, but not too bright (the ends and edges of leaves will turn brown). This bunch of plants looks like heck if you let them go their own way. Cut them back on a regular basis so they don't look like a hippy, dippy, do.

White-Velvet Tradescantia
(Tradescantia sellamontana)

You are inclined to pet this plant or put a leash on it and take it out for a walk. Its dark-green leaves are covered with a white fur, and the flowers are light purple. Grows fast if you place it in a cool, medium light location. Plant it in regular potting soil that you really water, and then don't water again until it's dry. Keep it away from litter boxes and fire plugs.

Yucca False Agave

This plant always looks so royal. Its leaves are sword-shaped, green, and sharp. The Yucca prefers a good bright light, regular potting soil, good air circulation on the dry side, and should be watered well and let run dry.

Zebra Plant *(Aphelandra)*

I am afraid this lady has been given a bad reputation by the growers. What you see and first buy, is not what you get after a few weeks in your home. The zebra plants are propagated from a cutting taken from the end, which accounts for its early beauty. It wants medium light, moist soil (Professional Mix). Keep dry and mist often. I seldom, if ever, recommend it!

3

Take Your Plants Shopping for Furniture
INTERIOR DECORATING WITH HOUSE PLANTS

I stated earlier that it is not a good idea to simply plunk a plant down in the center of a room just for the sake of having a house plant.

Each plant you select should be a part, not apart, from the entire room decor.

Plan Before You Plop!

To help you better understand the compatibility of specific plants, according to their shape, size, foliage, color, or texture, I asked Robert Vincent Sims, world-renowned horticultural explorer and interior landscape designer, grower, consultant, lecturer, and writer, also a good friend of mine, to classify the plant varieties included in this book as to the furniture style and decor they are most compatible with.

Mr. Sims now lives in Eustis, Florida, not too far from Orlando. Vince collects and sells one-of-a-kind plant specimens to arboretums, private collectors, and individuals for inclusion in the interior plantscapes. These clients pay hundreds of dollars to have a single plant to set on a special table, or accent an unusual decor. Interior designers for

SO WHAT IF AFRICAN VIOLETS DON'T LIKE CHIPPENDALE

both commercial and residential assignments ask his advice! You get free (well not quite, when you consider the price of this book) use of his valuable advice to help you get the most enjoyment out of your house plants.

IDENTIFY THE COMPANY YOUR PLANTS WILL KEEP

According to Vince, you must first understand the basic styles of furniture. Fewer folks than you think actually know by name the design of the three categories: Traditional, Provincial, Contemporary. So he has written a simple description of both the categories and the style names under each.

Traditional

This style furniture is without a doubt the most formal of the three, depicting the life style of royalty and the rich of Europe in the 18th and 19th centuries. Today, with modern manufacturing methods, this style is easily within reach of almost anyone. Within that category you will find the following:

Queen Ann

The graceful, pure Queen Ann design has extremely clean lines. The gentle curve of Queen Ann legs is beautiful, as well as being good sound engineering. It gives extra bracing at the top, where it is really needed, while the slippered foot puts extra wood on the bottom where the most wear occurs.

Georgian

This is the name given to the Queen Ann style when furniture designers began to add ornamentation to it. This highly carved and ornamental furniture was the transition from pure Queen Ann to Chippendale, and was called Early Georgian.

Chippendale

This was the in-style in the last half of the 18th century for the newly rich merchant class, and they wanted their own

LOVE THEM LEGS

style. Chippendale, a master carver of the times, gave it to them in the form of pierced carvings added to Queen Ann legs, and he changed the slippered foot to a claw and ball.

Louis XV

This was basically the same as Queen Ann, but the carver designers modified it with more delicate and fragile curves, which were carried in the overall styling of that piece of furniture.

Greek Revival

England, in the late 18th century, as a rule dictated the current fashions and styles throughout most of the civilized world. It became fascinated with the designer Robert Adams, who classically designed furniture inspired by both Greek and Roman architecture. It is column-topped legs with carved foliage and beaded bands around tables and the showy wooded parts of couches and chairs.

Hepplewhite

This style was a return to the more simple design and away from the elaborately decorated and ornate styles of previous generations. Hepplewhite is in the straight back, tapered leg, and shield back, and is seen rather extensively today in the Traditional furniture showrooms.

Sheraton

The same as Hepplewhite. Softer and a little more ornate, and is identified by the lyre back.

Duncan Phyfe

America got its first bit of recognition in furniture style setting with Duncan Phyfe's well-designed cabinets.

He was the first of the soon-to-follow famous cabinet makers. He was a great fan and student of Hepplewhite and Sheraton, and resembled to some extent these two great styles with a few variations. He used curved legs, and arms based on the ionic column.

Louis XVI

Again influenced by the style of Hepplewhite and Sheraton, but like most of the French designs uses more delicate and intricate decorative accents.

Empire

This style is also a Greek- and Roman-influenced design.

Ionic curves and Corinthian decorations were all combined to form the new style of the revolutionary society of France in the early 19th century.

Victorian

This style is a little of this and a little of that. The Victorian designers went to more heavy ornamentation.

Regency

This style is easy to spot because its designers use a great deal of bamboo trimmings and caned slats or backs, and called for a lacquer or gilded surface. It appeared in England after the Revolutionary War and was popular here for a very short while, under 40 years. It is often mistaken for oriental.

Provincial

Provincial is an indication from the designer that the pieces were inspred by the country, or in other words, was constructed of native wood, not imported like the furniture of royalty. The styles were copied from the styles at court, but with local flavor added.

French Provincial

This style appeared in the 18th century. Craftsmen were copying the styles of French kings, delicate and light designs with ornate and courtly styles. The early French Provincial had straight legs and simple lines, while later pieces had more curves and decorations. These styles are still popular.

Early Colonial

America's Early Colonial was far from the French Provincial, since it was not copied from the styles of court. America's early settlers were first concerned with sturdy and serviceable tables, chairs, chests, and storage benches. Utility was first, then comfort, and lastly, style.

Mid-Colonial

As the American colonies became more prosperous, they began to look for a little more style. American furniture craftsmen and designers did use the European styles, but had a style of their own. The Windsor chair became extremely popular both in America and Europe. It was durable, graceful, and yet, delicate. Most of America's furniture style prestige comes from a religious sect, the Shakers.

Spanish Mediterranean

This is a husky, massive style of dark natural woods, ornately carved and combined with rich textured fabrics and leather, that is one of the most popular styles still. It is also referred to as Western style.

Contemporary

Frank Lloyd Wright, Albert Kahn, and Eero Saarinen were not pleased with any of the then available furniture styles to complement their concepts of architecture, so they designed their own.

Modern

Modern is, as a rule, straight lines of very light colored woods, chrome, brushed metals, and plastic. The fabrics are bright and flashy, and tabletops are of glass, marble, or plastic.

Something to Go By

With this brief—very brief—lesson in architectural identification of furniture styles and designs, you should have a pretty good idea of your personal furniture's pedigree, and a picture of the plants and planters that would most likely be compatible.

The following chart indicates which of the three categories they are most likely to look good with:

PLANT SELECTIONS FOR INTERIOR DESIGN

Plant Name	Traditional	Provincial	Contemporary
African Violet		✓	
Aluminum Plant			✓
Areca or Butterfly Palm		✓	✓
Arrowhead Nephthytis	✓	✓	✓
Artillery Plant		✓	
Asparagus Fern (Plume, Plumosa, Spencer)	✓	✓	
Avocado		✓	✓
Baby's Tears (Irish Moss)		✓	✓
Balfour Aralia			✓
Bella Palm	✓		✓
Bird's-Nest Sansevieria			✓
Bloodleaf Achyranthus	✓	✓	✓
Boston Fern	✓	✓	✓
Bromeliads			✓
Buddhist Pine			✓
Burro's Tail			✓
Cactus			✓
Caladium	✓	✓	✓
Calathea	✓	✓	✓
Cape Primrose (False African Violet)		✓	✓
Century Plant (American Aloe)		✓	✓
Chenille Plant		✓	✓
Chinese Evergreen	✓	✓	
Chinese Holly Grape			✓
Climbing Fig			✓
Coffee Plant		✓	✓
Coleus		✓	✓

Plant Name	Traditional	Provincial	Contemporary
Copperleaf Plant		✓	
Coral Berry		✓	✓
Corn Plant (a Dracaena)			✓
Croton	✓	✓	✓
Crown of Thorns			✓
Date Palm			✓
Dracaena (Gold Dust, Warnecki, Janet Craig)	✓	✓	✓
Dragon Tree (a Dracaena)			✓
Dumb Cane (Giant, Spotted Golden)	✓	✓	✓
Elephant's-Foot Tree (Ponytail)			✓
Emerald Ripple Peperomia		✓	✓
English Ivy	✓	✓	✓
Euonymus			✓
False Aralia (Mock Cannabis)			✓
Fan Palm	✓		✓
Fiddle-Leaf Fig			✓
Fiddle-Leaf Philodendron (Panduraeforme)			✓
Fishtail Palm			✓
Flame Violet		✓	✓
Fluffy-Ruffle Fern		✓	✓
Gardenia			✓
Geranium		✓	
German Ivy (Parlor Ivy)	✓	✓	
Giant White Inch Plant			✓
Gold Vein Bloodleaf			✓
Gold Dust Ivy		✓	✓
Gold Dust Tree			✓

PLANT SELECTIONS FOR INTERIOR DESIGN (*Cont.*)

Plant Name	Traditional	Provincial	Contemporary
Golden Bird's-Nest Sansevieria			✓
Golden Pothos (Devil's Ivy, Hunter's Robe)	✓	✓	✓
Golden Trumpet			✓
Grape Ivy	✓	✓	✓
Hagenburger's Ivy		✓	✓
Hahn's Self-Branching Ivy	✓	✓	✓
Hastatum Philodendron		✓	
Hawaiian Ti			✓
Heart-Leaf Philodendron (oxycardium)	✓	✓	✓
Hibiscus		✓	
Holly Fern		✓	
Iron-Cross Begonia		✓	
Jade Plant	✓	✓	✓
Japanese Aralia		✓	✓
Japanese Littleleaf Boxwood			✓
Joseph's Coat	✓		
Jungle Geranium		✓	✓
Kangaroo Ivy	✓	✓	✓
Lantana		✓	✓
Lipstick Plant		✓	✓
Maidenhair Fern		✓	✓
Marble Queen Pothos		✓	✓
Medicine Plant (True Aloe)		✓	✓
Ming Aralia	✓		✓
Moon Valley Pilea			✓
Moses-in-the-Bullrushes		✓	✓
Narrow-Leaf Pleomele			✓

Plant Name	Traditional	Provincial	Contemporary
Natal Plum	✓		
Needlepoint Ivy		✓	✓
Norfolk Island Pine			✓
Orchid	✓		✓
Orange Tree			✓
Peace Lily			✓
Piggyback Plant		✓	
Pineapple			✓
Polka-Dot Plant		✓	✓
Polynesia			✓
Polypody Fern		✓	✓
Prayer Plant (Maranta)		✓	
Purple Heart			✓
Purple Waffle Plant			✓
Rex Begonia		✓	✓
Ribbon Plant (a Dracaena)			✓
Rosary Vine		✓	✓
Rose of Jericho			✓
Rubber Plant		✓	✓
Schefflera (Umbrella Tree, Shopping Center Palm)	✓	✓	✓
Screw Pine			✓
Sensitive Plant			✓
Shrimp Plant		✓	
Silver Lace or Table Fern	✓	✓	
Silver Tree Panamiga			✓
Snake Plant (Mother-in-law's Tongue, Barber Shop Begonia)	✓	✓	
Spider Plant		✓	✓

PLANT SELECTIONS FOR INTERIOR DESIGN *(Cont.)*

Plant Name	Traditional	Provincial	Contemporary
Split-Leaf Philodendron	√	√	√
Staghorn Fern	√		√
Strawberry Begonia		√	
Striped Inch Plant	√	√	√
Succulents (Kalanchoe Christmas Cactus)			√
Swedish Ivy	√	√	√
Sweetheart Ivy		√	√
Tahitian Bridal Veil		√	√
Tree Ivy (Aralia Ivy)	√		√
Tree Philodendron (Selloum)	√	√	√
Umbrella Plant			√
Variegated Balfour Aralia			√
Variegated Mock Orange			√
Variegated Peperomia		√	√
Variegated Swedish Ivy	√	√	√
Variegated Wandering Jew			√
Variegated Wax Ivy	√	√	√
Velvet Leaf Kalanchoe		√	√
Velvet Plant			√
Watermelon Peperomia			√
Wax Plant			√
Weeping Fig	√	√	
White-Nerved Fittonia		√	√
White-Velvet Tradescantia		√	√
Yucca (False Agave)			√
Zebra Plant	√	√	√

4

What's a Nice Plant Like You Doing in a Dumb Pot Like This?
CONTAINERS

I was being interviewed on the phone one morning by a garden editor from Orlando, Florida, and she said, "Your books are so easy to read and enjoy because you write like you talk. Your explanations are short and to the point. If it's a subject I am interested in, I can stop and read; if not, I can go on to a subject I am interested in and not feel that I have missed anything."

Well, here is your opportunity to test that philosophy.

WHAT'S SO IMPORTANT ABOUT A POT?

The subject of selecting containers to grow plants in does not seem to be high on the list of interest for most of you would-be "plantologists." (Don't look it up in Webster's book. It's not there. It's *my* word!) Most of you simply take it for granted that the pot your plant arrives in is the best; after all, it was grown in a greenhouse by a professional. On the other hand, some of you immediately do your new plant friend a favor (you think) and transplant it into a container twice the size it arrived in. Others transplant new

POTS AT WORK

arrivals into new containers because they like a different color, shape, texture, or material. Seldom is the true comfort, safety, or need of the plant considered. If you are any of the above, shame on you!

Selecting a proper container for a plant is as important as a location, comfort zone, menu, or water needs. A plant in an improper container will deteriorate as quickly as if you had over or under fed, watered, or lighted. I am absolutely serious, and your plant is dead serious if you're wrong.

Permanents and Temporaries

Wow! I think I just wrote myself into a corner on this one, but then the lady from Orlando said I write like I talk and it has been said that I can talk myself out of most anything, except taking the garbage out on Monday mornings. The first container a baby plant goes into is what we refer to as a temporary, organic container (better known to you as a peat pot). These we will discuss farther down the road when we talk about planting and transplanting. Right now, let's concentrate on working pots and dress containers.

When you go to the garden shop to buy a container for a new plant or one that has outgrown its present pot, you usually end up spending a few bucks, so give it a little more attention than buying a morning newspaper. I am getting ahead of myself, so let's get the permanent and temporary straight first.

Permanent Containers

This is a pot that a plant will be directly inserted into and surrounded by a planting media. There are two common and popular materials used: terra-cotta (clay) and plastic. Clay is a longtime favorite of most professional growers 45 years and older, while plastic-based pots are favored by the younger growers. Both containers have their good and bad points. Clay pots are heavier and breakable, while plastics are lighter and longer lasting. Clay is harder to keep clean and neat, while plastic is less apt to carry disease. Excess water and salts can escape from clay, while plastic can retain too much moisture and fertilizer salts. I am a 53-year-old clay man, but only because I like the terra-cotta look when my plants are not in their dress clothes.

I HAVEN'T MADE UP MY MIND YET

Temporary Containers

These are what I refer to as dress clothes. Glass, fiber, metal, wood, plastic (fancy), wicker, woven reed, and several other materials round out the type of wardrobe you can select for your houseplants. In most cases, as I pointed out earlier, they are not cheap, at least not the ones I want my plants to be seen in. No, I am not a plant snob! I want quality and appearance. No, I am not saying that if you don't spend a lot of money on a plant container you won't get a good one; just look for quality first.

The reason I refer to these decorative containers as temporary is because I move my plants from container to container, just like you and I wear a different combination of clothing from day to day. No, I don't change them every day (I have); in most cases, I change them once a month or so, and the reason is rather simple. Plants are like people when it comes to hygiene, and they like to look, feel, and smell fresh. When you remove a plant in its permanent container (clay or plastic) from its temporary container (decorative), you wash and spray both containers for insects and to control disease.

Here are a couple of tricks to protect and prolong decorative containers:

1. If they are fiber-coated, wood, wicker, bamboo, or reed, I spray them inside and out with two applications of a good fabric protector like Scotchgard or a similar product.

2. Good metal containers come coated inside with Rust-Oleum undercoat to prevent rust and salt damage from fertilizer salts.

These containers can now be washed with warm soapy water and sprayed with an insect spray or fungicide. Other washable containers should be scrubbed with soap and water with an ounce of bleach added per gallon and dried well before plants are returned.

Mismatched Planters Stick Out Like a Sore Thumb!

When you go to shop for a new dress or suit of clothes for your plants (that's right, we are discussing containers), keep

MISMATCHED PLANTERS STICK OUT LIKE SORE THUMBS

THE BIGGER THE BETTER'S NOT ALWAYS BEST

in mind the style of furniture, color of fabric, walls, and floor covering. No! I am not fooling. A plant container is the bridge between the plant and the room decor. You want harmony, not discord, when decorating with plants and containers.

The Bigger the Better Is Not Best!

It's just like buying clothes, my friend. Make sure the pants fit. A container too big for a small plant looks like the dickens and makes both you and the plant a laughingstock. By the same token, too small a container makes you both look silly. A container should never exceed two-thirds the size of the head of the plants. Most reputable merchants will allow you to return a container if it does not fit the plant or decor. Make sure both you and the plant are satisfied.

Room Dividers Are Something Special

As a rule, window boxes are permanent structures and their interiors should be constructed with timber that has been treated with a no-rot solution; same with room dividers. A heavy-duty plastic insert tray should be set in to hold the plants, which are left in their permanent containers of clay or plastic. This will permit the removal of the plants and tray so they can be cleaned and treated from time to time. Fill the tray up over the plant containers with a large-sized decorative bark that has been thoroughly sprayed and dried with an insect spray. Room dividers should have large, heavy-duty Shepherd casters hidden beneath so they can be moved for easy care and cleaning underneath.

Window Boxes Are an Old Standby

You don't see too many of these around much anymore. If you decorate with a window box, make sure you use several coats of undercoat on the inside and then seal it with a clear epoxy. Again, use a plastic tray (heavy-duty), not metal. Set plants, container and all, into tray; *do not* plant

SOME BREAK UP THE MONOTONY

SOME LIKE IT HOT

directly into tray. Since it will be necessary from time to time to remove plants from the window box for treatment, repair, or replacement, make sure you leave enough room above the window box to completely remove the pot and the plant without causing injury to other plants in the box. Whenever you set plants into a large container, make sure that you always use the lightweight, Hyponex Professional Planter Mix. This will protect the plants' roots and your back.

Plant Furniture Is on the Move

JUST MOVING AROUND

A piece of plant furniture to me is anything larger than a 10-inch pot, and then if you have ever tried to lift some of the 10-inch pots filled with ordinary potting soil and a large plant, your back would also consider them as devastating as any overstuffed chair. I either purchase with or attach casters or wheels to any type of plant-holding room divider I build or buy. The reason is simple: Like anything else that adorns a human occupied room, it gets moved from time to time for cleaning, decorating, or just the hell of it, and if it's got 60 or 70 pounds of soil and plant plus 75 to 100 pounds of lumber and nails in it, you are going to be a candidate for a hernia operation, and while you are recuperating they will have time to replace the torn carpet and scratched floors. I have found that the use of good-quality Shepherd casters (come in all sizes) for use on carpet or tile floors, is well worth the extra effort and investment. Out of doors, use heavy-duty casters. Make sure one set is a swivel type so you can guide the divider.

Restaurants, hair salons, and other commercial establishments are foolish if they don't insist that all plants be on moveable bases. Every piece of furniture in my home and office that I cannot comfortably pick up without my back objecting has casters under it. Any half-handy man or woman with a drill, hammer, and screwdriver can perform this transition.

The materials that are used to build plant stands, tables, room dividers, shelves, or boxes must be of *no-rot-treated* wood, or sealed and covered with attractive formica-type materials, or both. Be safe—not sorry a few months or years later when untreated materials would begin to decay from damp surroundings, warm rooms, and continued use of salty plant foods.

Tree Stumps and Bee Hives Make Great Planters!

Bird houses, abandoned bird nests, and any one of a dozen other imaginative and creative objects that will fit into your decorating scheme and that can safely hold a potted plant make great planters. There are a couple of cautions and tips that will keep you, your furniture, and your plants out of trouble. Most of the objects that fascinate most of us as possible planters are either from nature or are very old and aged looking. What they all have in common is that they are the homes, hiding, or nesting places of insects and little critters, and if they're not inspected, fumigated, cleaned, and protected, you may just end up with a distressed-wood piano, end table, or hutch from a post beetle that was asleep in an antique box or tree stump, that awoke and was sure it was in bug heaven when it saw all of your bright, shining, fragrant, and delicious-looking furniture, or the carpenter ant that joined in the feast; the fleas and ticks asleep or hiding in the old bird's nest that eye your pets as a feast of a dream come true, or a lethargic wasp that comes out of its dormant stupor in your warm living room, sure that it is in a combat zone and you and the kids are the targets. Unsuspecting mice, chipmunks, squirrels, and snakes have found themselves the center of unwanted attention while minding their own business in hibernation or just plain resting.

These are the steps I take before bringing any of my profound finds into the house:

1. Visually inspect, poke, prod, shake, tap, and otherwise make enough racket to wake the living dead.

2. Spray with a mixture of 10 drops of liquid soap, 2 teaspoons of chewing tobacco juice, 2 drops of onion or garlic juice, 5 drops of Methoxychlor, and 5 drops of Kelthane in a quart of warm water. Let dry.

3. Place the object inside a large, heavy-duty, dark plastic bag with one-half a pest strip. Seal the top and let set for 5 to 7 days.

ARE YOU SURE THE LAST TENANT MOVED OUT?

4. Open bag and insert a yellow plastic coffee can lid or plastic dish that has been rubbed with a liberal coat of vegetable oil. This will trap any insect that has not died.

5. Coat the exterior of nests with several coats of spray plastic. Other containers should be finished with an appropriate protective coating.

6. Constantly be alert for any signs of "reincarnation," and react immediately.

Bottles, Jars, and Jugs Are Real Standouts

I WOULD HAVE PREFERRED A THUNDERBIRD BOTTLE

Dress Them Up for Company

I am constantly amazed at the objects you folks come up with as superattractive planters. Coffee and tea pots, mugs, cups, pots, pans, bowls, buckets, and on and on and on. Some of the items I have witnessed have at one time been worth a great deal of money but after being used as a pot for a plant, with constant exposure to plant food, water, and insect control, they have become worthless.

Never, never, never use a valuable antique piece for a permanent planter. You can and should use them as decorative containers if steps are taken to protect their finish.

If I am using cup and saucer to display violets in, I place my plants into peat pots and then wrap them with aluminum foil so no water will leak. When watering, I remove them from the cup, remove the foil cover, water, feed, and recover.

All glass, metal, and ceramic objects should be washed monthly for their own protection with warm soapy water, and a few drops of bleach for glass and ceramics.

The more attention you pay to the container your plants are grown in, the more attention you will be paying your plants. When using plants in commercial offices and business establishments, I highly suggest the use of nonmundane containers. By the same token, the containers should be in keeping with the prestige and decor of the business.

We began this chapter by describing and discussing the permanent and temporary containers that plants are grown

WHY ALL THE FUSS?

and displayed in. Here we are simply bringing the two together. A permanent plant container, commonly referred to as a pot, is either clay (terra-cotta) or plastic (light weight). These two popular containers are used for greenhouse growing and shipping. The latter (plastic) is currently leading in popularity because it reduces the shipping weight by as much as 65%. That, my friends, is a great savings. But with the deregulation of the trucking industry, the weight factor is decreasing, and many growers are returning to clay growing containers. Nevertheless, we are concerned first with the plant's ability to grow and survive, and secondly with its esthetic compatibility with your current decor.

In the case of the commercial use of plants, the decorative display container (temporary) will be almost considered as a permanent, since it costs more to rotate plants from container to container. In your home or where smaller plants and containers are used, it will be much easier to rotate plant wardrobes. I am a great collector and saver of the woven, plastic-lined covers that come in natural and colors when gift plants are sent from flower shops. They resemble straw hats. I remove my plants from their current decorative covers, not disturbing them in their clay or plastic permanent growing pots, and insert them in one of these slightly oversized hat covers. By using an oversized one, I allow for more air circulation, evaporation, and drainage. When company is coming, I merely reinsert them into a clean, fresh, decorative cover. This may sound like a lot of extra work, but it's not! It takes the boredom of plant care out of everyday growing for both the plants and me. There are many other designs on the market today, as well as fabrics and colors in this same plastic-lined hat. Look for them.

One last point: Since they are plastic lined, be sure to pour off excess water after feeding and watering.

All Containers Aren't Dishwasher Proof, But Should Be!

It is so important to make sure that the containers plants are grown and shown in be kept clean, neat, and disease-free, that I just can't emphasize enough the necessity of constantly changing and washing both the permanent and the

MELT-DOWN TIME

temporary kinds. At least *every* 60 days my plants are removed from the permanent clay or plastic pot and inserted into a clean, washed, and sterilized pot of the same size for no other reason than to protect their health and my investment of time, money, and pride. "That's a lot of unnecessary work," you will say. Not when it is your hobby. I test pieces of material that will house my plants in the automatic dishwasher, and tend to go with those that pass this torture test. Clay wins hands down. Most of the metals, ceramic, glass, and some of the better plastic planters will also. Rubbermaid has gone out of its way to help you to help your plants. If you can't use the dishwasher, let the containers soak for a few days in a soap, bleach, Listerine, and tobacco-juice solution. Next, scrub, rinse, dry, and let them rest in a box or bag with a no-pest strip for company.

Just Let Them Hang Around for a While!

Hanging plants, or even one hanging plant, can do so much for a room or waiting area that it's a shame when they are forgotten by those who have chosen to use them in their personal environment. There are other places in this book where I have discussed the selection and care of plants for hanging baskets. I wish to acquaint you here with container uses and the hanging apparatus. There are six basic hanging containers; four are temporary and two are for outdoor or greenhouse growing. Both types can be converted to a decorative indoor display container. The four decoratives (temporary) are:

1. Clay with attached saucer
2. Plastic with attached saucer
3. Ceramic with no drainage
4. Metal with no drainage

The two outdoor hanging containers are:

1. Sphagnum-moss-lined wire basket
2. Sphagnum-moss-lined wood basket

There are also many variations of each of the wood, wire, and plastic container types. Yes, the wire basket is now available in plastic, and wood baskets are of wicker as well.

NO
LOITERING

WE'RE ALWAYS UP IN THE AIR

I must continue to drum the same beat. Set the plants that have been planted in the light-weight Hyponex Professional Planter Mix and are in plastic or clay pots into the decorative hanging containers.

In the case of the sphagnum-lined baskets, set a plastic saucer under the bottom of the moss to catch water. Now set the plant (pot and all) into the center of the moss. It looks great!

Out of doors you can plant directly into the sphagnum-and-planter-mix-filled basket. Remember to use one of the professional planter mixes. I use Hyponex Professional Planter Mix.

Care and watering of hanging baskets have always been a problem, as is distributing the light to all sides of the plants. There are all sizes of brass, chrome, steel, and copper pulleys available in plant and hardware stores to allow you to raise and lower your plants for care and tending, and fishing swivels of varying sizes are available to place between the hook on the ceiling and the hook on the hanging container to allow the plant to be turned 360° for balanced light.

When using hanging baskets and wicker or wire cages, you must be alert for permanent entanglements of the tendrils of vine-type plants, which will prevent you from removing these plants.

HOW THEY RATE IS
ONE MAN'S OPINION—MINE!

In this section I will try to sum up how I rate materials used for plant pots and containers. This is not to say that you can't and shouldn't experiment on your own, or that others haven't found to the contrary of my experience.

1. **Clay Pots** Clay pots are far and away my favorite. After a soap-and-bleach soaking and then a trip through the dishwasher, these pots are as attractive as a clean car on a Sunday drive.

2. **Plastic Pots** If I had a commercial greenhouse, I would go plastic; after all, the name of the game is profit and sales.

CLAY'S NUMBER ONE

3. *Metal Planters* You get what you pay for. Invest in to prolong their lives is to coat the interiors with an epoxy.

4. *Wood Planters* These containers, as a rule, have real class, but must be of the no-rot class and must be kept painted and coated.

5. *Glass* Glass containers are for looks only. Never put a plant into them.

6. *Ceramic* These run with the same crowd as glass. In both cases, make sure that they are of heavier material, since they will be supporting additional weight. KEEP THEM CLEAN!

7. *Fiber Pots* Pecan shells, sawdust, sisal dust, and coconut shell (crushed), are just a few of the fiber materials available. Treat them like wood and seal the inside. These must be handwashed and then sprayed for insect and disease control; use any plant bomb.

8. *Woven Reed* I make sure these containers have plastic linings or I tape a double layer or a heavy-duty garbage bag inside and use these containers as everyday coveralls for the working pots (clay).

9. *Woven Wicker* These are treated the same as wood, with one exception. I spray both inside and out with a material such as Scotchgard to prevent the wicker from softening up.

The longevity of any container is in your hands. To prolong its usefulness you must take the proper steps to keep it clean and protected. Science has come up with many, many good wood and fabric preservatives in the last decade, all of which preserve the quality of most materials against the elements. It is your job to see that it's done.

POTS MAKE THE PLANT

If you have gone to the trouble to read this section all the way to the end, neither I nor your plant needs to worry about its personal appearance.

I treat plants just as I would like to be treated. I am in the

public eye on TV and in personal appearances hundreds of times each year all over the world, and I make every attempt to put my best foot forward, and in so doing, I make sure the shoe is shined and always try to remember that clothes do make the man.

Always make sure that the clothes fit the plant, the plant fits the room, and the room matches the personality of the plant's friend. Next, make sure that the color, material, size, and shape are in harmony with the color and decor of the wall, floor, window, and furniture coverings.

It seems like a lot to remember, but it will become as natural to you as buying clothes or home furnishings as soon as you learn that plants are your friends.

5

The Light Side of House Plants
LIGHTING

I am always asked by interviewers, "What is the most asked question you receive from folks who are trying to grow healthy, happy, attractive plants in their homes and places of business?"

My answer to the question is, "The wrong one."

Because, while your concerns are pretty evenly divided between feeding and watering, what your plants wish you would ask about is the proper portions of light that they require to stay alive, let alone healthy.

Solitary Confinement Is Only for Punishment

You can give your house plants the right formula plant food, depending on their needs, at the right time and in the right quantities. You can also be letter-perfect on their water, temperature, and humidity needs and yet, to your continuing frustration, your plants, over the long haul, die.

It's enough to make most of you think that what little green thumb you might have had withered and went! Don't despair! I am about to shed some light on the matter, so you can soon see the bright side of house plant growing.

Light, without a doubt, is the single most important ingredient necessary for deep, rich, bright, attractive foliage, flowers, and fruit for indoor plants; then comes temperature, water, humidity, and food (and in that order).

No, I am not neglecting soil or insect and disease control. We will concentrate on them later.

Lights, Light! Right?

Plants, people, and animals all need light to some degree. Plants need light to assist them in processing the sugars and starches into chlorophyll and the green and other colors you expect from plants. Man and animals need the light source to manufacture vitamin D under their skin from the ultraviolet rays. Vitamin D encourages good bone growth.

Light can be both helpful and harmful to all of us, depending on its quality, quantity, and source. Sunlight is by

I WAS JUST KIDDING

WHERE ARE MY SUNGLASSES?

far the best quality of light. No, I am not taking anything away from the accomplishments of science in the field of artificial sources of light. These, as you will see later, are great substitutes for natural light. The sun delivers the full spectrum of color that is necessary for good growth potential of all living things. For your collection of trivia information, I am listing the colors found in light and their uses.

Sunlight, as we see it, is a combination of red, orange, yellow, and green. The colors we don't see are blue and violet. Red and orange promote the most noticeable effects on plants, such as flowers and shape. Yellow and green contribute little or nothing. Blue and violet promote foliage color and growth.

If this seems like a seventh grade botany lesson, it is. Once you understand the personality of the light source available to you, the quicker you will recognize problems and be able to react before it is too late for your plants.

If the permanent plants you have placed in your environment begin to show thinning of foliage and dropping of leaves and a change of vigor because of an erratic source of light, and you don't react quick enough, even the improvement of light will not save them.

Direct or Indirect Light—What Difference Does It Make?

It can mean the difference between life and death to some plants. Direct light is best described as the rays of the sun covering most of the plant from 3 to 5 hours on a bright, sunny day.

Indirect light, on the other hand, is that which fills a room from the north or south windows. It can also be described as the outside quantity of light that fills a space beyond the intended area in which it is placed (the farther reaches from the lamp on the table).

Obviously, the light unobstructed from its source (sun or lamp) produces the most direct effects, while to most flowering plants indirect light is like trying to suck up milk through a straw with a cut in it: You work twice as hard for half as much or less. Wait a minute! There are plants that prefer either one or the other or a mix somewhere in be-

MAKE UP YOUR MIND

tween. Here is a very brief description of the results from both too much or too little light:

Too Much Light The foliage will have spots (olive green to mushy brown). The foliage will be grayish green to yellow and curl up and bend over. If the tip and edges of the leaves turn brown, it can mean either too much light or lack of humidity, or a combination of both. An overabundance of light can also produce weak, soft, and thin foliage growth, with long distances between the leaves.

Not Enough Light When there is no new growth or it is slow appearing, with soft, weak small leaves and yellowing older foliage dropping off, you had better light up its life and pray like heck.

On almost every plant you purchase from a retail outlet, regardless of the store's size and specialty (plant store, grocery store, or K-Mart), you will generally find a care tag tied to or stuck in the pot. This tag gives you a rough idea of the comfort zone the plant needs for survival. Light, temperature, and water are usually noted. Please read and remember.

OPEN YOUR EYES!

There are people who can judge the quality and quantity of light, just by eyeballing. These are professional photographers and television and film cameramen. Since 1961, all three of these professional-type people have been an everyday part of my life. They photograph me, products, and plants for all of the media that I am involved with daily. I am absolutely amazed at the uncanny ability that some of them have of setting the f-stop on the camera (lens opening) just by looking at the light source and the subject's surface (will it reflect light or absorb light?). Then they set the lens! Next, they challenge their own talent. They always take out the light meter and mechanically measure the light's intensity. You will then hear, "I knew it without the damn meter," or "Close!" or "Boy, do I need glasses." What all of these pros did was check to be sure, because they are using a very sensitive, expensive film. Your plants display that same sensitive trait and deserve the same precautions.

SAY "CHEESE"

Keep the Meter Running!

Why not do as the professionals do, use a light meter? There are very simple, inexpensive light meters at the camera department, or you can purchase a plant light meter, which only differs in the face of the meter. Instead of f-stop openings, it states bright, medium, or dark, or may have numbers from 1 to 10 on its face and a chart on the back.

If you use a camera meter, here are what the f-stops (lens openings) mean:

f/5.6—Low light

f/8—Medium light

f/11—Good light

To check the light quality, take the reading when the room seems to be the brightest. You should take four readings a year: September, February, May, and July. This will give you an indication of the seasonal changes of light (shortening and lengthening of the days) and an opportunity to move the plants or add artificial light before the plants begin to deteriorate.

I don't care how good you are, eyeballing is not a very smart or safe way to protect your plants when it comes to light.

A LITTLE MORE TO THE RIGHT

Hangovers Make Everybody Uncomfortable

I am not referring to your plants' drinking habits here (that comes later). I am talking about roof overhangs and tree-limb obstructions that can affect both quality and quantity of light. As boring as this section is to most of you who are just growing a few plants, you will thank me farther down the growing path when your friends compliment you on the looks of your indoor green scene and call to ask you how to care for their plants.

When a garden writer recommends a window exposure (east, west, north, or south), they are referring to an unobstructed view—no roof overhang, curtain, shade, trees, buildings, or shrubs. They are using a 3-foot-wide by 5-foot-high window. Unobstructed means that the window

I NEED RELIEF

has an open view to the sky. An obstructed window is one that blocks out half the sky. They are also assuming that the top of the plant is at least a foot below the top of the window.

Here is what I use as a reference:

Low Light	*Window*
6 ft from unobstructed 4 ft from an obstructed	north
8 ft from unobstructed 6 ft from an obstructed	east or west
10 ft from unobstructed 8 ft from an obstructed	south

Medium Light	*Window*
4 ft from unobstructed	north
5 ft from unobstructed 4 ft from obstructed	east or west
8 ft from unobstructed 6 ft from obstructed	south

Bright Light	*Window*
3 ft from unobstructed 2 ft from obstructed	east or west
5 ft from unobstructed 4 ft from obstructed	south

Both obstructed and unobstructed exposures can be improved by supplemental lights or the use of sheer white Dacrons to reflect light farther into a room. In this situation keep plants 10 to 12 feet back from windows.

Remember to always check your hunches with a meter as my cameramen do, just to see how good you are.

SOMETHING FOR EVERYONE

The list of plants that I have selected for your consideration numbers 136 (see next section). This is a far cry from the total number available, but is the best balance in terms of shapes, textures, colors, sizes, and flowers. It does not include the seasonal and holiday plants, as these are covered in another section. Just remember, my good friend, that I have cautioned you several times before this that you must consider a lot more than just simple attractiveness before settling on a selection. My suggestion from here on is this: Take a piece of paper and jot down the name of a plant (or plants) that suits your fancy. Next to it, put down its light code, leaving room to add temperature and humidity needs and any other important factors for deciding which plants will join your decor as the green scene.

How Much Light to Shed on the Subject

Here are the basic light requirements for the most popular and available house plants for homes and offices. I have designated the degree of light as low, medium and bright, and then given you a cross-reference to the window direction that will make the most of this quality, unobstructed and unassisted by artificial light supplements.

LIGHT NEEDS FOR HOUSE PLANTS THAT THRIVE IN A NORTH OR EAST WINDOW EXPOSURE

Light Meter	House plants
L	Bella Palm
L	Bird's-Nest Fern
L	Boston Fern
L	Chinese Evergreen
L	Holly Fern
L	Maidenhair Fern
L	Peace Lily
L	Purple Waffle Plant
L	Rose of Jericho
L	Silver Lace or Table Fern
M	African Violet
M	Aluminum Plant
M	Areca or Butterfly Palm
M	Arrowhead Nephthytis
M	Artillery Plant
M	Asparagus Fern (Plume, Plumosa, Spencer)
M	Baby's Tears, Irish Moss
M	Bird's-Nest Sansevieria

Light Meter	House Plants
M	Boston Fern
M	Bromeliads
M	Buddhist Pine
M	Caladium
M	Calathea
M	Cape Primrose (False African Violet)
M	Chenille Plant
M	Climbing Fig
M	Coffee Plant
M	Coral Berry
M	Corn Plant (also a Dracaena)
M	Date Palm
M	Dracaena (Gold Dust, Janet Craig, Warnecki)
M	Dragon Tree (also a Dracaena)
M	Dumb Cane (Giant, Spotted, Golden)
M	Emerald Ripple Peperomia
M	Euonymus
M	False Aralia (Mock Cannabis)
M	Fiddle-Leaf Fig
M	Fiddle-Leaf Philodendron (Panduraeformé)
M	Fishtail Palm
M	Flame Violet
M	Fluffy-Ruffle Fern
M	Fun Palm
M	German Ivy (Parlor Ivy)
M	Giant White Inch Plant
M	Gold Dust Tree
M	Golden Bird's-Nest Sansevieria
M	Golden Pothos (Devil's Ivy, Hunter's Robe)
M	Grape Ivy
M	Hastatum Philodendron
M	Hawaiian Ti
M	Heart-Leaf Philodendron (oxycardium)
M	Iron-Cross Begonia
M	Japanese Aralia
M	Kangaroo Ivy
M	Lipstick Plant
M	Marble Queen Pothos
M	Moon Valley Pilea

LIGHT NEEDS FOR HOUSE PLANTS THAT THRIVE IN A NORTH OR EAST WINDOW EXPOSURE (*Cont.*)

Light Meter	House plants
M	Moses-on-a-Raft
M	Narrow-Leaved Pleomele
M	Norfolk Island Pine
M	Piggyback Plant
M	Polka-Dot Plant
M	Polynesia
M	Polypody Fern
M	Prayer Plant, Maranta
M	Rex Begonia
M	Ribbon Plant (a Dracaena)
M	Rosary Vine
M	Rubber Plant
M	Screw Pine
M	Sensitive Plant
M	Silver Tree Panamiga
M	Smoke Plant, Mother-in-Law's Tongue, Barbershop Begonia (All of the above are Sansevieria)
M	Spider Plant
M	Split-Leaf Philodendron
M	Staghorn Fern
M	Striped Inch Plant
M	Swedish Ivy
M	Tahitian Bridal Veil
M	Tree Philodendron (selloum)
M	Umbrella Plant
M	Variegated Mock Orange
M	Variegated Peperomia
M	Variegated Swedish Ivy
M	Variegated Wandering Jew
M	Variegated Wax Ivy
M	Wandering Jew
M	Watermelon Peperomia
M	Weeping Fig
M	White-Nerved Fittonia
M	White-Velvet Tradescentia
M	Zebra Plant

Light Meter	House Plants
B	Balfour Aralia
B	Bloodleaf Achyranthus
B	Burro's Tail
B	Cactus
B	Century Plant (American Aloe)
B	Chinese Holly Grape
B	Coleus
B	Copperleaf Plant
B	Croton
B	Crown of Thorns
B	Elephant's-Foot Tree (Ponytail)
B	English Ivy
B	Gardenia
B	Geranium
B	Gold Dust Ivy
B	Golden Trumpet
B	Gold Vein Bloodleaf
B	Hagenburger's Ivy
B	Hahn's Self-Branching Ivy
B	Hibiscus
B	Jade Plant
B	Japanese Littleleaf Boxwood
B	Joseph's Coat
B	Jungle Geranium
B	Lantana
B	Medicine Plant (True Aloe)
B	Ming Aralia
B	Natal Plum
B	Needlepoint Ivy
B	Orange Tree (also Lemon, Lime, and Grapefruit Trees)
B	Orchids*
B	Pineapple
B	Purple Heart
B	Schefflera, Umbrella Tree, Shopping Center Palm
B	Shrimp Plant
B	Strawberry Begonia

* Orchids thrive in an east window exposure only.

LIGHT NEEDS FOR HOUSE PLANTS THAT THRIVE IN A NORTH OR EAST WINDOW EXPOSURE (*Cont.*)

Light Meter	*House Plants*
B	Succulents (Christmas Cactus, Kalanchoe)
B	Sweetheart Ivy
B	Tree Ivy (Aralia Ivy)
B	Variegated Balfour Aralia
B	Velvet Leaf Kalanchoe
B	Velvet Plant
B	Wax Plant
B	Yucca (False Agave)

B = Bright (*f*/11)   M = Medium (*f*/8)   L = Low (*f*/5.6)

There's Light at the End of the Tunnel

GET THE BINOCULARS

Before we discuss the availability and uses of artificial light, let's talk a little bit about some ways that you may want to consider to let a little more material light into your homes. There is good reason for improving the natural light in an occupied room. First and foremost, it will help to keep your eyes healthy longer. Second, it has a positive psychological effect on one's mood. Finally, it allows you to see color closer to its natural hues. Thus, you will enjoy your decor more. Why not consider enlarging small windows. Many of our older homes were built with narrow, double-hung windows or short, sliding windows, which kept many of our bedrooms, kitchens, and dining rooms a bit on the dark side. The improvements in prefabrication of bow and bay window units (double- and triple-paned) has brought the prices within range of most of us to do it ourselves. Every weekend I see more do-it-yourself centers opening and offering classes and help at reasonable prices.

You might also consider having bids submitted for a window wall or extended window by an independent contractor (make sure you apply for a local permit). Your local building department and inspector can help to keep the quality of the project in line as well. One last consideration and the one that I have seen utilized the most lately is skylights, which can be used in any room with amazing results. These, too, are customer kits that can be installed very easily and quickly. Yes, you can do-it-yourself, but I do suggest that you have a roof man seal the installation to ensure no leaks.

These are just a few thoughts to help you get more use from the rooms you live in and add a little more natural beauty, through plants, into your life.

Tom Edison Turned the Tables on Mother Nature

AND LET THERE BE LIGHT

With the invention of the light bulb, a whole new world of indoor gardening opened up for us. Now, instead of a few shade-loving plants like ferns decorating the rooms of our great-grandparents' homes, an almost unlimited assortment of plants is available to you and me. An ordinary incandescent light bulb, which we use by the dozens each year in our lamps and overhead fixtures, gives off enough light to supplement the natural light in a room and extend the length of the growing cycle of most foliage plants in our homes and offices. If used in a proper way, the ordinary incandescent light has the same red and orange qualities as sunlight needed to keep our African violets in bloom. True, these rays are not as intense as sunlight, but they are better than no extra light in a dim room. Fluorescent lights, on the other hand, are heavy producers of the blue and violet spectrums that produce deep-color foliage, so in formerly drab offices and shops a whole new scene is unfolding. Waiting rooms, shopping centers, and restaurants resemble domed parks, with trees, waterfalls, and even birds, all because Edison did not let 1,600 failures deter his determination to develop a light source to replace the dangerous fumes of gas and the constant cause of life-taking fires from candles. I live just a few miles from Ford's Greenfield Village where Edison's lab now resides. I often visit the village and this building and always think, "Thanks, Tom!" as I stand about. If any of you get up this way, you must stop in Dearborn, Michigan, and visit Greenfield Village. It will take you two enjoyable days. It is a grown-up's Disneyland.

WHAT'S THE DIFFERENCE?

Let's Go Shopping for Lights to Grow By

There are real pros and cons on the need for specialty packaged lights for indoor growing. Some professional growers and avid hobbyists will tell you that a combination of cool-white and warm-white fluorescent lights at proper height and longevity (time on) are as good as the special lights, while others in these same categories swear by the special plant lights, as they are labeled.

What I have just done is put myself between a rock and a hard place, because you are depending on me to make everyday living and care of house plants fun, fast, and easy as well as economical.

My good plant friend, I have used lights labeled for plants with superior results. Then again, I have used nonlabeled cools and warms with the same high-quality results. I have also used them in combination (mix and match) with no noticeable difference. What I have found to be true of the major manufacturers of light bulbs—Westinghouse, Sylvania, General Electric, and Duro-Lite—is that they tell it like it is and let you make the choice. My personal advice is to try one of each and see for yourself.

You Could Be in a Real Fix Here

It becomes a real problem for most folks when it comes to hanging light fixtures to help them grow plants, and the reason is quickly apparent as soon as you see what's available. If I were to use one word to describe the fixtures available for holding light tubes, I would say, "Ugly." When I think of the time, effort, and money it takes to select all of the proper elements to have an attractive decor in one's home, office, or restaurant (like paint, wallpaper, floor covering and drapes, pictures, furniture, lamps and stained woodwork, planters, and plants) if I read that I had to place these mechanically sterile-looking light fixtures 10 to 12 inches above all my plants, my first reaction would be "Scratch planters and plants!" Hold on now, I am showing you both sides of the coin.

I'D LIKE AN 8 O'CLOCK WAKE-UP CALL, PLEASE

The manufacturers of light sources are well aware of this occurrence and have gone out of their way to design lamps (bulbs and tubes) that will fit into any and all of your present decorated light fixtures. So, relax and find just the right shape of bulb to grow your plants by. You will find that the inexpensive reflector shields with clamps for portable use will come in handy from time to time.

Lights Out!

With a couple of exceptions, most plants grown indoors need 16 hours of light a day in the winter and 14 in the summer. On the other hand, poinsettias, begonias, and Christmas cactus need 12 hours of undisturbed sleep (no light) if they are to show off in the proper season.

Remember what I said at the beginning of this chapter about a light meter of some type; well, here is where it comes in real handy. Measure the quantity of natural light at 10 A.M. and 3 P.M. Next, measure it with the incandescent bulbs on in your table lamps at 6 P.M. and again at 9 P.M. With this information in hand you can figure out how much and for how long supplemental light will be necessary.

Put the Clock on Them

There are so many timing devices on the market today (the prices range from cheap to expensive) that you should have no trouble finding one or two that will fit your pocketbook.

It's Cost Plus

It's cost plus your ability to pay higher light bills. You bet your bippy! Each tube, flood, spot, or bulb adds to your bill, so don't waste light. Here is a rough idea on how to figure the cost to operate each additional light you add. Mind you, this is just a ball park figure and not a figure to make a case with at the Public Service Commission.

Add up the watts figure on each bulb you are going to use. If a starter is needed, add another 20% to the watts, if not, leave it off. Now, multiply the watts by the number of

WE MEASURE UP

hours you intend to keep the new lights on. What you now have is the number of watt-hours. To find out how much they will cost, you reduce them to kilowatt-hours: 1,000 watt-hours equals 1 kilowatt-hour. Your current light bill will tell you what the light company is charging you per kilowatt-hour.

You're Now on the Spot

If you can see your way clear to use fluorescent and incandescent lights to keep your plants staying healthy, you must make sure they get close enough to benefit. As a rule, when the long and short tubes are used, your plants must be somewhere between 6 to 8 inches away. If incandescent lamps are used (reflector floods and spots), up to 6 feet away will benefit them. Most of the light manufacturers also have flexible fixtures for these lights that can well fit into your decor. Do not, I repeat, do not use old light fixtures for long periods of time with hot-base incandescent bulbs. It can be dangerous.

No Stone Has Been Left Unturned!

At least I hope none has, maybe a pebble or two, but then that's how we learn, through experiences; sometimes mistakes and even an occasional failure. I know I have, and learned from each. When you begin to use artificial lights for plant growing, you must keep your eyes on your plants for any change in their growing appearance and make immediate adjustments. This same caution goes for growing plants indoors, no matter what the light source is.

All Water Ain't Holy
WATERING

Whenever I start to write about the watering of plants, I always get the feeling that most of you think to yourself, "Water is water. Just fill up a glass and pour it into the pot."

If plants developed feet overnight, they would probably leave most of your homes, in search of the perfect water. Don't laugh! Look at all the fuss you folks make over the perfect beer, wine, or whiskey. Water is not just water—it's the difference between life and slow death to a plant. Most plants that I know can't stand the average tap water from public water systems because of the chlorine, fluoride, and other purifying agents that are used in it.

If you want a real eye-opener, do the same test on your drinking water you do on your swimming pool. You will be amazed.

The Taste Test

People spend millions of dollars each year on commercial bottled water, for both homes and business places. We want it clean, sweet, cold, and pure. Men search far and wide for unpolluted mountain streams, brooks, and natural wells for

DO I GET A FREE PRIZE?

the perfect glass of water and then pay an arm and a leg for it all the way from France. Why not give your plants the same pleasure? Following are the sources of water that your house plants and garden plants would prefer over a glass of tap water:

Air-conditioning water	Open-well water
Barnyard water	Rain water
Bar-rag water	Snow water
Bathwater	Spring water
Carbonated water	Sump pump water
Dehumidifier water	Swamp water
Lake water	Wash water

Quite a list, wouldn't you say? As a matter of fact, I would even say there are a couple of eyebrow raisers on the list. Let's look at the value of each one.

1. ***Air-conditioning water*** This is really a bonus from another comfort source. The moisture that is evaporated from our rooms on hot days runs out of a drain pipe at the bottom, and if collected and used on indoor plants and vegetable garden plants, performs magic

2. ***Barnyard water*** This is also known as "barnyard tea." This is moonshine to the plant world, and a little bit goes a long way.

3. ***Bar-rag water*** Your plants will line up early for a sip of this brew. Flat beer or whiskey mixed with water is an excellent organic base for mixing plant foods. Wash out beer bottles and cans as well as whiskey bottles.

4. ***Bathwater*** This is known as gray water and will help to soften up hard, dry soil, discourage bugs, and control many diseases.

5. ***Carbonated water*** If I am going to use any bottled water, it would be this, for the oxygen it provides as the bubbles burst. It's a great base, along with soap and tea for plant food watering.

6. ***Dehumidifier water*** This is the same as the air-conditioner, with one exception. If you are using calcium chloride bags for this purpose, don't make your plants drink it.

7. **Lake water** If there are no motor boats, septic fields, or industry on its shore, it will be acceptable. Beware of oil slicks on top.

8. **Open-well water** This water differs from deep-well water in that it, as a rule, does not have a heavy iron content and is totally comparable with rain and snow.

9. **Rain water** This one carries a large portion of natural nitrogen as well as a few man-made pollutants that most plants find acceptable. Why not purchase a good-quality oak barrel and place it under a downspout?

10. **Snow water** Melting of snow was a long-time practice by our forefathers and is still used by many of us. Water from snow has the same qualities as rain and both are excellent for washing your complexion, hair, and good linens.

11. **Spring water** I think you are all familiar with this thirst-quencher and its reputation of quality.

12. **Sump pump water** Here is a sleeper to most of you plant growers. This water has been filtered through several feet of soil, and though it loses its original nourishments, it picks up a whole new batch, plus some.

13. **Swamp Water** Rich and organic, sometimes even too rich.

14. **Wash water** Also known as a gray water. If you use a heavy nonchlorinated bleach, use sparingly.

I usually have several of these sources of water about in jugs and use them to vary my plant food concoctions.

Be darn sure that you label your jugs.

Now that you know the sources of good plant water, let's see what we can do with the tap water you have on hand.

No-Fuss Filters

You see TV, newspaper, and magazine ads for expensive attachments to hook on to your faucets to make your drinking water taste better. Well, you can make one just as good by cutting a hole in the top of a one-gallon plastic milk carton, big enough to get your hand through. Leave the top opening in place. Take an ice pick, nail, or knitting needle and poke twelve holes in a 4-inch circle in the center of the bottom. Next, cover the circle with a filter from a coffee maker and cover this with a box or package of charcoal that you buy in a pet store or garden shop. Cover the layer of charcoal with a heavy layer of crushed egg shells and top this off with two layers of marbles or well-boiled small stones.

You now have a superduper water filter. Run the water very slowly into the smaller top opening and allow it to pass through and out the bottom, collecting in a pan or jug for watering your plants.

The Right Time for Everything

I am sure that you have been told many times about the advantages of drinking an 8-ounce glass of water when you first arise each morning. Well, plants get more benefit from

NO-FUSS FILTER

an early morning watering and feeding. As a matter of fact, they should always be watered and fed before 11 A.M.

This allows them to take advantage of the remaining daylight hours to ingest and digest the beneficial elements in the water.

Plants should never be watered and fed just before the temperature and lights are turned down at night. They will have nightmares.

Even Plants Can Get Too Much of a Good Thing

There are a great many factors that go into determining how much and how often a plant should be watered.

The size of the plant, size of the pot, soil mix, time of the year, light source, temperature and humidity range, and the most important, the plant's own requirements, based on its natural habitat. I get so tired of hearing folks tell me that they water their plants once a week or twice a week only because that's what they have been taught.

The best method of determining a plant's water needs are with a water meter (ones with no batteries needed are best). These are available in all plant departments and are reasonably priced.

I use two different ones. One has a long shaft, the other a short set. This is so I can measure the needs in the big plant containers.

Want to Know What the Plants Prefer?

Here is a list of the most popular house plants available to most of you, along with their requirements for water.

ENOUGH IS ENOUGH

WANT TO KNOW WHAT PLANTS PREFER?

WATER REQUIREMENTS

Plant Name	*Watering Requirements*
African Violet	Moderately Moist
Aluminum Plant	Moderately Moist
Areca or Butterfly Palm	Very Moist
Arrowhead Nephthytis	Moderately Moist
Artillery Plant	Moderately Moist
Asparagus Fern (Plume, Plumosa, Spencer)	Moderately Moist
Avocado	Moderately Moist
Baby's Tears, Irish Moss	Moderately Moist
Balfour Aralia	Moderately Moist
Bella Palm	Moderately Moist
Bird's-Nest Fern	Very Moist
Bird's-Nest Sansevieria	Moderately Dry
Bloodleaf Achyranthus	Moderately Moist
Boston Fern	Very Moist
Bromeliads	Moderately Moist
Buddhist Pine	Moderately Moist
Burro's Tail	Moderately Dry
Cactus	Moderately Dry
Caladium	Moderately Moist
Calathea	Moderately Moist
Cape Primrose (False African Violet)	Moderately Moist
Century Plant (American Aloe)	Moderately Dry
Chenille Plant	Moderately Moist
Chinese Evergreen	Moderately Moist
Chinese Holly Grape	Moderately Moist
Climbing Fig	Moderately Moist
Coffee Plant	Moderately Moist
Coleus	Moderately Moist
Copperleaf Plant	Moderately Moist
Coral Berry	Moderately Moist
Corn Plant (a Dracaena)	Moderately Moist
Croton	Moderately Moist
Crown of Thorns	Moderately Dry
Date Palm	Very Moist
Dracaena (Gold Dust, Janet Craig, Warnecki)	Moderately Moist

Plant Name	Watering Requirements
Dragon Tree (a Dracaena)	Moderately Moist
Dumb Cane (Giant, Spotted, Golden)	Moderately Dry
Elephant's-Foot Tree (Ponytail)	Moderately Moist
Emerald Ripple Peperomia	Moderately Dry
English Ivy	Moderately Moist
Euonymus	Moderately Moist
False Aralia (Mock Cannabis)	Moderately Moist
Fan Palm	Very Moist
Fiddle-Leaf Fig	Moderately Moist
Fiddle-Leaf Philodendron (Panduraeformé)	Moderately Moist
Fishtail Palm	Very Moist
Flame Violet	Moderately Moist
Fluffy-Ruffle Fern	Moderately Moist
Gardenia	Moderately Moist
Geranium	Moderately Dry
German Ivy (Parlor Ivy)	Moderately Moist
Giant White Inch Plant	Moderately Dry
Gold Dust Ivy	Moderately Moist
Gold Dust Tree	Moderately Dry
Golden Bird's-Nest Sansevieria	Moderately Dry
Golden Pothos (Devil's Ivy, Hunter's Robe)	Moderately Moist
Golden Trumpet	Moderately Moist
Gold Vein Bloodleaf	Moderately Moist
Grape Ivy	Moderately Moist
Hagenburger's Ivy	Moderately Moist
Hahn's Self-Branching Ivy	Moderately Moist
Hastatum Philodendron	Moderately Moist
Hawaiian Ti	Very Moist
Heart-Leaf Philodendron (Oxycardium)	Moderately Moist
Hibiscus	Moderately Moist
Holly Fern	Moderately Moist
Iron-Cross Begonia	Moderately Moist
Jade Plant	Moderately Dry
Japanese Aralia	Moderately Moist
Japanese Littleleaf Boxwood	Moderately Moist
Joseph's Coat	Moderately Moist

WATER REQUIREMENTS (*Cont.*)

Plant Name	Watering Requirements
Jungle Geranium	Moderately Moist
Kangaroo Ivy	Moderately Moist
Lantana	Moderately Dry
Lipstick Plant	Moderately Moist
Maidenhair Fern	Very Moist
Marble Queen Pothos	Moderately Moist
Medicine Plant (True Aloe)	Moderately Dry
Ming Aralia	Moderately Moist
Moon Valley Pilea	Moderately Moist
Moses-in-the-Bullrushes	Moderately Moist
Narrow-Leaved Pleomele	Moderately Moist
Natal Plum	Moderately Moist
Needlepoint Ivy	Moderately Moist
Norfolk Island Pine	Moderately Moist
Orange Tree	Moderately Dry
Orchids	Moderately Moist
Peace Lily	Very Moist
Piggyback Plant	Moderately Moist
Pineapple	Moderately Moist
Polka-Dot Plant	Moderately Moist
Polynesia	Moderately Moist
Polypody Fern	Moderately Moist
Prayer Plant (Maranta)	Moderately Moist
Purple Heart	Moderately Dry
Purple Waffle Plant	Moderately Moist
Rex Begonia	Moderately Moist
Ribbon Plant (a Dracaena)	Moderately Moist
Rosary Vine	Moderately Dry
Rose of Jericho	Moderately Moist
Rubber Plant	Moderately Moist
Schefflera (Umbrella Tree, Shopping Center Palm)	Moderately Dry
Screw Pine	Moderately Dry
Sensitive Plant	Moderately Moist
Shrimp Plant	Moderately Dry
Silver Lace or Table Fern	Moderately Moist
Silver Tree Panamiga	Moderately Moist

Plant Name	Watering Requirements
Snake Plant (Mother-in-Law's Tongue, Barbership Begonia) (All Sansevieria)	Moderately Dry
Spider Plant	Moderately Moist
Split-Leaf Philodendron	Moderately Moist
Staghorn Fern	Moderately Moist
Strawberry Begonia	Moderately Dry
Striped Inch Plant	Moderately Moist
Succulents (Christmas Cactus, Kalanchoe)	Moderately Dry
Swedish Ivy	Moderately Moist
Sweetheart Ivy	Moderately Moist
Tahitian Bridal Veil	Moderately Dry
Tree Ivy (Aralia Ivy)	Moderately Moist
Tree Philodendron (Selloum)	Moderately Moist
Umbrella Plant	Very Moist
Variegated Balfour Aralia	Moderately Moist
Variegated Mock Orange	Moderately Dry
Variegated Peperomia	Moderately Dry
Variegated Swedish Ivy	Moderately Moist
Variegated Wandering Jew	Moderately Dry
Variegated Wax Ivy	Moderately Moist
Velvet Leaf Kalanchoe	Moderately Dry
Velvet Plant	Moderately Moist
Wandering Jew	Moderately Moist
Watermelon Peperomia	Moderately Dry
Wax Plant	Moderately Dry
Weeping Fig	Moderately Moist
White-Nerved Fittonia	Moderately Moist
White Velvet Tradescantia	Moderately Dry
Yucca (False Agave)	Moderately Dry
Zebra Plant	Moderately Moist

Very moist: Keep wet at all times; Moderately moist: Keep evenly moist; Moderately dry: Let dry out from one watering to the next.

Making Water Wetter

How can you make water wetter? By adding any liquid soap to it, also known as a wetting agent. Always add 10 drops per quart, 1 ounce per gallon, or 1 cup per 10 gallons.

What this does is remove or break through the static barrier that is caused by warm, dry air in our homes. I also want you to add 1 tea bag per quart and three to the gallon. Used bags will be OK. The tannic acid will help the plant's digestive system much as a dish of sherbet, between each course we eat, helps us.

Give Them a Drink, Don't Drown Them

Every one of us has a technique or style in each job we attempt. Some are good, some are bad. When it comes to watering plants, we are usually in a hurry and have very little consideration for the plant's comfort, and in most cases we expect them to chug-a-lug, and they just aren't prepared. First off, their drink must be at room temperature (70°) as cold water gives them cramps. Next, water from the top of the soil and let the water run all the way through.

I CAN'T SWIM, BUT I LOVE THE WATER

BELIEVE IT OR NOT!

One of the worst mistakes you can make is to lightly water plants, often. What this does is give you a false security. You feel the top of the soil and it feels damp, but way down deep in the pot where the roots are, your plants are reliving "Death Valley Days."

After you have finished, return in a half hour and pour off or extract the excess water with an old turkey baster.

Do not let plants sit in a tray of water.

Another way to water is to completely submerge the pot in water and let it sit until the bubbles stop, remove, and drain.

Placing plants in the shower is also a good way, if they aren't too big or heavy. Make sure that the foliage is dry before putting back into the light and make sure the water is 70°.

Plants drink more and eat more when they are in active growth and during warm dry weather, or when the air-conditioning is running full tilt. Air conditioners are not a refrigerator as many people think. Air conditioners draw moisture out of the air, walls, rug, furniture, your skin, and especially the leaves and soil of your plants. Don't be lulled into that false security that your plants don't need watering because the room feels cool.

On the other hand, plants need and drink less when the weather is cool and damp and the days are shorter. You must, however, be cautious, because the type of heat and your temperature preference can change this rule.

Electric and gas heat tend to dry out rooms very fast. Oil and space heaters are not so bad, but they deposit a thin film on foliage that slows up their ability to transpire.

Steam heat is the best for your plants and you.

Wood stoves that are now so popular and fireplaces dry a room, your skin, that cat's fur, and your plant's leaves out quicker than the wink of an eye.

Leave It Up to Your Plants

There are several types of self-watering planters on the market today. They have wicks that are inserted into the soil through the bottom and then an inch or so of the wick sits in a reservoir of water and food below, allowing the plant to help itself. You must make sure that the bottom of the pot does not sit in the water. You can make any pot (plaster or clay) self-watering with a small length of cotton rope. I must advise you that I am not a big fan of this type of watering, unless you are a serious hobbyist or going on vacation.

Now We Have a Drip to Contend With

No, I am not talking about an obnoxious bore, I mean drip irrigation. This is the automatic way greenhouses feed and water large numbers of plants.

A black plastic tube, the size of your thumb, runs down the middle length of a plant bench and is attached to a water and food source. Hundreds of small thin tubes are inserted into the bigger pipe and then these thin tubes are set on top of the soil of each plant. (A small lead weight is attached to each tube to anchor it.)

This system is attached to a timer that automatically turns the water on and off.

There are small drip systems available for home gardeners, but these are impractical indoors, except for those with a greenhouse or a large number of plants close together.

Before we move on, let me again remind you that it is important that you take watering seriously or all your work and money are down the tube.

7

House Plants All Suffer from Anorexia
FEEDING

"What are you feeding your plants with?" I asked the caller on the phone. "Nothing, just water," they replied.

This is the dialogue in seven out of every ten conversations or in correspondence I have with you folks regarding the feeding of house plants. Most of you are so afraid you are going to overfeed that you don't bother to feed at all. Next to overwatering, underfeeding accounts for the most plant deaths, followed by lack of humidity and improper light. Temperature, believe it or not, is seldom the direct cause of the demise of our house plants.

There are plant foods in pill, tablet, capsule, stick, granule, powder, liquid, and gel form. There are fast-acting, slow-acting, time-released, and water-soluble. You apply some plant foods through the leaves, while others prefer soil application. It's no wonder you're confused—and who suffers? Your plants do, and that's a rotten shame.

UNDERSTANDING THE PLANT FOOD MAZE

The three numbers you see on the boxes, bags, cans, cartons, and bottles of plant foods are not the odds on whether

YOUR GUESS IS AS GOOD GOOD AS MINE

your plants will live or die. It is describing to you what the contents contain. The first figure is always nitrogen. Nitrogen stimulates foliage growth. The second or middle number indicates the amount of phosphate available. Phosphate is responsible for the bloom show and root mass. The third and last number is potassium. Potassium ensures strong stems and a resistance to disease. These three are the major nutrients that your plants all need, and depending on what they are best known for (flowers, fruit, berries, nuts, vegetables, or foliage—all-green, variegated, or multicolored), their need (diet) for the quantities of these three will vary. For your further information, but not confusion, you should know that in addition to these three primary nutrients, there are three secondary nutrients that plants prefer: calcium, magnesium, and sulfur. Take a deep breath and relax for a minute. That's a lot to comprehend in one dose.

Back to class. Just as we have a minimum daily requirement (see the listing on the side panel of a cereal box), so plants also need an abundant number of micronutrients. They are: boron, chlorine, copper, manganese, iron, and zinc. So now you understand why when you say to me you're just feeding them with water, I cringe.

To boil it down, plants that are best known for foliage need more nitrogen; while flowering plants order lower amounts of nitrogen and bigger helpings of phosphorus and potassium. For dessert they may order a bit of sulfur, magnesium, or calcium, and as an after-dinner drink, iron and water will round out the meal.

The objective of this book is to make house plant care fun, fast, and easy. If you understand the whys, hows, whens, and what-withs, it will accomplish my goal.

Some Plants Are Health-Food Nuts

There are two different types of plant food: natural, known as organic, and manufactured, described as chemical. There are plant owners who wouldn't think of using the latter, and vice versa. Personally, I am a mix-and-match plant food user. For my cactus, succulents, orchids, geraniums, mums,

IT TAKES ALL KINDS

and begonias I would never think of using anything but Super K-Gro Fish Emulsion (5-1-1), an organic.

Liquid fish plant foods are rich in most of the needs for these and all other plants, and can be purchased in any garden department. This type of food does have one drawback, as do most of the other organic plant foods that are either manure base, decomposing vegetation, processed sewage, or seaweed—they stink!

Other Plants Don't Much Care What the Source Is

Chemical plant foods, as a rule, are cleaner and seldom have any odor; therefore, more folks use them. Chemical plant foods are also faster acting, thus more dangerous to the plants, and must be used sparingly. I prefer a plant food in either a liquid form or water-soluble powder. I use Super K-Gro Water Soluble Plant Food (15-30-15) for nearly all of my other green plants, and Plantabbs Water Soluble African Violet Food (11-15-20) for most all of my blooming house plants and variegated or multicolored foliage.

BOTTOMS UP, BABY

In the past three days, my wife, Ilene, and I have gone out to eat at a different one of our regular restaurants each day. We both had the same complaint. We were bored with the same old menu. If they could talk, your plants (indoor and out) would complain about the same thing with their day-in and day-out menu. I have a solution; as a matter of fact, a couple of different solutions (some of my critics call them concoctions) that I serve up to my plants as a variation to their regular menu from time to time. Most of you, who have known me through my books, television, and radio, know the first.

GRANDMA PUTT'S HOMEMADE PLANT FOOD

To a gallon of good water (rain, well, river, pond, melted snow, air conditioner, or dehumidifer) you add the following:

1 tbs. household ammonia	the heads (unburned) of a book of matches
1 tbs. baking powder	
1 tbs. saltpeter	1 rusty nail
2 tbs. Epsom salts	2 tbs. liquid soap

Mix 1 cup of this plant food with another gallon of good water and use in place of your regular plant food, once or twice a month, during your plants' growing period. I also use this mixture as a sort of "chicken soup" in place of a regular plant food until I can figure out what is ailing a plant.

The second homemade plant food is made as follows:

ORGANIC VEGETABLE PUNCH

Into a blender place the following ingredients:

Carrot tops, peels, and pieces, potato peels (raw), lettuce, cabbage, spinach, beans, onions, green beans, and banana peels	1 cup of good water
	1 cup dissolved gelatin powder
	2 bottles of beer

I HAVEN'T DECIDED YET

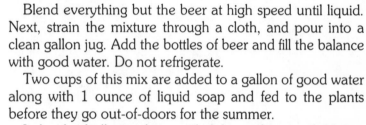

Blend everything but the beer at high speed until liquid. Next, strain the mixture through a cloth, and pour into a clean gallon jug. Add the bottles of beer and fill the balance with good water. Do not refrigerate.

Two cups of this mix are added to a gallon of good water along with 1 ounce of liquid soap and fed to the plants before they go out-of-doors for the summer.

I also feed all my plants with fish emulsion and African violet food once or twice a year. Fish just after they go outdoors and violet food for the last meal before coming indoors. I also place a Super K-Gro Plant Stick in each pot before it comes indoors in the fall so the plants have something to nibble on during the winter (one a season is all I use).

Key to Feeding Schedule

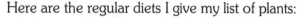

Here are the regular diets I give my list of plants:

1. Super K-Gro Water Soluble (15-30-15);
2. Plantabbs Violet Food (11-15-20);
3. Fish emulsion (5-1-1);
4. Super K-Gro Plant Sticks (13-4-5);
5. Super K-Gro Liquid Plant Food (10-10-5).

I'M NOT PARTICULAR

FEEDING SCHEDULE

Plant Name	Foods
African Violet	2,3
Aluminum Plant	2
Areca or Butterfly Palm	1,3,5
Arrowhead Nephthytis	1,5
Artillery Plant	1,3,5
Asparagus Fern (Plume, Plumosa, Spencer)	1,3,5
Avocado	1,3
Baby's Tears, Irish Moss	3
Balfour Aralia	1,5
Bella Palm	1,3
Bird's-Nest Fern	3
Bird's Nest Sansevieria	1,2,3,5
Bloodleaf Achyranthus	2,3
Boston Fern	1,5,3
Bromeliads	3
Buddhist Pine	1,5
Burro's Tail	3
Cactus	3
Caladium	2,3
Calathea	2
Cape Primrose (False African Violet)	2
Century Plant (American Aloe)	3
Chenille Plant	2,3
Chinese Evergreens	5
Chinese Holly Grape	1,5
Climbing Fig	1,5
Coffee Plant	2,3
Coleus	2
Copperleaf Plant	2
Coral Berry	2,5
Corn Plant (a Dracaena)	1,5
Croton	2
Crown of Thorns	2
Date Palm	1,3,5
Dracaena (Gold Dust, Janet Craig, Warnecki)	1,5
Dragon Tree (a Dracaena)	2,3
Dumb Cane (Giant, Spotted, Golden)	1,3,5
Elephant's-Foot Tree (Ponytail)	2,3

Plant Name	Foods
Emerald Ripple Peperomia	2,3
English Ivy	1,5
Euonymus	1,5
False Aralia (Mock Cannabis)	1,5
Fan Palm	1,3,5
Fiddle-Leaf Fig	1,5
Fiddle-Leaf Philodendron	1,5
Fishtail Palm	1,5,3
Flame Violet	2,3
Fluffy-Ruffle Fern	1,3,5
Gardenia	2,3
Geranium	3
German Ivy (Parlor Ivy)	1,2
Giant White Inch Plant	1,5
Gold Dust Ivy	1,5
Gold Dust Tree	2
Golden Bird's-Nest Sansevieria	1,2,3,5
Golden Pothos (Devil's Ivy, Hunter's Robe)	1,2
Golden Trumpet	2
Gold Vein Bloodleaf	2,3
Grape Ivy	1,5
Hagenburger's Ivy	1,5
Hahn's Self-Branching Ivy	1,5
Hastatum Philodendron	1,5
Hawaiian Ti	2,3
Heart-Leaf Philodendron (oxycardium)	1,5
Hibiscus	3,5
Holly Fern	1,3
Iron-Cross Begonia	2,3
Jade Plant	3
Japanese Aralia	1,5
Japanese Littleleaf Boxwood	1,2
Joseph's Coat	2
Jungle Geranium	2
Kangaroo Ivy	1,5
Lantana	1,5
Lipstick Plant	2
Maidenhair Fern	1,5
Marble Queen Pothos	1,2
Medicine Plant (True Aloe)	3

Plant Name	Foods
Ming Aralia	1,5
Moon Valley Pilea	2,3
Moses-in-the-Bullrushes	2
Narrow-Leaved Pleomele	1,5
Natal Plum	2,3
Needlepoint Ivy	1,5
Norfolk Island Pine	1,5
Orange Tree	2
Orchids	3
Peace Lily	1,5
Piggyback Plant	1,5
Pineapple	3
Polka-Dot Plant	2,3
Polynesia	2,3
Polypody Fern	1,3
Prayer Plant (Maranta)	2
Purple Heart	2,3
Purple Waffle Plant	2
Rex Begonia	2,3
Ribbon Plant (a Dracaena)	2,3
Rosary Vine	2,3
Rose of Jericho	2,3
Rubber Plant	1,5
Schefflera (Umbrella Tree, Shopping Center Palm)	1,2,3,5
Screw Pine	1,5
Sensitive Plant	2,5
Shrimp Plant	2
Silver Lace or Table Fern	1,3
Silver Tree Panamiga	2,3
Snake Plant, Mother-in-Law's Tongue, Barbershop Begonia (All Sansevieria)	1,2,3,5
Spider Plant	1,5
Split-Leaf Philodendron	1,5
Staghorn Fern	1,3,5
Strawberry Begonia	2,3
Striped Inch Plant	2,3
Succulents (Christmas Cactus, Kalanchoe)	3

Plant Name	Foods
Swedish Ivy	3,5
Sweetheart Ivy	1,5
Tahitian Bridal Veil	2,3
Tree Ivy (Aralia Ivy)	1,2
Tree Philodendron (Selloum)	1,5
Umbrella Plant	1,5
Variegated Balfour Aralia	2
Variegated Mock Orange	2
Variegated Peperomia	2,3
Variegated Swedish Ivy	3,5
Variegated Wandering Jew	2,5
Variegated Wax Ivy	2,3
Velvet Leaf Kalanchoe	2
Velvet Plant	2
Wandering Jew	1,3,5
Watermelon Peperomia	2,3
Wax Plant	2,3
Weeping Fig	1,5
White-Nerved Fittonia	2,3
White Velvet Tradescantia	2,3
Yucca (False Agave)	1,3
Zebra Plant	2,3

Plant Baby Food? You've Got to Be Kidding!

No, I am not kidding! It is known as vitamin B root stimulator from Dexol and is found in most garden shops. It is used when you transplant or pot new seedlings to minimize transplant or new-plant shock. New or old plants should be held in a 65°, dark holding area after they are fed with this solution only. Do not feed for at least 10 days afterward.

Never Feed After 11 A.M.— Breakfast or Brunch Only

That's it folks! Plants only eat during daylight hours and should never be allowed to eat in bed. When the lights are

UMM-UMM-GOOD!

turned down or off and the heat lowered for the evening, plants' ingestion and digestion systems slow down. Late feeding opens up the possibility of fertilizer burn.

Don't Just Feed Your Plants

What I am telling you is that plants should be fed and watered simultaneously. Every time you water your plants, you must feed them just as it is done in the greenhouse. In most professional greenhouses you will notice that the water coming out of the hose is generally dark blue. This color indicates fertilizer is in the water. Plants can ingest and digest only small amounts of food at one time, depending on whether they are in production or at rest.

When watering and feeding your plants, always add 10 drops of any liquid soap per quart, 1 ounce to the gallon or 1 cup to each 10 gallons. What the soap does is allow better penetration into the soil and roots. If the ends of the leaves suddenly turn brown, remove the fertilizer and only water with the soapy water. Plants should never be fed when the soil is dry.

THANKS! I NEEDED THAT

Can Plants Really Eat Through Their Skin?

This is referred to as foliar feeding and many a plant food makes this claim, but, in fact, very little food value gets into the plant's blood stream from manufactured plant foods. There is one exception and that is by spraying the foliage with a warm soapy solution of ordinary tea water with household ammonia. Add 10 drops of soap and ammonia to a quart of warm weak tea and mist spray every three days. The reason your plants can accept this is that the soap opens up the pores and the ammonia gas passes through. Try this for a couple of poor looking plants for a couple of weeks and watch the difference.

A Shot and a Beer Never Hurt a Plant

I am always asked about feeding my plants with beer and whiskey. If you're wondering if I really do, the answer is yes. From time to time, if there are no parties with leftover drinks (no sweet ones) or beer bottles and cans to rinse out, I will simply add a can of beer or shot of bourbon, scotch, vodka, or gin to a gallon of room temperature water with an ounce of soap and let it set for half a day or so, and then add my plant food and feed. If I catch a plant wobbling, I cut off its drinks. What the yeast in the booze seems to do is rejuvenate the old soil in the pot.

Getting Hot Under the Collar Just Makes People and Plants Old Quicker

TEMPERATURE, HUMIDITY, AIR CIRCULATION, AND FRESH AIR

THE NEAR-PERFECT COMFORT ZONE

If you and your plants are to be healthy, happy, and comfortable, and if your furniture, floor, and wall coverings are to last any length of time, you must have a well-controlled and balanced combination of four things inside your home: temperature, humidity, air circulation, and a fresh-air source.

Most folks only consider setting the thermostat on the wall; up in the morning, down at night, and that's it. The floor and door squeaks because of lack of humidity (moisture) in the air. You wake up with dry skin, your lungs feel like you slept through a sand storm, and your eyes feel like you might have peeked at it—all because of lack of humidity (moisture).

Are you getting the picture? Or, do I have to hit you with a rain storm? Humidity—relative humidity—is the invisible water vapor in the air, and without the proper amount combined with the temperature, most everything is uncomfortable, especially the plants that you have invited to live in

I'M TOO OLD FOR THIS

your home or place of work. With you and me, dry heat draws the moisture out of our skin and bodies. To replenish this loss, we simply go to the faucet for a drink, and thus we avoid dehydration. Pets can do the same as you and I. Plants can't!

If plants could walk, they would—probably right out of your home. Most plants must be given a 40% to 60% humidity range, if they are to have even half a chance to survive in our homes.

Be a Rainmaker

I try real hard to look for ways to help you get more enjoyment out of home gardening, both indoors and out. Therefore, I am always looking for good, simple information in my research for the exact amount of humidity the different plants like. I went to a noted authority on greenhouse growing to help me. His answer: "There is very little humidity data for most kinds of plants, and unless you have been to the natural habitat of most of your plants, you will have to play it by ear!" This was a lousy answer, so I went to a man who has been all over the world collecting plants, Robert Vincent Sims, who taught us about interior designing with the proper plants.

Vince assures me that I am not wrong when I tell you that in most cases (9 out of 10), you can grow just about all of the plants, in your homes, that are presented for sale in the plant sections of stores. I know what you are thinking: African Violets like 75% humidity, while cactus want 30%. Both of these plants will adapt to a range of 50% to 55%.

You can and should pinpoint humidity for different plants, and this can be done with an investment of under $10 for a cool-water vaporizer, used for children's rooms. A room humidifier that you fill with water or a humidifier that adapts to your present furnace are the mechanical ways of providing humidity.

Pebble beds kept damp under your plants, wet sponges in cake pans in front of hot-air registers, and aquariums all add to the relative humidity. An excellent investment is a couple of inexpensive hygrometers (meters that measure the relative humidity in your home), which can be purchased in most hardware and plant departments.

Things Are Heatin' Up

I said that we must have a proper mix of four elements for the perfect physical environment. Temperature is next.

NO, YOU DON'T HAVE TO WEAR FEATHERS AND DANCE

I'M ROASTING!

KEEP 'EM HAPPY

It's true that you can use any source of heat to control temperature; however, different heat and fuel sources give you different qualities of heat. In most homes today, we find forced air powered by gas (natural or bottled). This is an extremely dry source of heat and must have a good humidity source attached to it. New condos and apartments are electric-baseboard heated, which makes it necessary to add a good source of humidity.

Electric heat is a more level and constant heat and does not dry quite as quickly. Steam heat is a very good source of heat, and it puts a little moisture into the room's air, but you will again have to supplement the humidity.

Wood stoves and fireplaces, even though energy conserving, tend to dry out everything—person, pet, or plant—in sight and beyond. You must have an obvious source of moisture in conjunction with wood or coal.

Space heaters powered by fuel oils are not my favorite, unless they are the type that does not let the excess fumes into the room; otherwise, they pollute the air and clog up plants' growing apparatus.

Take a Room's Temperature

I have both an indoor and outdoor thermometer (none was more than $5) in the four plant rooms and as I said before, a hygrometer in each room helps to keep my plant crowd comfortable. I also have a maximum-minimum thermometer that I from time to time use to find special spots in a room for special pots. You must remember! You cannot keep changing the temperature of a growing room every few hours; your plants will soon complain.

A Gentle Breeze, Not a Gale

We have covered two of the four necessities for the near-perfect comfort zone. This third factor is nearly ignored totally, although it is really needed for our plants' comfort in the winter when the heat is on full blast.

In the summer, we think of our own comfort and hunt for or manufacture our own breeze. You got it! Air circulation is a must for good, healthy people or plants.

Stale, stagnant, greasy, dusty, smoke-laden, dry, hot air can do more harm to your skin, hair, eyes, nose, and respiratory system than you would believe. Moving the air down and around will keep the humidity on the move and all of us a little bit happier.

SWING AND SWAY THE PLANT'S WAY

Fan Out

This is not a baseball term but a good old-fashioned growing hint. Turn on the summer oscillating fan or overhead ceiling fan and get the air on the move. Set the fan either up on top of a cabinet or bookshelf, or aim the floor fan up.

Do you know that in addition to improved comfort, you will reduce your heating bill because you will reduce the heat loss?

Cool It, Friend!

Even in the winter months, in the greenhouse, we bring cool, outside air into the slipstream plastic tunnels that run the full length of the 100-foot building, mix it with the hot air from the blower, and force it into the interior. This is fresh, clean air, a real necessity.

You can do the same by closing the door of an unused

IT'S C-C-C-C-C-OLD IN HERE

bedroom, turning off the heat, and opening the window. The cold, fresh air will be taken in through the cold-air return to the furnace, mixed, heated, and forced into the rooms where the humidity is being added to the temperature and moved about by the fan. You now have the perfect blend for a comfortable comfort zone.

A PLANT'S TASTE IN HUMIDITY AND TEMPERATURE

Plant Name	Humidity	Temperature
Aluminum Plant	Medium	60°—85°
Arabian Coffee	Medium	60°—85°
Areca Palm	Low	60°—85°
Arrowhead Nephthytis	Low	60°—85°
Artillery Plant	Medium	60°—85°
Baby Doll Dracaena	Medium	60°—85°
Baby's Tears	High	55°—70°
Balfour Aralia	Medium	60°—85°
Bella Palm	Low	60°—85°
Bird's-Nest Fern	Medium	55°—70°
Bird's-Nest Sensevieria	Low	55°—70°
Bloodleaf Achyranthus	Medium	55°—70°
Boston Fern	Medium	55°—70°
Bromeliads	Medium	60°—80°
Buddhist Pine	Low	40°—65°
Burro's Tail	Low	55°—70°
Cactus	Low	65°—85°
Caladium	Medium	60°—85°
Calamondin	Low	55°—70°
Calathea	Medium	60°—85°
Candle Plant	Medium	60°—80°
Cape Primrose	Low	40°—65°
Century Plant	Low	55°—70°
Chenille Plant	Low	60°—85°
Chinese Evergreen	Medium	60°—85°
Chinese Holly Grape	Medium	55°—70°

A PLANT'S TASTE IN HUMIDITY AND TEMPERATURE
(Cont.)

Plant Name	Humidity	Temperature
Cluster Fishtail Palm	Low	60°—85°
Coral Berry	Medium	55°—85°
Corn Plant	Medium	60°—85°
Creeping Fig	Medium	60°—85°
Crown of Thorns	Low	60°—80°
Dragon Tree	Medium	60°—85°
Dumb Cane	Medium	60°—85°
Elephant's-Foot Tree	Low	55°—70°
Emerald Ripple Peperomia	Medium	60°—85°
English Ivy	Medium	40°—65°
Euonymus	Medium	40°—65°
Fan Palm	Low	55°—70°
False Agave	Medium	55°—70°
Fiddle-Leaf Fig	Medium	60°—85°
Fiddle-Leaf Philodendron	Medium	60°—85°
Flame-of-the-Woods	Medium	65°—85°
Flame Violet	Medium	60°—85°
Fluffy Ruffle Fern	Medium	55°—70°
Giant White Inch Plant	Medium	55°—70°
Gold Dust Dracaena	Medium	60°—85°
Gold Dust Ivy	Low	40°—65°
Gold Dust Tree	Medium	40°—65°
Golden Bird's-Nest Sansevieria	Low	65°—85°
Golden Dieffenbachia	Medium	60°—85°
Golden Pothos	Medium	60°—85°
Golden Trumpet	Medium	60°—85°
Giant Dumb Cane	Medium	60°—85°
Grape Ivy	Medium	60°—80°
Hahn's Self-Branching Ivy	Low	40°—65°
Hastatum Philodendron	Medium	60°—85°
Heart-Leaf Philodendron	Medium	60°—85°
Iron-Cross Begonia	Medium	60°—85°
Jade Plant	Low	55°—70°

Plant Name	Humidity	Temperature
Janet Craig Dracaena	Medium	60°—85°
Japanese Aralia	Medium	40°—65°
Japanese Littleleaf Boxwood	Medium	40°—65°
Kangaroo Ivy	Medium	60°—80°
Lipstick Plant	High	60°—85°
Maidenhair Fern	Medium	60°—85°
Maranta	Medium	60°—85°
Marble Queen Pothos	Medium	60°—85°
Medicine Plant	Low	55°—70°
Ming Aralia	Medium	60°—85°
Moon Valley Pilea	Medium	60°—85°
Moses-in-the-Bullrushes	Low	55°—70°
Narrow-Leaved Pleomele	Low	60°—85°
Natal Plum	Medium	55°—70°
Needlepoint Ivy	Low	40°—65°
Norfolk Island Pine	Medium	55°—70°
Parlor Ivy	Medium	60°—85°
Peace Lily	Medium	60°—85°
Piggyback Plant	Medium	60°—85°
Pigmy Date Palm	Low	60°—85°
Pineapple	High	60°—85°
Plumosa Fern	Medium	55°—70°
Polka-Dot Plant	Medium	60°—85°
Polynesia	Medium	60°—85°
Polypody Fern	Medium	55°—70°
Purple Heart	Medium	60°—80°
Purple Waffle Plant	Medium	60°—85°
Rex Begonia	Medium	60°—85°
Ribbon Plant	Medium	60°—85°
Rockford Holly Fern	Medium	55°—70°
Rose of Jericho	Medium	40°—65°
Rubber Plant	Medium	60°—85°
Schefflera	Medium	60°—85°
Screw Pine	Medium	60°—85°
Sensitive Plant	Medium	60°—85°

A PLANT'S TASTE IN HUMIDITY AND TEMPERATURE
(Cont.)

Plant Name	Humidity	Temperature
Shrimp Plant	Medium	55°—70°
Silver Tree Panamiga	Medium	60°—85°
Snake Plant	Low	60°—85°
Spider Aralia	Medium	60°—85°
Spider Plant	Medium	55°—70°
Split-Leaf Philodendron	Medium	60°—85°
Spotted Dumb Cane	Medium	60°—85°
Sprenger Asparagus	Medium	55°—70°
Staghorn Fern	Medium	60°—80°
Strawberry Begonia	Medium	40°—65°
String-of-Hearts	Medium	55°—70°
Striped Inch Plant	Medium	55°—70°
Succulents	Low	65°—85°
Swedish Ivy	Medium	60°—80°
Sweetheart Ivy	Medium	40°—65°
Tahitian Bridal Veil	Medium	55°—70°
Trailing Velvet Plant	Medium	60°—85°
Tricolor Dragon Tree	Medium	60°—85°
Tree Ivy	Medium	40°—65°
Tree Philodendron	Medium	60°—85°
Umbrella Plant	Medium	55°—70°
Variegated Balfour Aralia	Medium	60°—85°
Variegated Mock Orange	Medium	55°—70°
Variegated Peperomia	Medium	60°—85°
Variegated Rubber Tree	Medium	60°—85°
Variegated Wandering Jew	Medium	55°—70°
Variegated Wax Ivy	Medium	60°—80°
Velvet Leaf Kalanchoe	Medium	55°—70°
Velvet Plant	Medium	60°—85°
Victoria Table Fern	Medium	60°—80°
Warnecki Dracaena	Medium	60°—85°
Watermelon Peperomia	Medium	60°—85°
Wax Plant	Medium	55°—70°

Plant Name	Humidity	Temperature
Weeping Fig	Medium	60°—85°
White Velvet Tradescantia	Medium	55°—70°
Zebra Plant	Low	60°—85°

Bah, Humbug to Dehumidifiers and Air Conditioners!

When a plant comes into your home and sees either of the above, it cringes.

Neither an air conditioner nor a dehumidifier cause a plant a direct injury: it's the indirect action that gets them.

Both of these items remove moisture from the air (humidity), and while they are at it, they get the moisture from the tissue of the plants as well.

For some reason, folks seem to think of an air conditioner as a unit that refrigerates the *air;* it merely removes the moisture and returns it to the room.

Wilt Pruf Your House Plants

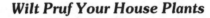

This product does just what its name implies. It keeps your nonflowering house plants from wilting by coating the foliage with a clear, flexible, transparent film that holds the moisture in the foliage longer while reducing water loss.

Wilt Pruf is a must when you are going on vacation and the usual watering schedule will be interrupted. Wilt Pruf is safe, organic, and biodegradable. If you use this material, half your plant problems will go away.

IT'S PLANT BODY LOTION

No Plant Wants to Live in a Bughouse

INSECT IDENTIFICATION AND CONTROL

No one on this earth can grow plants, indoors or out, without having to go a couple of rounds with an insect or two.

When insects invade our green scene and attack our poor defenseless plant pots, it's our job to protect them. How you spray and dust, dip, gas, and swat does make a lot of difference in how the battle ends. If you use the wrong ammunition in the wrong weapons, all you probably do at the time is win the little battles, but you end up losing the war.

Choose Your Weapon

Aerosol Sprays There are sprays on the market that use a propellant (type of gas that's safe) that is mixed in with the chemical control. There are other types that use a pressure filling bag that forces the chemical out when the valve is pushed. Both of these are expendable after use.

Aggravants These are usually very sharp materials applied to the surface of the soil or mixed in it, or dehydrants and expandants. Swimming pool powder, ashes, and soot round out this group, and are used against snails, slugs, and worms.

Baits These are tasty tidbits placed on the soil surface to attract such insects as slugs and snails.

Compression Sprayers These are reusable sprayers of metal or plastic. You simply mix the chemical with water in the base, screw on the pump top and nozzle, then hand-pump air into the base container of chemical mix. Pull the trigger and you release the spray.

Dipping Here is a method I often recommend and describe on TV and radio for smaller plants I can handle. Using heavy cardboard, I first make several disks the size of the inside circumference of my containers. I make a hole in the center to allow for the stem, then cut a slot from the outside edge of the center of the hole so I can slip the disk around the plant. I use them to hold the soil in when I tip the plant upside down into a bucket of warm chemical solution. Always use longsleeved shirts and plastic throwaway gloves when using chemicals.

Drenching This method is to apply the chemical in liquid form to the soil only, not the foliage.

Drinking This is a variation of the drenching method, which is used for potted plants you cannot lift. Submerge the pot, soil and all, into the chemical mix until the bubbles stop. Remove the plant and let drain well.

DRAW!!

Dusters These are either a rubber-ball-type base with a plastic stem and nozzle or a prefilled plastic container whose sides you squeeze to make the dust come out.

Fumigation This method of insect control is done with gas or fumes and, when possible to use safely, really works. One method is to eradicate most soil insects from your potting mix by treating it out-of-doors with a material so designed and indoors with a recommended method (such as pest strips).

Systemics As a rule, these have been used only professionally in the past, but now several consumer product companies have made them available for home use. The chemicals are applied to the soil surface and then taken up by the plant through the roots when the plant is watered. Now the entire plant is poison to the bugs. But never use on edible food plants.

The above ten insect weapons are the handiest and most economical available to you today.

You Don't Have to Be a Thrill Killer to Win the Bug War!

You are now aware of the types of applicators available for house plant care and protection. Now let's look at the ammunition available to get the job done.

Right here and now I want to go on record as having advised you that no matter what else you wish to accomplish with your plants, *SAFETY IS ALWAYS FIRST!* Don't take chances with your or anyone else's health or safety.

- Always wear plastic throwaway gloves.
- Wear longsleeved shirts.
- Cover your eyes and nose, no matter how dumb you may look.
- Spray, dust, dunk, drench, and dip in a well-ventilated room—without spectators.
- When plants can't be treated in a safe area, cover them with a paper or plastic bag, tear or cut a hole to spray through, and tape shut when done. Or, use a closed cardboard box.

WHO SAID IT'S A FRIENDLY GAME

- Do not buy more chemicals than you need for the battle.
- Wash your hands, face, and arms with Ivory bar soap after working with chemicals.
- Wash your clothes before you wear them again. We use old-fashioned Fels' Naptha for decontamination.

In my business we are always playing it safe because we have friends that are sorry that they weren't safety conscious with plant chemicals. Insecticides and pesticides don't pollute. People pollute through misuse and abuse. Don't be one of them.

Not-So-Secret Weapons

Here are 16 recommended house plant insect controls available to you:

Bacillus Thuringiensis Berliner (Thuricide) The name alone is enough to scare the heck out of most worms and caterpillar pests. It is extremely safe for home use. It controls by paralyzing the stomach of the insect.

Baits These are chemicals that are mixed with an attractant that constitutes a natural food for these insects. There are baits on the market for snails, slugs, sow bugs, cutworms, earwigs, fleas, and ants. As a rule, a chemical called Mesurol is used in slug and snail bait, while Sevin is mixed for the other listed insects.

Chewing Tobacco Juice This is another insect aggravator. When sprayed with liquid soap or as an addition to regular chemicals, it makes bugs wish they hadn't been born.

Di-Syston A systemic insecticide for house plants as well as outdoor plants. This can be applied to the soil in the pots of house plants. It is odorless, dustless, and needs no mixing when in granular form. Di-Syston at a ratio of 2% can protect your plants from aphids, thrips, leafhoppers, whiteflies, mealybugs, spider mites, and more, for up to 6 weeks.

Dursban A drench-and-dunk control for soil insects both before and after you use potting soil.

USE PROVEN WINNERS

Insecticidal Soaps Here is a perfect example of an old wives' tale: Always throw your wash and dishwater out on the shrubs and roses and dip your house plants into warm, soapy water because this discourages the insects. This old wives' tale, in the form of insecticidal soap, is now considered a scientific breakthrough. It costs more, but gets the same result. Insecticidal soap effectively controls whiteflies, aphids, scale, mealybugs, spittlebugs, thrips, wooley aphids, psyllids, crickets, earwigs, and grasshoppers.

Kelthane You can use Kelthane to control over 25 different species of mite, red spider being the most common indoors. It kills on contact and lasts for a long time, but will not harm the good bugs.

Malathion This quickly kills scale, aphids, spider mites, thrips, and dozens of other insects indoors and out. Malathion is one of the oldest and most reliable insecticides, is extremely effective, and won't harm the environment. On bugs it's another story. It attacks the nervous system in three ways: (1) if the chemical touches them, (2) if they walk on it, or (3) if they eat a leaf with it on.

Methoprene This is an insect growth regulator that is environmentally sound. This control blocks the area in the bug's brain that tells it to move on to the next stage of growth. Affects whiteflies, mealybugs, aphids, mites, and more.

Nicotine Alkaloid Orchids, ferns, begonias, and fuchsias love this relief. Nicotine stops insects when they breathe it. Aphids, thrips, spider mites, orchid scale, and fungus gnats go bye-bye.

Pentac Here is another control that interrupts the life cycle of the insect. It is an ovicide, destroying the metabolism, and the direct kill of the unborn results in the death of the adult. Aphids, mealybugs, whiteflies and mites are affected, as are other insects.

Piperonyl Butoxide Another of the organic insect controls for control of insects both indoors and out. Aphids, flea beetles, whiteflies, and leafhoppers are well controlled by it.

Resmethrin (Synthetic Pyrethrine) If the word gets out to insects that you are defending with this material, they won't fly anywhere near. Resmethrin has quick knockdown power on more than 24 house plant insects. Whitefly, mealybugs, mites, and aphids are on the list.

Sevin This insect control comes as both dust and a liquid. I prefer the specifically formulated liquid for contol of aphids, worms, scale, beetles, leaf rollers, leafhoppers, mealybugs, and psyllids.

Tetramethrine You African violet growers will appreciate this bug weapon for combating on contact whiteflies, mealybugs, aphids, and spider mites.

Vapona I guess you would refer to this as a gas. You know it as a no-pest strip. I use these strips as recommended around the house, as well as placing them in among infested plants. Cover with a plastic bag or sheet. This method gets most of the flyers.

There are many more chemicals available at your plant department, and many of those listed above control more bugs than are indicated. However, these are the ones I have seen them control.

Before you turn to the use of an insecticide, miteside, or pesticide, however, try the good cultural practice of washing with soap and water. If that fails, use the proper controls as recommended, safely. The chemical controls are available in many brand names at your garden centers, often times as part of a combination spray, so read the labels.

Supercharge Your Insect Control

I have found that spraying the foliage of a plant (both top and bottom) with 10 drops of liquid dish soap per quart of warm tea water, and then waiting 10 to 20 minutes before applying the chemical recommended, makes it work quicker and more effectively.

Caution! You must read all labels before you use a chemical to make sure that the manufacturer does not warn against its use on certain plants.

WHO DO YOU CALL?

THE INSECT ENEMY AND THE PROPER AMMUNITION

Insects / Chemical Controls	Ants	Aphids	Caterpillars	Centipedes	Cockroaches	Crickets	Cutworms	Earthworms	Earwigs	Leaf Miners	Leaf Rollers	Mealybugs	Millipedes	Mites	Nematodes	Red Spiders	Scale	Slug and Snail	Sow Bugs	Springtails	Thrips	Whitefly
Bacillus Thuringiensis			✓																			
Baits	✓				✓													✓				
Di-Syston		✓									✓	✓		✓		✓						✓
Dursban	✓				✓	✓		✓	✓					✓						✓	✓	✓
Insecticidal Soap					✓				✓					✓		✓	✓				✓	✓
Kelthane														✓		✓						
Malathion		✓						✓						✓		✓					✓	
Methoprene		✓										✓		✓		✓						✓
Nicotine		✓								✓		✓	✓	✓							✓	✓
Pentac		✓										✓		✓		✓						✓
Piperonyl		✓																				✓
Resmethrine	✓										✓	✓	✓	✓		✓					✓	✓
Sevin		✓									✓	✓		✓					✓			
Tetramethrine		✓										✓		✓		✓						✓
Tobacco		✓												✓		✓	✓				✓	
Vapam	✓			✓			✓	✓	✓					✓	✓					✓	✓	
Vapona		✓							✓	✓	✓			✓		✓					✓	✓

Here Comes the Enemy

There are several million species of insects, it is true, and science is naming more all of the time, but you only need to worry about a few around your home and plants:

Ants I really never gave much thought to ants as a pest on or around house plants, until I found a colony of carpenter ants housed in the planter with my 6-foot schefflera. Ants, as a rule, do no damage to plants, but they carry mealybugs and aphids from plant to plant. The latter insects will thus produce more of the sweet honey dew as they suck the life out of your plants, and the ants love this sweet sticky material.

Aphids Masses of small, green insects covering new young buds and leaf terminals are a sure sign of aphids. Aphids are also honey-dew-makers and sap-suckers that stunt growth and make your plants look like they have the flu.

Caterpillars These fuzzy little worms may be cute to children, but not to plant growers. They have an appetite that would put a horse to shame and they eat everything but the pot. You usually find caterpillars in the summer and fall when you first bring plants indoors.

Cockroaches Most folks find it hard to believe that roaches bother house plants. Cockroaches are usually thought of as around food. They eat leaves on plants, and hide and dine in terrariums.

Crickets If a cricket moves into one of your planters, you will know it. It will keep you awake worrying about whether it is going to eat your carpet, sweaters, cereal, fruit in the bowl on the kitchen table, and will (if they find a plant they like) eat up a plant in nothing flat.

Cutworms If a cutworm moves in on your plant collection, you will know it because a few stalks will be lying there, cut off at the soil. Keep alert.

Earthworms These guys are just klutzes. They undermine the soil in the pots and clog the drainage holes. In some cases, they make a big enough mess out of a pot of soil to cause the roots to dry out. If you submerge the pot in warm water and let it set for 10 or 15 minutes, Willy the worm will come up for air and you can put him in the compost pile where he belongs.

Earwigs I can tell you that earwigs really do exist. A lot of you may never see most of these insects we talk about, but it's a good idea if you can recognize them. Earwigs have pinchers in the tail and each foot. They pinch dozens and dozens of holes through leaves overnight. You can find them in dark, dry spots—like my bed when I lived in England.

Fungus Gnats It's the babies that do the damage. On top of that, they are ugly. The little brown maggots are always hungry and eat root tissue, so the plant wilts or catches some other darn disease, like root rot.

Leaf Miners Foliage appears to be blistered and transparent when the sow fly lays her eggs and the babies begin to tunnel between the layers of leaves. Indoors it's usually mums and azaleas that get staked out by the leaf miners.

Leaf Rollers These small worms or caterpillars roll one or more leaves around it for protection and then proceed to eat its protection up. If you see leaves curled up, unroll them and look for yourself.

Mealybugs When this little critter is around, you know it from the cottonlike cover it has over it on stems and under the leaves. This is the most common of the house plant insects and, as a rule, wins out over most of you because you give up too easily.

Millipedes Boy, these guys are a real pain in the pot to many a house plant gardener. Millipedes are found around some compost piles that are not kept fresh and turned. They eat roots and screw up young seedlings. It is true that the millipedes eat some insects, but the damage they do doesn't make up for their superficial good guy image.

Mites You talk about little. These tiny tigers are only one sixtieth of an inch, and with a chip on their shoulder. They are sap-suckers, and you have to look close—look under the leaves. Mites like it in a cool, moist area.

Nematodes Wow! What a problem these almost invisible microscopic worms have caused through the Southeast. Almost every pot has its share of nematodes. They get into the roots and stunt the growth and slow down the plant's vigor. If they are in the roots of your plants, you can see it.

Red Spider Mites There is a difference between these and other mites. These guys and gals like it brown or somewhere in between. They never stop eating, breeding, and make a tangled, sticky, dusty mess out of most plants they pitch their tent over.

I KNEW I SHOULDN'T HAVE HAD
THAT LAST DRINK

Scale Here is a plant pest that can do more damage quicker than a swarm of locust on a wheat field. Scale appears on the stems and undersides of leaves in the shape of tiny shells or bumps. Scale also sucks the fluid from the plants and excretes a sticky honey dew that can cause a fungus growth, which is yet another problem.

Slugs and Snails These slimy jerks darn near eat the paint off the side of the garage if you let them. They are not as easy to control as some folks would have you believe. You all know what they look like—the snail has a shell and the slug is naked. The only good snail is boiled in hot butter and garlic.

Sow Bugs There are several bugs called sow bugs, but the most common is the pill bug. The pill bug is found in and around greenhouses or damp plant benches. The pill bug eats young roots.

Springtails This is the story of most of us garden guys and gals: There are over 2,000 species of springtails and only one eats the roots and chews holes in the leaves, and they show up at our houses. Springtails can't last around relatively dry soil, and if you are watering well and then let it almost dry out, odds are you won't see them. If you have a heavy hand with the watering can, you will see them.

Thrips These are mean little cusses when it comes to your plants. Their rough mouths rip and tear foliage, while the female causes foliage to blister where she lays her eggs.

Whitefly This is a troublesome little white mothlike insect that almost seems indestructible. Between the adults and the green larva on the underside of the leaves, sucking the sap and leaving a sticky honey dew that attracts ants (who carry them from plant to plant), they set the scene for disease.

YUM!

PLANT MENU FOR BUGS

Insects / Common Plant Names	Ants	Aphids	Caterpillars	Centipedes	Cockroaches	Crickets	Cutworms	Earthworms	Earwigs	Leaf Miners	Leaf Rollers	Mealybugs	Millipedes	Mites	Nematodes	Red Spiders	Scale	Slug and Snail	Sow Bugs	Springtails	Whitefly	Thrips
Aluminum Plant												✓		✓								
Arabian Coffee																						✓
Areca Palm	✓	✓										✓	✓		✓		✓					
Arrowhead Nephthytis		✓										✓										✓
Artillery Plant														✓			✓					✓
Baby Doll Dracaena	✓											✓		✓	✓							
Baby's Tears		✓										✓										
Balfour Aralia	✓	✓												✓		✓	✓				✓	
Bird's-Nest Fern	✓	✓										✓					✓	✓			✓	✓
Bird's-Nest Sansevieria																	✓					
Bloodleaf Achyranthus												✓										
Boston Fern	✓	✓										✓					✓				✓	✓
Bromeliads	✓																✓					
Buddhist Pine																	✓					
Burro's Tail	✓											✓						✓	✓			
Cactus	✓											✓					✓	✓	✓			
Caladium		✓																				✓
Calamondin												✓		✓			✓					
Calathea	✓											✓										
Candle Plant	✓								✓	✓							✓				✓	
Cape Primrose														✓		✓	✓					
Century Plant												✓										
Chenille Plant		✓																				
Chinese Evergreen	✓											✓										
Chinese Holly Grape	✓	✓										✓		✓		✓	✓					
Cluster Fishtail Palm	✓	✓										✓	✓		✓		✓					
Coral Berry		✓										✓					✓					

PLANT MENU FOR BUGS (*Cont.*)

Common Plant Names \ Insects	Ants	Aphids	Caterpillars	Centipedes	Cockroaches	Crickets	Cutworms	Earthworms	Earwigs	Leaf Miners	Leaf Rollers	Mealybugs	Millipedes	Mites	Nematodes	Red Spiders	Scale	Slug and Snail	Sow Bugs	Springtails	Thrips	Whitefly
Corn Plant	✓											✓		✓		✓						
Creeping Fig												✓					✓				✓	
Crown of Thorns												✓				✓	✓					
Delta Maidenhair Fern	✓	✓										✓					✓				✓	✓
Dragon Tree		✓												✓		✓						✓
Dumb Cane	✓	✓										✓		✓								
Elephant's-Foot Tree												✓		✓								
Emerald Ripple Peperomia		✓																				✓
English Ivy	✓	✓										✓		✓	✓		✓					
Euonymus																	✓					
European Fan Palm	✓	✓										✓		✓	✓		✓					
False Agave												✓										
Fiddle-Leaf Fig	✓	✓										✓		✓			✓				✓	
Fiddle-Leaf Philodendron														✓								
Flame of the Woods												✓		✓								
Flame Violet		✓										✓										
Florida Ruffles Fern	✓	✓										✓				✓					✓	✓
Giant White Inch Plant		✓										✓		✓		✓						
Gold Dust Dracaena	✓											✓		✓								
Gold Dust Ivy	✓	✓										✓		✓			✓					
Gold Dust Tree												✓		✓			✓					
Golden Bird's Nest Sansevieria																	✓					
Golden Dieffenbachia	✓	✓										✓		✓								
Golden Pothos												✓					✓					
Golden Trumpet												✓		✓			✓					
Giant Dumb Cane	✓	✓										✓		✓								
Grape Ivy	✓	✓										✓		✓			✓					

Insects / Common Plant Names	Ants	Aphids	Caterpillars	Centipedes	Cockroaches	Crickets	Cutworms	Earthworms	Earwigs	Leaf Miners	Leaf Rollers	Mealybugs	Millipedes	Mites	Nematodes	Red Spiders	Scale	Slug and Snail	Sow Bugs	Springtails	Thrips	Whitefly
Hahn's Self-Branching Ivy	√	√										√		√			√					
Hastatum Philodendron		√										√		√								
Heart-Leaf Philodendron		√										√		√								
Iron-Cross Begonia	√	√									√										√	
Jade Plant	√											√						√	√			
Janet Craig Dracaena	√											√		√								
Japanese Aralia	√	√												√			√				√	
Japanese Littleleaf Boxwood														√		√	√					
Kangaroo Ivy		√	√									√		√			√					
Lipstick Plant		√																				
Maranta		√										√		√								
Marble Queen Pothos												√					√					
Medicine Plant	√											√						√	√			
Ming Aralia	√	√												√			√				√	
Moon Valley Pilea	√	√											√									√
Moses-in-the-Bullrushes												√		√	√							
Narrow-Leaf Pleomele	√													√							√	
Natal Plum												√					√					
Neanthe Bella Palm	√	√										√		√	√		√					
Needlepoint Ivy	√	√										√		√			√					
Norfolk Island Pine	√	√															√					
Parlor Ivy	√	√										√		√			√					
Peace Lily	√								√			√										√
Piggyback Plant																						√
Pigmy Date Palm	√	√										√		√	√		√					
Pineapple	√																√					
Plumosa Fern	√	√										√					√				√	√
Polka-Dot Plant												√		√								√
Polynesia												√		√							√	√

PLANT MENU FOR BUGS (*Cont.*)

Common Plant Names \\ Insects	Ants	Aphids	Caterpillars	Centipedes	Cockroaches	Crickets	Cutworms	Earthworms	Earwigs	Leaf Miners	Leaf Rollers	Mealybugs	Millipedes	Mites	Nematodes	Red Spiders	Scale	Slug and Snail	Sow Bugs	Springtails	Thrips	Whitefly
Polypody Fern	✓	✓										✓					✓				✓	✓
Purple Heart	✓											✓		✓								✓
Purple Waffle Plant	✓	✓										✓		✓								
Rex Begonia	✓	✓									✓										✓	
Ribbon Plant	✓	✓									✓		✓									
Rockford Holly Fern	✓	✓										✓					✓				✓	✓
Rose of Jericho	✓	✓																				
Rubber Plant												✓		✓			✓				✓	
Schefflera	✓	✓										✓		✓			✓					
Sensitive Plant												✓		✓								
Shrimp Plant	✓	✓										✓										✓
Silver Tree Panamiga												✓										
Snake Plant																	✓					
Spider Aralia												✓					✓				✓	
Spider Plant	✓	✓										✓										
Split-Leaf Philodendron												✓										
Spotted Dumb Cane	✓	✓										✓										
Sprenger Asparagus	✓	✓										✓					✓				✓	✓
Staghorn Fern	✓	✓										✓				✓						
Strawberry Begonia	✓										✓										✓	
String-of-Hearts												✓		✓								
Striped Inch Plant		✓										✓		✓								✓
Succulents												✓							✓	✓		
Swedish Ivy												✓					✓				✓	✓
Sweetheart Ivy	✓											✓					✓				✓	✓
Tahitian Bridal Veil	✓	✓										✓									✓	✓
Trailing Velvet Plant	✓	✓								✓		✓		✓	✓							
Tricolor Dragon Tree	✓	✓												✓							✓	✓

Common Plant Names	Ants	Aphids	Caterpillars	Centipedes	Cockroaches	Crickets	Cutworms	Earthworms	Earwigs	Leaf Miners	Leaf Rollers	Mealybugs	Millipedes	Mites	Nematodes	Red Spiders	Scale	Slug and Snail	Sow Bugs	Springtails	Thrips	Whitefly
Tree Ivy	✓	✓										✓					✓				✓	✓
Tree Philodendron														✓								
Umbrella Plant	✓	✓												✓	✓	✓						
Variegated Balfour Aralia														✓			✓					
Variegated Mock Orange	✓	✓										✓		✓	✓	✓	✓					✓
Variegated Peperomia		✓																				✓
Variegated Rubber Tree	✓	✓										✓		✓			✓				✓	
Variegated Wandering Jew	✓	✓										✓		✓						✓	✓	
Variegated Wax Ivy	✓											✓			✓							
Veitch Screw Pine												✓										
Velvet Leaf Kalanchoe	✓	✓							✓			✓		✓	✓							
Velvet Plant	✓	✓							✓			✓		✓	✓							
Victoria Table Fern	✓	✓										✓					✓				✓	✓
Warnecki Dracaena	✓											✓		✓								
Watermelon Peperomia		✓																				✓
Wax Plant	✓											✓			✓							
Weeping Fig	✓	✓										✓		✓			✓				✓	
White-Velvet Tradescantia	✓	✓										✓		✓						✓	✓	
Zebra Plant	✓	✓										✓		✓			✓					✓

Don't Get Caught with Your Plants Down!

Just because you see a large number of squares not marked under the names of some of the insects, don't think that these insects cannot take a liking to any of the above-listed plants. I could have put a mark in every square for most plants for caterpillars, centipedes, cockroaches, crickets, earthworms, earwigs, millipedes, sow bugs, and springtails, because these guys show up when you don't keep your house plants' home and clothes clean. Remember, a clean plant is a safe and happy plant.

It's Your Own Damp Fault
If the Bugs Win the Battle

IT WAS THE UPPER CUT

I can tell you how to recognize the signs that insects are at work in your plant play area. I can show you pictures of the dizzy dastards that do these dastardly deeds to your poor defenseless plants, but I can't look over your shoulder every minute to chide and scold you into keeping your tools, benches, cupboards, shelves, floors, pots, and soil clean and fresh. I would constantly remind you not to pile bags, boxes, and boards up where insects can hide and breed. So, you must practice neatness for your plant's sake. Over 90% of all insect- and disease-connected plant deaths were the direct result of carelessness on the part of the grower.

10

And You Think Herpes Is Bad!

DISEASE CONTROL

Fungus infection diseases are passed from one plant to another by air circulation, hands (yours), dirty pots, planters, and baskets.

Fungus infections, as a rule, get a start because you get lax in your everyday care and plant comfort conditions. You let the temperatures run above 75° or below 50° for long periods of time and allow the humidity to get above 60%. Other causes are overwatering, not enough light, pots too close together, and poor air circulation.

If house plant care becomes as much a part of your everyday routine as your daily chores, odds are you won't have these problems.

As a rule, damage caused by these fungus diseases turns the plant tissue soft and mushy, rots leaves and turns foliage gray or brown, fuzzy, and powdered white. With some of the fungus diseases, spots, dents, and depressions appear. If you don't treat these diseases right away, they will end up killing your plants.

HELP IS ON THE WAY

It's Life or Death—Emergency Steps to Take

1. Remove the plant from its present position and location to a room with 70° daytime and 60° nighttime temperatures, and a steady 50% humidity factor.
2. Remove the plant from its current pot and place into a clean, sterilized clay pot of the same size.
3. Drench the soil and spray the foliage with a solution of 1 tablespoon liquid soap and 1 tablespoon Listerine mouthwash in one gallon of warm, weak tea.
4. Remove all disease-damaged foliage and throw away from the area.
5. Wash hands often with Fels' Naptha soap.
6. Spray or dip foliage and drench soil with the recommended fungicide. Always read labels before use.

All Plant Diseases Are As Bad As They Sound

Half the battle for recovery after a bout with a fungus disease is based first upon recognition and then the proper use of the right medication, for the proper period of time and recommended dosage. Here is a brief description of the most common plant diseases you and your plants are likely to encounter on your growing journey.

Anthracnose

You can identify this communicable disease by the sunken spots on the tops of leaves; centers will be dark and dry. You will also see the ends of the leaves turn brown and shrivel up. Anthracnose is usually an indication that you continuously overwater. Plants in the rubber tree family and some succulents like the jade plant, citrus, and other fat-leaved plants are particularly susceptible.

Botrytis

Sometimes we know where plant diseases come from, other times we are at a total loss to explain, and you really can't

I'M A GONER

get mad at your plants. The only thing you can do is give them the cure and keep your eye on them.

Botrytis is a highly contagious disease that infects African violets, velvet leaf, and other hairy-leaved plants. Botrytis is a gray-white growth that appears on the uppermost leaves. If you spot this moldy growth, isolate the plant or plants immediately and cut off the affected foliage and destroy it. Spray the plant with Zineb and keep the plant isolated. If any new foliage becomes infected, remove it. When the plant appears healthy, return it to the group. Botrytis is a result of plants being crammed together and touching one another and having poor ventilation and air circulation. Cigarette smoke has been suggested as a cause. Wash your hands after smoking.

Crown or Stem Rot

If I had to guess the most common cause for plant deaths in winter months, I would have to say a combination of overwatering, too hot or cold temperatures, and too much humidity without proper ventilation.

Otherwise you invite a disease called "crown rot." Its people disease comparison is consumption (progressive bodily wasting away). Crown rot (also called stem rot) occurs when the stem gets soft and mushy from the above combined conditions. The first step to correct it is to lay off the water, get the air circulating around your plants, set your temperature at 70°, and keep your cotton-picking hands off the thermostat. The sick plant should go into surgery immediately. Cut the infected area away with a clean razor blade, brace the stem with a firm stick, and dust the infected area with a plant medicine called Perbam, available at most garden shops. Crown or stem rot can attack any plant that is exposed to the conditions I mentioned.

Damping Off

I got a frantic call from a friend of mine the other day. "Come quick, Jer! They're all falling down, they're going to die." He was sure telling the truth. When I got there, they were all DOA—not one had survived. Oh! I'm sorry—I didn't mean to panic you; my friend had started a whole group of house plants, herbs, and vegetables from seeds, and they had all succumbed to a fungus disease we refer to in gardening as "damping off disease." Damping off disease only attacks new-born plants that have been started in heavy, unsterilized soil that stays too wet and too warm. Prevent this from happening to any of your baby plants by using a light planter mix, or a starter mix purchased at the plant shop. Keep the temperature at a constant 70° and dust with Perbam at the first sign of a cough.

Leaf Spot

Plants get acne! That's right, plain old-fashioned acne—as described by Noah Webster, a skin disorder marked by inflammation of skin glands and hair follicles, causing pimple formations.

On plants I call acne "leaf spot." It's an infection caused by lack of certain vital elements or too much of certain ones; much like too many sweets for young people. The leaf spot description sounds like acne. The blemishes on the leaves have a yellowish margin, while the centers are white, brown, or black. How's that grab you? The treatment: Spray the foliage with Zineb, increase the light, and wash the foliage weekly with soap and water. One last caution: Don't squeeze the spots, or scarring will occur. Don't worry! Your plants will grow out of it.

Mildews

Now that you have had a chance to grow a plant or two for a while, you know it isn't all smooth sailing. You have probably discovered by now that most plant diseases are caused by not keeping your plants clean and comfortable. Oh! I know lots of you have bitten off more than you can chew in plants, because they're all so darn attractive. You keep adding to your plant family, and then you run out of time. Baths get put off, or the morning tea and showers; the heat gets moved up and down, or your forget to turn their pots; the timer on the lights got unplugged by mistake. Besides, it's more fun to talk to them and play than work.

Shame on you plant mommies and papas! All talk and no action causes plants to get mildew that coats the leaves, keeping light from the thin tissue, thus causing them to get sick. Just start bathing the foliage if any signs of mildew are apparent. Bathe the foliage with the soap, water, and Listerine mouthwash spray. Spray with Zineb or any one of the other plant fungicides available in the garden shop labeled for house plants.

Mold

I bet you didn't have as much botany in school as you have had since you began listening to me, but it is absolutely necessary if you are to have happy, healthy, productive, and attractive plants around you.

The odds are in your favor that you, or your plants, will never come in contact with most or any of the plant health problems that I have been describing for the past few paragraphs, but an ounce of prevention sure beats the cost of a pound of cure. I want to bring a few more plant diseases to your attention (forewarned is forearmed). One is mold. The black powdery mold that forms on the sweet sticky stuff mealybugs, aphids, and scale excrete. Plants are also bothered by an icky gray-white mold that shows up on the soil. It is caused by overwatering. Check the bug chart for all of the plants that aphids visit and keep your eyes open for mold.

A warm soap and water bath will wash away the black powder, and Malathion spray will control the bugs. Zineb on the soil will stop the icky one.

Root Rot

Athlete's foot is the most aggravating condition a body can think of. You never can get comfortable, and you need a good fungicide to relieve the itching and burning.

You got it, friend! No, not the athlete's foot. I mean plants can get it. Yes! Athlete's foot on plants is called "root rot." If it gets bad enough, your plants will end up with a naked stem, leaves will turn brown, shrivel up, and drop off. It comes from wet, warm soil. Sound like a familiar condition?

Remove plant from present pot, remove soil from root, cut off damaged roots and repot in light planter mix. Apply Thiram to the new soil, be more cautious on the watering, and keep the pot away from warm spots. Plants that have been ill should not be made to eat for at least a week.

Good Plant Parents Keep Their Eyes on Their Plant Kids

I am the guy who first wrote that plants are like people, and I recommend that you talk to your plants. I only hope that they hear and understand what it is that I am talking about. With my own children (the human ones), I always told them not to talk to strangers, accept a gift, or get into a car. I informed them to run like the dickens and scream at the top of their voices. These are the same instructions I give both my little and big plants when it comes to Freddie Fungus. Here are a few of the plants that are most likely to be affected by certain diseases. With ants, aphids, and mealybugs around, you have to watch them all.

African violets and other hairy-leaved plants are the victims of: root rot, crown or stem rot, leaf spot, mildew, and Botrytis.

Aloe and the succulents from the desert are fair game for: root rot and stem rot. Especially watch your cactus in the winter and do not overwater.

The begonia family should ring the wagons and watch for: root rot, crown or stem rot and Botrytis.

Our friends from both the fruit belts and citrus plants are a favorite of: anthracnose.

Dracaenas, the quiet pretty plants, seem almost too tough to be bothered by anything, but leaf spot pays them a visit from time to time.

The Dumb Canes (Dieffenbachia) will not be happy with: stem or crown rot.

Geraniums growing indoors are a target for: leaf spot, and stem or crown rot.

Gesneriacae, of which Gloxinia is the most famous big flower, dare not let down its guard or root rot, crown or stem rot, or leaf spot will be a huffin' and puffin' to blow the door down.

Kalanchoe and other fat-leaved plants are stuck with: anthracnose and root rot.

Palms are aggravated by: root rot and anthracnose.

Philodendron wish crown or stem rot would rot away.

The rubber tree, creeping fig, and old Fiddle-Leaf fig are troubled by: anthracnose, mold, and mildew.

YOU'RE DARN RIGHT I'M OVERPROTECTIVE

The Cures
Cost Like H

The Rx for these diseases is as expensive as any antibiotic your doctor prescribes for you, and should be purchased in small sizes, as they don't seem to have good shelf lives.

The Cause	The Cure
Anthracnose	Maneb
Botrytis	Benomyl
Crown or stem rot	Truban
Damping off	Truban
Leaf spot	Benlate
Mildews	Phaltan, Benomyl
Molds	Soap and water, Benomyl
Root rot	Truban

Prevention Is Always Cheaper

Dishpan Hands Save Plants

I can't for the life of me see why good gardeners should have dirt under their fingernails. The reason I say this is because I usually have my hands stuck in warm, soapy water with bleach and Listerene mouthwash in it scrubbing up my old pots so that they are ready for immediate use. I never let dirty, moldy, salty pots lie around, because you are just asking for trouble. I use a scouring pad on clay and one of those sponges that are soft on one side and rough on the other side for plaster, metal, glass, and ceramics.

SCRUB...SCRUB...SCRUB, ALL THE
POTS IN THE TUB

Grandma Putnam's Pot Soak

Into a large 20-gallon container (washtub in her day) half full of real warm water, add: 1 cup bleach, 1 cup Listerine, 1 cup shaved Fels' Naptha soap (or liquid dish soap), and 2 tablespoons of boric acid. Stir well and let pots soak in it overnight. The next day, mix up a gallon of fresh soak in another bucket and scrub each pot, one at a time, and rinse them in a clean bucket of water. This simple step will keep your plants free from most plant disease, provided you become a good house plant keeper.

YOU SHOULD SEE WHAT SHE PUTS JUNIOR IN FOR A POISON IVY CURE

11

Would You Like to See My Incision? Or, Let Me Slip into Something Comfortable
PROPAGATION AND PLANTING

Plant propagation was probably one of the most boring things I had to study in biology when I was a youngster. I can remember having to draw pictures of plant cells and learn the parts of a flower and describe the steps of plant reproduction step by step. What a drag that was. Years later, here I am with tweezers, magnifying glass, camel's hair brush, air duster, and scalpel, hunched over a beautiful little defenseless African violet or other flowering or foliage plant, pollenating, air layering, or grafting, all for the sake of increasing the plant population—and enjoying every minute of it. I enjoy it now because I can understand the necessity of knowing if I am to have healthy happy plants.

In the only children's book I have written, *Plants Are Like Kids,* I explained that there are boy plants and girl plants and that they had reproductive organs and that for new babies to be born, the male had to fertilize the egg (seed). There was some objection by parental groups, but plant sex education won out.

Continuing Your Plant's Family Tree

I get the biggest kick out of visiting a friend of mine who was bound and determined that he was not cut out to be a green thumb person; it seemed to him that *every* plant he touched withered and went.

I am going to tell you the same thing I told my other plant friend, and especially before you tackle plant propagation, because you are bound to have a setback or two. I still do.

To begin, there are no magic potions or lotions! That's right, my friend. No secrets or magic, just good old-fashioned pride, patience, persistence, and practice. That's how you develop a green thumb.

Don't always be in a big hurry with your new baby plants. If one takes hold sooner than another, just spend a little more time with the pokey one.

If something goes wrong with a plant friend, don't give up, start over again. You will soon be like my friend who has so many new baby plants growing and going that I can hardly move in his house.

Why Go to the Trouble of Growing My Own?

There are several reasons for starting your own plants at home. The least of the reasons is not having to buy new plants. Then there is growing new plants from an old and aging plant (for gifts and trading) of a variety that you can't purchase. All are good reasons for propagating new plants.

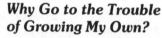

WE GO ALL THE WAY BACK TO EDEN

JUST A SNIP OFF
THE OLD POP

HOW NEW PLANT BABIES ARE BORN

Again, I will say that there are several ways plants are born in your home, and you are the midwife:

From seed You can purchase several house plant seed varieties from such popular seed companies as Ferry Morse or Park Seed:

Asparagus—Plumosus

Asparagus—Sprengeri

Browallia—Bluebell

Coleus—Saber Pineapple

Dracaena—Cordyline indivisa

Dracaena—Draco (lleaceae)

Jerusalem Cherry

Ornamental Peppers

Polka-Dot plant

Ponytail Palm

There are many more varieties, but these will give you a feel for this fast, easy, and fun way to increase your plant collection.

Steps to Seed Success

1. Always soak new seeds in a warm solution of very weak tea for 8 to 10 hours.
2. Fill a clean clay pot with very moist Hyponex Professional Planter Mix. Do not use potting soil to start seeds.
3. Place seeds one at a time just a little way under the soil and press lightly, but firmly. Leave enough room between seeds that you can remove them by hand for transplanting.
4. Cover the pot with clear plastic wrap.
5. Place in good lighted area, but not in direct sunlight.
6. Keep room at 70°, but not over 75°.
7. Don't get restless. It will take 14 to 16 days for germination, and in some cases even longer.
8. When seedlings emerge, remove plastic and keep damp but not wet.
9. When seedlings are 2″ tall, carefully remove them and transplant into 2¼″ damp peat pots filled with damp Hyponex Professional Planter Mix, and then slip the peat pots into clean, damp 2½″ clay pots.
10. Watch your new babies carefully and feed with a very mild soapy fish-emulsion solution (5 drops of soap and 5 drops of liquid fish emulsion per quart of water).

Steps to Air Layering

This method scares the dickens out of most everyone who tries it the first time because you are generally air layering a big rubber tree or dumb cane, Dracaena, or Monstera. Air layering works best on thick-stemmed plants.

1. Wash the stem with a weak tea solution of warm soap and water, with 5 drops to the quart of Listerine mouthwash. You only need to work 4 to 6 inches above and below where you are going to make the incision.

2. With a clean, sharp, sterilized razor or knife blade (alcohol or whiskey will do to sterilize the blade), cut an inch wide band one-half way around the stem, not more than 4 inches below a leaf.

3. Make a plastic cylinder from a plastic bag and plastic tape and place around the stem.

4. Secure the bottom of the plastic bag around the stem firmly with a twistem, but not enough to cut into the stem.

5. Fill the plastic cylinder with damp sphagnum moss and seal with a twistem.

6. Keep moss damp and give plant normal care.

7. It will take a month or two before you see a considerable number of roots through the plastic.

8. Remove bag and cut just below where the lower tier was.

9. Pot the newly rooted top in a peat pot filled with damp Professional Planter Mix.

10. Care for new top and old bottom, and they will both surprise you.

I really want you to try once and have it work, because that's when you can say you are a real green thumber.

Steps to Soil Layering

This one is child's play, and one you should encourage them to try right along with you. Almost all trailing and climbing plants with long flexible stems can be done this way. However, it takes a long time. Spring is the best time to try this, and outdoors is the best place to try it (eastern exposure).

1. Fill damp 2¼" peat pots with damp Hyponex Professional Planter Mix.

2. Set the filled peat pot into a damp clay pot.

3. Set the parent plant on the ground and place the filled small pots underneath each runner.

4. Make small pins from light wire coat hangers.
5. Pin the stem down firmly into the planter mix.
6. Keep damp, and feed the mama.
7. When roots have set in pot, cut loose from mama.

Steps to Rooting Plantlets

Here is another one that is child's play. For plants that have small plants on the end of their stems, such as spider plants, follow these steps:

1. Fill a damp peat pot full of damp Professional Planter Mix.
2. Place the filled peat pot into a damp clay pot the same size.
3. Set plantlet into soil and pin down.
4. Keep damp.
5. When roots have taken hold, cut the cord.

Steps to Rooting Offsets and Pups

Some of our house plants produce little plants off to the side at soil level of the main stems. Bromeliads, succulents, and cacti are good examples.

1. Fill a damp peat pot with damp Professional Planter Mix.
2. Cut offset plant or pup from the mother plant with a clean, sharp blade, making sure you keep any root available.
3. Plant into the damp mix like any other cutting.
4. Set peat pot and plant into a damp clay pot.
5. Do not overfeed or drown.

Steps to Planting Divisions

This is what we refer to as a family gathering of plants around the mother, like clumps. African violets, ferns, San-

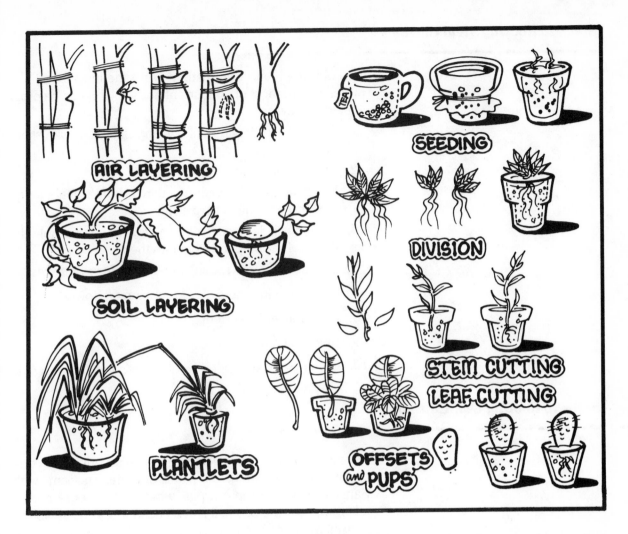

sevieria, and Maranta are just a few. Steps to planting divisions:

1. Tap the plant from the pot gently.
2. Gently take some of the planting media away from the roots, so you can see where these plants are connected.
3. Cut with sharp blade at connection.
4. Half fill a damp peat pot with Professional Planter Mix and press down.
5. Set new plant into one-half-filled pot and continue to fill and press out all air pockets.
6. Do not overwater.

Steps to Rooting Stem Cuttings

This old, tried, and true method is still the most favorite of professionals. Most of our current house plants can be propagated this way:

1. Take a 2- to 3-inch nonflowering stem. Cut with sharp blade.
2. Strip lower foliage.
3. Fill damp peat pot with two-thirds Professional Planter Mix and one-third sharp sand.
4. Use your little finger or clean stick to poke a hole the depth of the stripped stem into the mix.
5. Dip dry stem into rooting powder and tap off excess.
7. Place stem into hole. Avoid rubbing off powder.
8. Press mix around stem.
9. Keep soil damp.
10. Cover plants and pot rim with plastic bag for humidity.

Steps to Rooting Leaf Cuttings

Here is where you really get your money's worth. From one begonia leaf you can get 10 plants or more. The same with Sansevieria and Streptocarpus, when you only use part of a leaf. In the case of small-leaved begonias, African violets, Gloxinias, and Peperomias, you insert stem and leaf. For both types, you begin with the same potting media.

1. Fill a damp peat pot with two-thirds Hyponex Professional Planter Mix and one-third sharp sand.
2. Insert into damp clay pot.
3. For leaf cuttings, dip stem into rooting powder. Poke hole with stick or little finger.
4. Insert stem to just above mix.
5. When you plant partial pieces, use 2-inch pieces with a rex begonia. Cut it like a piece of pie.

6. Use a knife blade to make a wedge in mix and insert one-half the piece.
7. Press firmly and keep damp.

Steps to Rooting Canes

If you once try this, I won't be able to stop you. The ti plant, dumb cane, Dracaenas, and Cordyline, or any, or at least many, of the thick-stem cane-type plants, can be multiplied this way:

1. Fill a damp peat pot full with damp Hyponex Professional Planter Mix.
2. Insert peat pot into damp clay pot.
3. Cut a piece of the cane with one nodule attached.
4. Place the cut piece on top of the mix with the leaf bud (little lumplike pimple) up, and press half into mix.
5. Keep damp.

RULES TO PLANT BY

It used to be that in 1960 when this whole new house plant green scene began, there were very few growing media on the market. Dirt piles were secured and then put into plastic bags, sealed, and sold to you. No consideration was given to the plant's needs.

As the interest and volume increased, the universities began to experiment with safer, lighter mixes, and came up with the professional planter mixes. Hyponex Company, among others, blends these clean, disease- and insect-free mixes for professional growers, golf courses, and home gardeners.

When propagating, I only use the professional mix with about a third sharp sand for leaf and cane cuttings and succulents. But for transplanting, I use the Hyponex Regular Potting Soil, or half and half. Always make sure the pots are clean and damp. Hands and bench should be clean also. If the mix or soil is dried out, add 10 drops per quart of liquid

THESE ARE NOT TO BE BROKEN

soap and mix with dry medium until it is damp and crumbly, before using.

Give your plants an even chance for successful growth. Make sure their feet are comfortable.

When the Toe Comes Out the Hole in the Bottom—Transplant

TIME FOR A NEW POT

I have always said that you folks have transplantitis. When you first get a plant home, you dump it into a pot it gets lost in, and then wonder why it won't grow.

1. Transplant all new plants into a clean, damp clay pot the same size it is now in.

2. When transplanting, only move the plant up one pot-size larger, and add damp, clean Professional Planter Mix.

3. Only plant, transplant, and take cuttings after 7 P.M. in the evening.

4. Never plant a plant directly into a decorative planter. Only set the plant in its clay work pot into a decorative planter.

5. Never feed a newly planted or transplanted plant for at least a week.

12

Glasshouse Gang!

HOME GREENHOUSE GROWING

LET ME INTRODUCE YOU TO THE GLASSHOUSE GANG

Growing seedlings, cuttings, cut flowers, orchids, herbs, vegetables, shrubs, and even ornamental trees in the controlled climate of a greenhouse can be a fun-filled and exciting hobby. It will also allow you to easily grow all sorts of exotic ornamental and flowering plants that have special needs and requirements when it comes to light, heat, and humidity. A good working greenhouse can provide your home with a continuous supply of colorful plants and flowers day-in and day-out, all year round!

While it's true that greenhouses were once the playthings of the very rich, like expensive cars and color television sets, this is no longer the case. Today, different styles of greenhouse come in many sizes and shapes that are well within the price reach of most middle-income families. Nevertheless, I get pretty serious about greenhouse gardening since your investment is more than a packet of seed or even a new lawn mower; let me lay it all out for you and then you decide if you are willing to invest the time as well as the money.

Lord and Burnham, a leading manufacturer of commercial greenhouses, informs us that there are basically two types of greenhouse, **attached** and **freestanding.** There are also two basic designs, **lean-to** and **open-** or **even-span.**

Attached greenhouses are joined to the outside wall of your home or another building on your property. They can be of either **lean-to** or **open-span** design. One advantage of attached greenhouses is that they are often easier to hook up to heat, water, and electricity. Attached greenhouses work best when they have a south, southeast, or southwest exposure.

Freestanding greenhouses are all of the open-span design. They are separate and individual structures. They have two sides, two ends, and a door at one end or side. They may have a door at each end. They may be permanent, with concrete or masonry floors and partial walls, or they may be temporary and movable with walls entirely of glass, fiberglass, or vinyl. Most experienced greenhouse gardeners recommend the glass-to-ground greenhouse, because of its having so much more growing room. One advantage of freestanding greenhouses is that they can be located where the plants you raise inside of them will get the best possible exposure to the sun. Make sure you pick a site where water, gas, and electricity can be made easily and economically available.

The two most common styles of greenhouse design are the **curved-wall** and the **straightline-wall.** You should pick the style that most appeals to your taste and that will most complement the architecture of your home. Recent research, however, indicates that the curved-wall style permits the entry of the maximum amount of solar energy.

Whichever type, design, and style you select, begin gradually, but plan for the future. By that I mean, don't spend a fortune on the most expensive greenhouse structure that money can buy without first learning a few of the "how-tos" that can only come from firsthand experience. By the same token, don't start out so small and so inexpensively that you will soon have to tear down your original structure

WHAT A CHOICE

and build one twice as large and twice as costly. Modular, or add-on, greenhouses are a good bet for the beginner.

Location

Finding the best location for your greenhouse is the first important step toward growing success. Your location depends on the amount of sunlight that will be needed by the kinds of plants you intend to grow. The reason most flowering plants don't do well in your home is because they don't get enough sunlight. This is especially true in winter when most homes are dark for a good part of the day. If you plan to grow flowering pot plants in your greenhouse, find a location with a southern or eastern exposure. That way, your plants will get the first warming rays of the morning sun, and they will be in sunlight for the major part of the day. Check your planned location to make sure no trees, shrubs, walls, or buildings obstruct or interfere with the low winter sun.

Only a few flowering plants, such as African violets, other gesnerads, and orchids will grow well without direct sunlight. If you plan to grow these, you can choose a west or northern exposure.

You may find yourself limited as to where you can place your greenhouse. Keep in mind that any location can be improved with the addition of artificial lighting. If electricity is available, you can locate your structure where it's most attractive and convenient. If not, do your best to find a location that will supply maximum sunlight. If there is too much sun, you can always decrease the amount of light with shading.

Shading

In the old days, greenhouse gardeners used to shut out the sun's hottest rays by applying a coat of paint from a white powder or paste. You can still get the fixin's for this paint and apply it in the spring and summer when the sun's rays are hottest, but most modern gardeners agree with my friend (?) who says this gets to look like bird droppings in a few weeks, after the rain washes most of it off. Instead, today's gardeners seem to prefer shades or slatted blinds made of wood, aluminum, or plastic. Removable aluminum slats can be put inside the greenhouse in summer and taken down in winter. One advantage of these slats, which are sold by Greenhouse Distributors, is that they can be used to shade specific areas. For shading your entire greenhouse, I suggest inexpensive rolled plastic shades that can be raised or lowered on the outside roof and walls to let in, or shut out, as much light as you desire. Outside the greenhouse, these shades are less likely to be harmfully affected by excessive moisture. They will also serve the double duty of providing protection from hailstones. These shades come in various lengths for porches, patios, and greenhouses, and can be obtained at most garden centers.

Drainage, Foundations, Floors and Doors

Good drainage under and around your home greenhouse is just as important as in your potted plants or garden. Check the ground below and around the site where you plan to put your greenhouse to be sure that the drainage is good. Use my Grandma Putt's "old-fashioned rain barrel test." That is, pour a barrel or galvanized tub full of water out onto the ground where your greenhouse will be placed. If the water takes more than 30 minutes to drain off, you have poor drainage in this area and will have to install drainage tiles. Do this *before* erecting your structure. If you don't install drainage tiles, you are almost certain to get a water-logged growing area inside your greenhouse and a spongy, "swampy" condition in the grounds immediately outside. In the winter and the spring rainy season, you may be the victim of flooding.

Placing your greenhouse on a firm and even foundation is also essential. This will prevent the structure from sagging under its own weight. You can use concrete blocks for foundation footings, or poured concrete.

If you don't plan to use the ground-level borders inside your greenhouse for growing (tomatoes, chrysanthemums, etc.), you can set your greenhouse on a concrete slab with a center drain tile. Concrete slab floors are a good idea for any greenhouse structure, but they are especially needed if you attach your structure to your home or garage. You can add to the attractiveness of an attached greenhouse by tiling the floor with flagstones, slate, or one of the many types of ceramic and composite flooring materials currently on the market. Freestanding greenhouses are often provided with gravel floors by their owners. Pea gravel is attractive, easy to maintain, and economical. It also allows for excellent drainage. Other floorings that allow good drainage are planks, unmortared flagstone, and wood chips—or a combination of two or more of these.

Your greenhouse should have at least one door. Attached greenhouses usually need two, so they can be reached from the outside as well as the inside. Make your outside door large enough so that you can easily move benches, wheelbarrows, etc., in and out. Sliding doors are practical for this purpose, but are often too expensive.

Augment with Artificial Lighting

If you have located your greenhouse in a shaded part of your property, you may be obliged to add to the light supply with incandescent or fluorescent lighting. In a greenhouse, each of these has its own particular uses and good points.

Fluorescent lighting is used primarily to increase the *intensity* (the how-much) of light required in your greenhouse. Incandescent lighting is used mostly to increase the *duration* of periods of light, as they usually don't emit enough blue rays (in the light spectrum) to promote new growth. However, the "day-glo" incandescent bulbs that have recently become available are proving that they can be used economically for increasing intensity and duration. These bulbs emit both the blue and red rays necessary for plant growth.

Scientists have done a great deal of research to find out how much light various plants need to carry out the process of photosynthesis, which turns light into chemical energy needed so they can manufacture their own food and carry on other necessary functions.

Another field of study and experimentation of a phenomenon called *photoperiodism* has yielded valuable information about how different plants respond to varying lengths of "daylight." Most types can now be categorized as long, neutral, or short-day plants. Neutral day-length plants can thrive in varying periods of light and darkness.

In addition to this, it is now known that certain plants demand a corresponding length of darkness within each twenty-four-hour period to balance their exposure to light. These are called intermediate or balanced day/night-length plants.

A list of plants, with information regarding their requirements as to light intensity levels and day-length durations, is included at the back of this book.

These two areas of scientific inquiry have taken a lot of the guesswork out of home greenhouse gardening under artificial lights.

How Much Lighting Do You Need?

Here is a helpful way of figuring the amount of artificial lighting you will need in your greenhouse. For a growing area 2 feet by 4 feet, use one commercial fluorescent light unit with reflector and two 40-watt bulbs. If they are to be used in addition to partial sunlight, burn them each afternoon and evening from 4 to 10 P.M. This kind of lighting is excellent for growing annual flowers that require plenty of light. It is also useful during the short days of fall and winter for growing plants that require "long days."

As I mentioned earlier, incandescent lighting is also useful for increasing the duration of your greenhouse "days" during fall and winter when sunlight is at a minimum. They are especially useful for growing flowers that require long periods of sunlight.

For every 4 feet of bench space, use a reflector with a 60-watt incandescent bulb. If you don't want the burden of remembering to turn these lights on every evening at 5 P.M.

and off at 10 P.M., purchase an inexpensive automatic timer to do the job for you.

Incandescent lighting can be very helpful to speed up the normal growing time for young seedlings until they bud and open.

Heat and Temperature Maintenance Are Critical

Most modern greenhouses are designed to trap the sun's energy and use it as *heat* as well as light. Because of this, heating your home greenhouse to the proper day and night temperature range for the plants you choose to grow there may, or may not, pose a problem.

Experts tell us that temperature during the night is the most critical factor in plant growth. Many beginning greenhouse gardeners fail to take the time to find this out early in the growing game. As a result, they don't score many successes until Ol' Man Experience hits them over the head a few times! African violets are an excellent example of this. They need a daytime temperature in the low 70s, but will not set blooms and may even perish, if the nighttime temperature falls even a few degrees below 65°. It's most critical, then, that these warmth-loving plants get controlled heat at night.

Before you purchase any plant and bring it into the controlled climate of your greenhouse, it's tremendously helpful to first find out what are the best day and night temperatures for it. Although each plant has its own individual temperature likes and dislikes (like people), most of them can be placed in one of the following categories for greenhouse culture:

1. Hothouse plants requiring 75° or higher during the day, and not less than 65° at night.
2. Warmhouse plants requiring 65° day and 55° night.
3. Coolhouse plants requiring 55° day and 45° night.

Since the whole idea of growing plants under glass is to provide a place for them that has more light, heat, and humidity than they can get in your home or garden, you will have to select plants that will thrive in one of the three temperature-range categories listed above. Attempting to grow plants from two or more separate categories in one greenhouse is like trying to play with snowballs in Hell. Don't try it, or you are certain to learn a sad and expensive lesson!

The category of greenhouse you decide to maintain depends on the type of plants you prefer to grow and on the amount of time you have to spend in your greenhouse. Hothouse plants require a lot more work, watering, and watching out for diseases and insect pests than plants suited to the other two categories.

To Heat or Not to Heat

Since your greenhouse will most likely be installed without any heating system other than the sun's natural energy, let's consider what kind of results you can expect should you choose to operate it this way. An almost unlimited number of plants will grow in this type of greenhouse in summer. In winter, you will still be able to grow many plants from among the hardy and semihardy annuals and perennials. This list, of course, lengthens if you happen to reside in Hawaii, Southern Florida or California, or certain parts of the South and Southwest. Also, many bulbs, herbs, vegetables, and fruits do well under unheated glass. In Southern California, truck farmers grow tons of lettuce, asparagus, cucumbers, tomatoes, and flowers in huge plastic greenhouses that are unheated except for a period of several weeks during the winter. These growers experience more problems with cooling and ventilation than heating. In cooler areas, you can protect your greenhouse plants from frost by covering the glass or plastic with polyethelene film. Be careful when you do this, as the film also cuts down on the amount of sunlight your plants will get. Double-glazed greenhouses are available on the market, but are used mostly by orchid specialists.

After a year or two growing in a "cold" greenhouse, you may want to expand your plant variety. To do this, you will need to install a heating system. If your greenhouse is the attached type, your home heating system may be hooked up to it. The first problem with this is that you and your plants may not be on the same wavelength when it comes

SOME ARE BETTER THAN OTHERS

to deciding what's a comfortable living temperature! You may want to augment your greenhouse heating with a space heater. If yours is a freestanding greenhouse, hooking in with the home heating system may turn out to be too difficult or expensive. In that case, you will need to purchase a heating unit or system. The factors you will want to consider before purchasing a heater for your greenhouse are:

1. *Outside temperature conditions in winter and summer*. If the winters become very cold, you will need a heavy-duty unit. The difference between the coldest weather your area has experienced in the past 10 or 20 years, and the highest temperature you want to operate your greenhouse at, will give you, in degrees, an idea of the amount of heat your system will have to put out.

   If the winters get cold and the summers get very hot, you may decide on obtaining a heater/cooler. A good evaporator/cooler can reduce the temperature inside your greenhouse by as much as 30° in the hot summer months.

   If the temperatures are mild most of the year round, your heating needs are minimal at best.

2. *The size of your greenhouse*. It should be obvious that heating a glass or plastic enclosed area is somewhat complicated, and becomes more of a problem as the size of the area increases. Multiply the length × the width × the height of your structure to arrive at the number of cubic feet you need to heat it. Then, using the three plant categories above, select a heater that's adequate to do the job. There are other factors, like heat loss, involved, so I usually recommend that you purchase a system that's capable of heating twice your present space at the temperature range for hothouse plants. That way, if you should want to enlarge your greenhouse, or move on to making tropical plants your specialty, your system will not have to be replaced. A larger capacity heater will also come in handy if your particular greenhouse is located where it's exceptionally windy, made of a high heat-loss material, or if there happen to be any unusually cold winters.

3. *Fuel availability and cost*. You should take care to consider the long-range availability and cost of each type of fuel in your specific area when selecting the heating system for your home greenhouse.

   Up until the present time, electric heating was generally more costly to install and operate, but much easier to control automatically. Automatic controls will help you realize some savings in your day-to-day operations.

   Experienced greenhouse operators recommend a warm-air, overhead heating system. When these use natural-gas fuel and are controlled automatically to distribute the air through plastic heating ducts, they will combine low cost with excellent air distribution.

   A forced-air oil heater offers a third alternative. Like the gas units, they should be housed outside the greenhouse to prevent harm from coming to your plants from any noxious emissions.

4. *Your present and future needs.* This is just a reminder that while you may have modest heating requirements at first, most greenhouse hobbyists soon discover these increase as their knowledge and interest expand. Don't be penny-wise and pound-foolish when you estimate your long-range heating needs.

It's usually very useful to take the time and trouble to consult several heating specialists before selecting any type or size of heating unit. It's also helpful to find heating men who have worked on greenhouse heating systems before.

Ventilation

Plants, like people, need fresh air to live. The adequate circulation of fresh air, warmed to the proper temperature and containing the proper humidity, inside your greenhouse is essential to healthy plant growth. Without proper ventilation, the air in your greenhouse will tend to become stagnant and will layer-out, or stratify. The hot, humid air will rise to the ridge line, and the cool, drier air will lie at ground level. This inhibits the proper distribution of heat and moisture. In order to overcome this stagnation, and to get your air circulating correctly, you will have to take steps to supply good ventilation.

If yours is a small greenhouse, which you attend regularly, the constant opening and closing of the door should be enough to introduce fresh air and generate good circulation.

Think of this kind of greenhouse as being roughly opposite to your refrigerator. If you are constantly opening your refrigerator door, too much warm air will be introduced, and you will have to lower the thermostat setting to make the box cooler. If you keep your refrigerator door closed too long, the air becomes stagnant and stratifies. In your small greenhouse, too much opening of the door will introduce too much cold air and possibly harmful drafts. If you leave the door closed too long, the air may become too hot, humid, and stagnant inside, and you will probably have to lower the temperature setting on your heater.

In a small greenhouse, ventilation and circulation are very much dependent on how much you use it. If you put yourself on a regular schedule, you will have the best results.

Larger greenhouses aren't as subject to radical changes in air circulation as are smaller ones, nor is the air as likely to become stagnant and stratified. Generally, the larger the greenhouse, the better the circulation. Still, adequate ventilation is always a problem in any enclosed growing space. Long periods of very hot, sunny weather can create enormous amounts of heat and humidity that may "force" weak, leggy growth in your plants. To release this heat and humidity, most medium and large greenhouses are equipped with vertical ventilation. Movable vents or windows which can be opened and closed either manually or automatically, are located along the ridgeline. At certain times of the year, when it's windy and the temperature changes constantly, you may find yourself opening or closing your vents as often as two or three times a day. If you fail to do this, your plants can be badly damaged. For this reason, automatic ventilation that is thermostatically controlled can be a godsend. It's usually to your advantage to have an automatic system included in the package when your greenhouse is installed. That way, the cost is slightly lower and more easily absorbed. If the price of such an automatic system is prohibitive, don't despair. The majority of greenhouse gardeners get by just fine with hand-operated vents. They will make you pay a little more attention to your plants and also give you the experience that will allow you to become a good judge of temperature and humidity. Until you gain that experience and judgment, it's a good idea to have a maximum/minimum thermometer and consult it regularly. These thermometers need to be reset on a regular schedule.

Another form of ventilation, called horizontal ventilation, can be supplied by exhaust fans mounted near the top of the ends of your greenhouse. These can be useful when large amounts of hot, humid air collect along the ridgeline and have to be removed. Whether you actually need one, two, or none of these fans depends primarily on the size of your greenhouse. Operators of larger greenhouses generally have the most need for them.

When these fans are operating, you must keep your vertical vents closed, or the two forms of ventilation will be working against each other.

If you install an exhaust fan yourself, make sure it is adequate to do the job. These fans are rated in cubic feet per minute (cfm), the amount of cubic feet of air they can move per minute.

Make sure the fan you purchase has a cover that raises when the fan is in use and lowers when it is not. Keep this cover closed at all times when the fan is not operating.

These exhaust fans also come equipped with thermostatic controls for automatic operation. This can remove some of the responsibility for proper maintenance of good ventilation from your shoulders.

Another form of ventilation, which I touched upon briefly in the earlier section on heat and temperature control, is called *fan and pad ventilation*. This method cools the outside air as it is drawn into your greenhouse. This is done with evaporator/cooler systems. The units in these systems are basically composed of a fan and a pad. As it is pulled into the greenhouse, the air passes through a pad that is saturated with moisture. The moisture in the pad cools the air. (Humid air is considerably cooler than dry air.)

These systems work best in nonhumid regions of the

country where the outside air is relatively dry. They can effectively decrease the temperature of hot, dry air as much as 30°.

One important thing relating to proper ventilation is that tobacco smoke can be very harmful to growing plants. Never smoke in your greenhouse.

Humidity and Staging

Most greenhouse plants, excluding cacti and some succulents, grow best when the air immediately surrounding them is relatively moist. If you live in a dry area, you will be constantly looking for ways to increase the amount of moisture in the air at the lower levels of your greenhouse as the temperature rises. Moisture content in air at any given temperature is measured in percentiles. These readings are referred to as *relative humidity*. An inexpensive hygrometer will help you check the amount of relative humidity in your greenhouse at any given time.

One method you can use to increase the humidity in your greenhouse is to spray the inside walls with water. The sun's rays, hitting the outside walls will cause the water to evaporate into the greenhouse atmosphere.

Raising your plants up from the floor or bench level of

TO EACH HIS OWN

your greenhouse on different "stages" can be very helpful in giving them more humid conditions. Proper staging, plus damping down the floor with water, should be a routine morning procedure on hot, sunny days.

Staging for growing, displaying, and supporting greenhouse plants can be built by you do-it-yourselfers, or purchased, in two types—open or closed.

The term "open staging" simply means that the material on which your plants stand is open to allow the warm, humid air in the greenhouse to circulate freely to the bottom of the pots. Open staging also allows you to have a greater amount of control over the drainage of your plants.

The most commonly used open staging is made of wood slats nailed to 1″ × 4″ framing of redwood or aspen that's been treated for moisture resistance. Although the slats are separated by from one-half to three-quarters of an inch, moisture will eventually swell them closer together. Arranged in steplike terraces, with the widest at the bottom, this type of plant support can be a very attractive and practical space-saver.

In addition to wood, metal grill work treated with fiberglass is a good material for open staging.

"Closed staging" is usually of noncorrosive metal racks or pipes on which high-lipped metal trays are laid. The trays, about 1 or 2 inches deep, can be filled with tiny pea gravel or sand, which is kept moist. This is excellent for African violets, which many gardeners feel should be watered from the bottom.

Benches

Greenhouse benches and display staging can be obtained from manufacturers and suppliers if you don't care to build them yourself. Whatever your source, it's extremely important that they are both sturdy and comfortable for you to work at.

Most greenhouse benches are 36 inches high and 30 inches wide. This is wide enough so that you can easily put four rows of medium-sized flowerpots or two seedling flats back to back. The height off the ground should be adjusted to your height so that you can work on the plants at the back conveniently. Most manufacturer-installed benches are set at 36 inches, but if you are as tall as me, and the benches are on adjustable pipes, raise them another 4 to 6 inches. If you are short in stature, lower them 4 to 6 inches. Setting their level at the most comfortable height will save you from many a nagging backache!

Wood benches should be treated with a moisture-inhibiting preservative and reinforced with steel braces.

Bench tops may be open or closed. If open, place moist burlap or newspaper down on new tops before planting. Later on, this won't be necessary as the moisture in the greenhouse will swell the wood and move the slats closer together. If the tops are closed, you can lay down corrogated plastic or aluminum sheeting. This can be filled with moist sand for drainage and bottom watering of your potted plants, or it can be planted on directly.

Wood benches often have a 2″ × 6″ board facing that creates a 4-inch depth. Deep benches like this can be useful in many ways. They hold pots and flats from falling, they can be filled with gravel and sand for drainage, and they can be filled with soil for direct planting.

Some bench framing is made with galvanized iron or aluminum pipe. This can be especially good if your greenhouse is of the glass-to-ground design. Pipe framing will not block so much sunlight, if you should decide to plant under the benches.

All benches and staging should be situated slightly away from the glass walls to allow the air to circulate freely.

Storage

Most greenhouse pots, soil, fertilizers, and equipment can be stored neatly under benches or put in storage bins under benches. I have found 15-gallon plastic garbage cans to be excellent for sand, soils, compost, and fertilizers. They are sturdy and lightweight and have tight covers. If you use one of these for sand, make a frame with wheels or rollers for the bottom.

Hand tools can be hung on a rack at the end of a bench.

If you find yourself accumulating too many tools and other unsightly paraphernalia, you can build a handy portable storage closet on wheels. A very practical design for such a carryall is described on page 83 of the Sunset *Garden Work Centers* book.

Pesticides and any other potentially dangerous tool, liquid, or compound should be locked up or stored on high shelves out of the reach of children and visitors. Remember, kids aren't the only ones who have accidents!

Tools, Gadgets, and Greenhouse Equipment

Most hobbyists go half-crazy when it comes time to stock up on the tools and trinkets for their particular pastime. We all know people with tons of camera equipment who can't take a decent snapshot. Well, so it is with greenhouse gardeners. A greenhouse full of gadgets won't necessarily make you a super gardener, and believe me, there are enough "handy" gimcracks available on the market to move you out of house and garage! Go slow. In the beginning, buy only what is necessary. Over the first year, add to your tool inventory only as you need to.

Here is a list of "nice, but not so necessary," and "necessary" tools and equipment:

Nice Tools and Equipment, But—

Assortment of watering cans
Capillary watering system
Dibber
Dibber board
Gardener's measuring jug
Hose-end sprayer
Hudson mister (cordless)
Presser and tamper
Propagating case
Pump-sprayer
Several plant water and insecticide sprayers
Sieves and seed strainers
Soil sterilizer
Tensiometer

Necessary Tools and Equipment

Assorted tin cans
Bamboo plant stakes
Bucket
Flower pots and flats
Fork
Garden hose
Hygrometer
Knife
Marking pen and labels
Maximum/minimum thermometer
Old flatware setting and tablespoon
Old Windex spray bottle
Pruner
Scissors
String
2-pint measuring cup
Trowel
Watering can with long spout "rose" and "coarse"
.attachments
Wooden plant sticks
Work gloves

Heat Your Soil the Electrical Way

As you get more expert in your new hobby, you may want to try soil-heating cables. These are excellent when it comes to starting cuttings and seedlings in a greenhouse bench, or in the greenhouse ground-soil under a bench. A standard electric soil-heating cable will supply even "bottom heat" to a propagation area of 36 square feet. Smaller ones are available to use in flats.

Add a Clock Radio to Your Equipment List

One thing that's really handy to have in your greenhouse is a clock radio. Maybe one of the reasons you go in there is to forget time, but a small clock with an alarm can be helpful to remind you to begin or end a number of gardening chores. Also, as everybody should know by now, plants grow better to music! A soft musical background will serve to relax you and make your time in the greenhouse all the more enjoyable.

Try to get in the habit of putting all your tools and equipment back where they belong before you leave your greenhouse every time you work there. If you keep a neat and orderly work and growing area, your greenhouse will be much more pleasant whether you come to work or just to look!

YOUR PLANTS WILL
WARM UP TO ME

Water

A source of water in, or near, your greenhouse is a must. If your structure is small and portable, you can probably give your plants the watering and moisture they need with a watering can, mister, and garden hose.

If your greenhouse is larger and more permanent, you should take the trouble and expense to have water pipes hooked up to it. I say water pipes because warm water is best for growing plants.

It's also a good idea to equip your greenhouse with a janitor's deep-sink or laundry tub with a mixing faucet. A friend of mine has an old sink taken from his kitchen when he remodeled.

Because most faucets allow the water to come out with too much force, you might want to install an adapter and tiny cutoff above the faucet, to which you can hook up a rubber tube for watering seed trays and small plants.

An excellent supplemental water source is from an old-fashioned rain barrel that can be placed just off one corner of the greenhouse roof. Rain water is high in nitrogen and other life-giving trace elements.

When and How Much to Water

Before you purchase any plant and bring it into the controlled climate of your greenhouse, it's tremendously helpful to first find out what its requirements are for light, heat, humidity, and watering.

Plants that come from a tropical habitat will require frequent and regular waterings. Plants that come from the temperate zone will need regular watering about twice a week. Plants, like cacti and succulents, which grow mostly in the arid and semiarid regions, will need very little watering. There are no hard and fast rules, however. Because of the humid and moist atmosphere of your greenhouse, watering will probably not have to be done as often as it would in the dry, warm climate of your home. The best way to handle the watering problem for your plants is to set up a regular schedule. Then, before each watering, check the soil around each plant with your forefinger or a tensiometer. If the soil is dry, or the tensiometer indicates watering is necessary, go ahead. If the soil is moist, skip watering this time. If you find that certain plants need watering less or more often, adjust your schedule accordingly. In time, you will get to know each of your plants as an individual and you will have a good idea of its watering needs.

I generally recommend watering your plants and seedlings in the morning. This will moisten the tiny root hairs and fortify them for the hotter parts of the day ahead. If you water from above, soak the soil thoroughly and allow the water to drain off. Shallow watering inhibits healthy root growth. If you water from below, you will probably have to water more often or use a constant-drip capillary system. This consists of a length of small-gauge plastic hose set out on fiberglass bench trays. The hose has tiny openings that keep the sand in the trays constantly moist. This constant-drip system has proved to be one of the best ways for watering plants like African violets and Gloxinias. It's usually a good practice to wait a few days after repotting a plant or transplanting seedlings before trying to adapt them to a capillary watering system like this. Repotting and transplanting will cause some shock to the tiny root hairs of your plants, and it will take several days before these tiny root structures are healed enough to take in water by themselves.

Certain plants, like ferns, azaleas, and orchids, require a very moist atmosphere. For these plants you can use a hand mister, a child's vaporizer, or one of the many automatic misting suppliers.

Seedlings and cuttings also need near-continuous moisture. To provide it, you can create some temporary "terrariums." Do this by placing clear plastic bags over potted seedlings and cuttings. The bags may be punctured with your dibber or a pencil to allow some air circulation. Or, place a glass pane over seed trays to hold moisture. The pane should be turned over once a day to provide fresh air and to eliminate drops of moisture, which have a way of forming on the inside of the glass. If not eliminated, this moisture can cause a fungus disease called "damping off" that is almost always fatal to young seedlings. To get the seeds started, place a single layer of newspaper over the glass. This may be removed as soon as new growth begins to show. Keep seedlings out of direct sunlight or they may dry out.

Pots, Flats, Seed Trays, and Bulb Pans

Now that you have become a greenhouse gardener, one thing you will notice right away is that there never seem to be enough pots!

Pots can be of clay or plastic, depending on your preference. Plastic pots are lightweight and hold moisture longer. Clay pots, while somewhat heavier, are porous and "breathe."

Pots come in sizes of 2½, 3, 4, 5, 6, 8, and 10 inches. Stock up on an adequate supply of each size. Most operators stock a lot more smaller pots than larger ones because of the number of cuttings and seedlings they turn out. Pith pots in the smaller sizes are very good for transplanting seedlings. They fit inside the clay "seedling pots."

Seedling flats come in a standard size of 16″ × 22″ × 3″. They are made of wood, plastic, or fiberboard. There are also square seedling trays that fit inside the wooden flats. These come in several sizes and are real space-savers.

Three-quarter pots are also very nice to have. They are used most often for the culture of African violets and azaleas, as those are shallow-rooted plants. Three-quarter pots are so called because they are only about three-fourths as deep as other pots of a similar size.

Tulips and daffodils are often "spring forced" in shallow pots called *bulb pans*. These pots, which are only half the size of standard pots of a similar size, are also used for other shallow-rooted plants, such as African violets and fibrous-rooted begonias.

No greenhouse grower should fail to put a couple of plants in tubs or to dress up his enclosure with several hanging baskets. Tub culture in your greenhouse is a good way to grow tomatoes, miniature citrus fruit trees, tree roses, camellias, flowering maples, and other ornamentals. Hanging baskets make good growing receptacles for ferns, azaleas, begonias, succulents and orchids.

Soil Mixtures and Feedings

As a beginning greenhouse gardener, you will probably begin to take a greater interest in the potting and planting soils you use for the residents of your new structure. This is good because while most plants will do all right when potted in a general-use mixture, a little more care and attention to a specific plant's soil requirements will increase your growing success to a remarkable degree.

The plants you purchase for your greenhouse at most garden centers, florists, or nurseries have probably been grown in the best medium for them. But, before long you will find they are outgrowing their pots and require repotting in larger containers. Or, you may want to raise some new plants from seeds or cuttings. When that time arrives, it's useful to have a good basic knowledge of the several different soil mixtures that are suitable for a specific plant's needs.

Soil is one of the most mysterious materials on our planet. It is made of numerous particles, elements, and microorganisms in complex and varying amounts. It's an axiom in agriculture and gardening that no two soils are exactly alike. Sometimes there are marked differences in two soils found just a few feet from each other on the same farm or garden. Years of painstaking experimentation and research have gone into finding the basic qualities of a good growing medium for your plants.

Soil is made up of sand, silt, clay, and humus. Sand is the gritty-feeling material in the soil. Sandy soil is loose and fast draining. Silt is the powdery substance in the soil. Clay is the heavy, sticky material you feel. A clay soil is tight and holds moisture. Humus is the organic material in soil that is the end product of a process that breaks down vegetative and animal matter. It is generally light and coarse in texture, brown or black in color, and sweet-smelling. Humus contains millions of tiny microorganisms that work to change the elements in the soil into usable forms that plants can absorb as nutrients.

A good greenhouse potting mix for most plants will break down first into two-fifths sand, two-fifths silt, and one-fifth clay. To this mixture, add an amount of humus equal to one-quarter of the total volume.

Since inexpensive potting mixtures are available at most garden centers, I suggest you begin your adventure in greenhouse growing by purchasing several different types of commercial soils and soil additives to have available for your potting and repotting operations.

A Sowing Mix

This is a special formula developed commercially for growing plants from seeds. It has all the nutrients to aid seed germination and beginning growth without burning out tender new seedlings.

A Growing Mix

This is a heavier soil mixture containing more clay than the sowing mix. It has been designed as a general mix suitable for most plants, and contains the proper texture and nutrients to provide comfortable growth from the seedling stage on through maturity. I usually add a teaspoon of bone meal or other slow-acting fertilizer to the bottom of the pot when transplanting or repotting with this mix.

Some of the best-known general potting mixes, or growing mixes, available commercially are based on formulas developed by Cornell University, the University of California, or, in England, by John Innes. They are sold under many labels, often as "African Violet Mix," "Potting Mix," or "Greenhouse Soil." The two best things going for these commercial mixes is that they are relatively inexpensive and are presterilized. One negative quality is that they are usually too finely pulverized for the tastes of most experienced greenhouse gardeners. This drawback can be overcome by adding humus or vermiculite.

Commercial general potting mixes are a good base if you should want to mix various soils for potting plants with more

HOW SWEET IT IS!

specific soil requirements. Here are some easy-to-acquire growing-medium additives that will help make it easy for you to manufacture specific potting mixtures of your own.

Agricultural charcoal	This groundup charcoal will filter out harmful salts.
Agricultural lime or chalk	Will "sweeten" acid soil.
Eggshells	Supplies some needed roughage and contains the trace element calcium.
Fir bark	Also for orchid culture, comes in coarse, medium, and fine grades.
Horticultural perlite	Is a presterilized synthetic sand substitute.
Humus	A commercial compost that comes presterilized.
Leaf mold	Harder to get, but many old-timers say it's the best humus.
Old coffee grounds	Will make soil more acid.
Osmunda fiber	Excellent growing medium for orchids.
Sand	Use presterilized, sharp, horticultural sand if at all possible.
Sphagnum peat moss	This organic additive comes in shredded, chopped, and milled form. Milled peat moss is best for general potting mixtures.

With the above listed ingredients you can mix an excellent growing medium for just about any plant in the world. Here are five of my favorite "soil" mixtures.

BAKER'S MIX NO. 1

This is an excellent general growing mix for greenhouse benches and most fruiting, flowering, or foliage pot plants. Mix thoroughly:

1 quart of commercial growing mix

1 quart of perlite, or sharp sand, mixed with finely broken eggshells

1 quart of milled peat moss (moistened in warm water and wrung out damp)

1 tablespoon of agricultural lime or chalk

3 tablespoons of bone meal

BAKER'S MIX NO. 2

This mix is especially good for members of the cactus and succulent families. Mix thoroughly:

1 quart of commercial growing mix

2 quarts of perlite, or sharp sand, and eggshells

BAKER'S MIX NO. 3

For India rubber plants and other large, leafy ornamentals mix the following:

1½ quarts of commercial growing mix

1 quart of peat moss (soak in warm water and wring out damp)

1 quart of perlite, or sharp sand, and broken eggshells

4 tablespoons of bone meal

BAKER'S MIX NO. 4

For most orchids and Bromeliads, use one part osmunda fiber, unshredded sphagnum moss, or fir bark (fine).

If you should have the time and good fortune to be able to maintain a compost pile in your garden, you will want to use the "black gold" of your homemade humus in your borders, benches, and potting mixtures. Light, well-aerated soil, with lots of the organic roughage contained in compost is particularly helpful in keeping bench and border soils from becoming compacted from the high moisture content in the greenhouse atmosphere. Border and bench soil often has to be replaced after a year of cultivation under glass unless compost is continuously added. Starting out with a well-composted soil will let you delay this major task for at least another year. Here are two mixes that incorporate compost.

BAKER'S MIX NO. 5

Mix thoroughly in these portions:

2 quarts of commercial growing mix or garden loam

1 quart of compost or leaf mold

1 quart of sharp sand or perlite

This is a very good general growing mixture for greenhouse benches, borders and most pot plants, fruits, and vegetables.

BAKER'S MIX NO. 6

Mix thoroughly in these proportions:

1 quart of commercial growing mix or garden loam

1 quart of sharp sand or perlite

1 pint of compost

1 pint flowerpot shards or crushed brick

1 tablespoon of bone meal

1 tablespoon of agricultural limestone

This is a fast-draining, gritty growing medium for most cacti and succulents.

It's almost impossible to consider the texture and structure of your soil without also considering the availability of the elements in those soils that supply nutrients to your plants.

Good soil contains all the elements necessary for your plants' healthful growth. The three most important of these are nitrogen, phosphorus, and potassium or potash. Other necessary elements, but less critically so, are boron, calcium chlorine, iron, nickel, maganese, etc.

Simply, nitrogen supplies healthy, green foliage, while phosphorus produces abundant flower buds and strong stems. Potash gives added grow power to the root structure.

If you use one or more of the soil mixtures mentioned above, heavy feeding of your greenhouse plants shouldn't become a major problem.

I usually mix a small amount of bone meal (a teaspoonful) with the bottom layer of soil in my pot plants. Foliage plants need it no more than once every 6 months. Foliage plants need phosphorus for sturdiness, so use any liquid, powder, or tablet form house plant food that comes in a 5-10-5 or 10-20-10 ratio. Use as directed on the label. For younger plants, feed every 4 months but at half the prescribed dosage on the fertilizer container. Flowering plants have feeding requirements that vary from family to family. Generally speaking, they like a 20-10-10 house plant food and should be fed only after new growth or blooming has begun, never in their dormant or resting stage.

If flowering plants seem to be producing too much foliage

FOUR-STAR RESTAURANT

and no flowers, cut down on the nitrogen in your plant food. If they continue to behave in this way, stop feeding them entirely until blooming begins.

If you did not use any of the soil mixes suggested above, and your greenhouse benches and borders contain old soil, you can take a few samples to the agricultural station in your area and they will check its nutrient content and for the presence of acidity or alkalinity. The acid or alkaline content in your soil is measured on what is commonly called a pH scale. The scale has a range of 14 points, with 7 as neutral pH. Some plants, like African violets, azaleas, and camellias, need slightly acid soil. Cacti and succulents usually require slightly alkaline soil.

Fertilizers that incorporate the necessary amounts of nitrogen, phosphorus, and potash are sold under many trade names. Some are designed for foliar feeding, others for root feeding. Some are slower acting organic types, like blood meal and fish emulsions. Faster acting inorganic types are also available and are preferred by many growers because of the quick results they produce and the lack of odor that is associated with the organic types. Select the type of plant food that works best for your plants and your style of greenhouse gardening.

PROPAGATION

Soon after you begin to use your greenhouse in earnest, you will discover that buying new plants to increase your stock can be a very expensive proposition. The most rewarding and satisfying way to avoid these costs and to increase your supply of plants is to experiment with one of the several methods of propagation. Plant propagation can be easily accomplished from seeds, cuttings, air layerings, and root divisions.

Seeds

Seeds are the fertilized embryos of new plants. Inside the seed coat, there are "seed leaves" and enough stored food to begin growth as soon as the necessary amount of moisture is present to activate the enzymes contained there. As these enzymes begin to break down, they release the stored food elements and the baby plant begins to grow.

Before long, the "new individual" is too big for its "baby carriage" and the seed coat breaks open. To get this whole process to take place, you will have to provide moisture, subdued light, and favorable air and temperature conditions. Most seeds need temperatures of 65° to 70° to germinate, but there are certain ones that require much higher temperatures. Most seeds purchased from reliable seed companies will come with information on the particular condition required.

Sow your seeds in late winter or early spring in wooden or plastic seed trays. If you are not using new trays, be sure the ones you are using are clean and disease free. Before putting in your soil mixture, cover the bottom slit with pot shards to ensure proper drainage. Plastic seed trays usually have small holes all over the bottom area for drainage.

Sterilizing, Sprinkling, and Storing

Before filling your seed trays with soil, it's a good idea to sterilize it. For this you can use a commercial soil sterilizer, or you can place the soil in a pie tin or roasting pan and bake it. I usually lay a potato on top and bake it and the soil together. Set your oven at 200° and leave the soil there until the potato is done. You can then remove the container, use the soil for potting, and enjoy eating the potato! The reason you sterilize the soil is to kill harmful disease organisms—especially that "childhood killer" of young seedlings, the dread "damping off" fungus. Actually, effective sterilization of harmful organisms will take place if the soil temperature is kept at 180° for 20 minutes. After baking, never mix this soil with unsterilized soil or your work will have been in vain.

If you don't want to take the trouble to sterilize your soil, you can purchase a presterilized sowing mix in various-sized plastic bags. This mixture contains the proper amount of nutrients to get your new seedlings off to a good start without burning them. You can also use vermiculite, a sterilized nonorganic growing medium, or milled sphagnum moss.

Milled sphagnum is my favorite, as it provides a hostile environment for the damping off fungus.

Use the sowing mix or sphagnum to fill your containers, loosely, right up to the top. Remember, sphagnum moss must be presoaked and wrung out a couple of times in hot water, as it is non-water-absorbent.

Now, sprinkle your seeds thinly on the surface of the soil. Don't feel you have to use all the seeds in a seed packet. One tray of seedlings, even after thinning, should be enough to satisfy even the most avid collector. Store extra seeds with cotton in airtight containers. I use baby food jars because we always seem to have such a good supply. Label the jars with the plant's name, the age of the seed, and planting instructions. Also include color of the flower, temperature required for germination, etc. Seeds can be stored for several years this way.

Seed Trays

Label your just-planted seed tray so you won't forget your babies' names, place it in a loose-fitting plastic bag that's sealed to retain moisture, and put it in a location where it will get warmth and subdued light, but no direct sunlight.

If the tray is placed over a child's vaporizer, you can have germination in about a day and a half! These seedlings will then need direct sunlight quickly or they will become "stringy" from stretching toward the light.

If you don't use the vaporizer, you will begin to see green in your trays in several days. These are not true leaves, but are the seed leaves, which die out and are followed by true leaves. Move the tray near a window—but still out of direct sunlight. Since the milled sphagnum is hostile to damping off, don't worry about excess moisture collecting in the bag, but do open the bag every once in a while to let in air. If the atmosphere looks dry, mist lightly. Otherwise, leave the setup intact.

When the second or third true leaf appears, remove the tray from the plastic bag. Prick off or thin out the weakest seedlings with long-bladed manicure scissors. Now, move the tray to a cooler spot (about 65°). After the fourth true leaf appears, you can transplant the seedlings into 1½-or 2-inch pitch pots which fit inside plastic or clay pots. Keep your seedlings in small-sized labeled pots in a moist growing medium. Don't give their roots too much room.

You may now want to leave the young plants in your greenhouse or move them to their permanent location in your home or garden. If they are outdoor plants, be sure the last frost is past before moving them.

Feed young seedlings with a mild-solution liquid fertilizer about once a month.

The seed tray and milled sphagnum may be reused for more seeds. Propagating plants from seeds isn't the quickest or the most reliable way to reproduce true color or shape. Many of the most common and popular plants are the products of numerous hybridizations. Plants grown from the seeds of such hybridized specimens usually revert to the flower color and foliage shape of one of the original strains from which they've sprung. To reproduce exact duplicates of your favorite plant pals, you will have to use one of the several methods of vegetative plant propagation. These are the ones most often used in greenhouse growing: cuttings taken from stems and leaves, air layering, and root divisions.

Cuttings

A small piece of the stem or leaf of a plant is all that is needed to propagate a plant from "cuttings." The most usual cuttings consist of the terminal portion of a healthy stem. When making such a cutting, use a sharp pruning knife, X-Acto tool, or a razor blade. These tools will make a clean cut and eliminate excessive damge to the cells, which will otherwise be slow to recover from the shock. Remember, plants are like people. You wouldn't want a surgeon to operate on you with a jagged scalpel or a hacksaw!

Cuttings should be kept moist until you are ready to plant them. This may be up to about 5 weeks from the time they are taken from the "mother" plant.

A hormone "rooting compound," such as Rootone, will help promote rooting in many normally "hard-to-root cuttings." Simply dip the cut end into the substance about a quarter inch deeper than you intend to plant it in the growing medium. Tap off any extra powder and insert the treated cutting in a hole in the growing medium that is a little larger than the cutting. Make sure it is resting on the bottom of the hole, and that there is no trapped air pocket that will dry out the new roots before they can get started. Next, pack the soil around the cutting, not too tight—but firmly enough to hold the "new plant" upright.

This type of stem cutting is called a terminal cutting. Terminal cuttings are commonly used to propagate a wide variety of plants, including begonias, carnations, chrysanthemums, Coleus, English ivy, Euphorbia, geraniums, Impatiens, Pyracantha, Salvias, Violas, yew, and many others. Label your cuttings for easy identification later.

Sectional cuttings are made from small sections of a single stem. Each section is cut just above and just below a node, and the resulting cutting is about an inch long. It's important to remember which is the top and which is the bottom of your sectional cuttings. If you plant them upside down, they won't root. A few of the plants that can be reproduced from sectional cuttings are: Diffenbachia, Dracaena, and Philodendron. Hawaiian ti "logs," the curious plant souvenirs of our fiftieth state, are also examples of stem sectional cuttings that will grow into new plants. When you pot your sectional cuttings, you may place them in their new home in a horizontal or vertical position.

Leaf cuttings are obtained by slicing off a leaf and treating the cut edge with a commercial rooting hormone before inserting it in moist sand, vermiculite, perlite, or potting soil. Potting soil should be sterilized.

Gesneriads such as African violets and Gloxinias are easy to propagate from leaf cuttings. Begonias, Kalanchoes, Peperomia, Sansevierias, and most succulents are also reproduced this way. By laying a rex begonia or Sansevieria leaf on the surface of your growing medium, you may obtain several new plants from the single leaf.

Leaf cuttings are often water-rooted. Water-rooting is a time-honored way to treat both leaf and stem cuttings, although the former are more usually treated this way.

To water-root a leaf cutting, fill a jar or glass with water. Put wax paper over the open end of the container and secure it by a rubber band. Slit the paper with a knife or sharp scissors—just enough to allow the cutting to be pushed down through, until the cut end is covered with an inch of water. Some easy plants to water-root are: African violets, Chinese evergreen, English ivy, oleander, Pandanus, Philodendron, pothos, and wandering Jew. It's a good idea to treat these cuttings with rooting hormone, also, before inserting them in water.

Whether you root your cuttings in water or a growing medium, they should now root quickly if their immediate atmosphere is saturated with moisture. You can create these essential moist conditions with a plastic food bag. Place the bag over the pot. This should be held up and away from the foliage with bamboo plant supports or plastic soda straws. Put pot and all in a location where it will get some light, but escape the direct rays of the sun. For non-water-rooted cuttings, an alternative method of creating proper growing conditions can be provided by a propagating case. This is a closed case, large enough to hold cutting trays or pots. Sometimes propagating cases come supplied with their own bottom heating and automatic watering or "misting" systems. Misting has been found to be a way to avoid giving your cuttings too much moisture. Such a case helps create an ideal moist and warm environment that promotes the successful growth of new cuttings and seedlings.

Air-Layerings

Certain plants like Ficus elastica, the India rubber plant, can be propagated from air-layerings.

If your rubber plant has become "leggy" because of dim indoor lighting, it's just right for such an operation. Lay the plant on its side on a fully opened newspaper. Pick a spot about 10 or 12 inches from the growing tip and cut a notch upward one-third of the way into the stalk or stem. Pull off the cambium layer around the cut, but never all the way around the stem. Wipe away any healing fluid that the plant sends to the wound and dust the cut with rooting compound.

Now surround the stem with a large wad of moist sphagnum moss at the cut area and wrap this with plastic food wrap to hold in the moisture. You can leave a small opening at the top in case water has to be added later. Check the air-layering every few days to see it's not getting dry. Water the parent plant sparingly.

It may take as long as 7 or 8 weeks, but eventually roots will fill the sphagnum. When you are satisfied that you have a healthy root system, cut off the new plant and its root ball. Plant it carefully in potting soil (mixture #3).

Spring is the best time of the year for air-layering. After the main stem has been successfully air-layered, the parent plant will produce several side shoots, which in turn may be air-layered to produce new plants.

Plants like Codiaeum (Crolton), Diffenbachia, Dracaena, most varieties of Ficus, and Philodendron can be easily air-layered.

Division Is Another Commonly Used Method for Propagating Plants

African violets, Armus, Aspidistras, chrysanthemums, Cyclamens, dahlias, ferns, Gladiolus, Heleniums, Marnatas, orchids, Sansevieria, and tuberous begonias are all good subjects for *simple division*. Simple division consists of breaking up a mature plant that has developed multiple crowns or roots into two or more smaller plants.

Division is usually done in the fall. Select a time when new growth is apparent, but the plant you wish to divide is not in blossom.

Lay down several thicknesses of fully opened newspaper and remove the plant from its pot. Very carefully—so as to injure as few of the root hairs as possible—pry the individual crowns apart. For some plants, you will find this very easy to do with a minimum of pulling. For others, it will be necessary to use a sharp knife to do some cutting.

After the divisions are made, pot the new plants in a soil mixture that's best suited for their needs. Water them sparingly. If yours is a glass-to-ground greenhouse, put them under a bench where they will get subdued light. Otherwise, shade them from direct sunlight.

For some plants, like Aspidistras, division is very beneficial. You should divide them every 3 years or so.

Whether you grow new plants from cuttings, air-layerings, or divisions, you should treat each new individual with the same respect for, and attention to, its cultural requirements as you would its "parent" or "mother" plant. Talk to your new plants and give them a name. Use a label and felt-tip pen. Although they will require subdued light and lots of moisture at first, in a few weeks you will have to see that they are *hardened off*. This means that you will gradually prepare them to move into the conditions where they will be permanently located. Moving them from a moist to a drier atmosphere, from warm to cooler temperatures, and from subdued to direct sunlight (depending on a plant's needs) should be done in gradual steps, so as not to cause a severe shock from which it cannot recover.

Another thing to consider when propagating is that it can be overdone. When a new gardener has success, he often begins reproducing everything in sight. Remember, this is just one of the many, many exciting and satisfying ways to enjoy your greenhouse.

DISEASE AND PEST CONTROL

Theoretically, there are an almost limitless number of insects, fungi, and disease organisms that could wipe out an entire greenhouseful of plants. But, if you limit your greenhouse stock to plants that are best suited to one of the three environments described earlier, you will be able to severely limit the types of insect and disease organisms that might attack your plants. And, if you keep your greenhouse clean, water your plants properly, give them space to grow in, and maintain the proper conditions of light, heat, humidity, and ventilation, very few of these plant enemies will be able to get a good foot hold. Then, if you develop a keen observing eye and set up a routine control program, you should be able to effectively dispose of any that do appear.

Most harmful pests and diseases are introduced into your greenhouse when you bring in new plants. For this reason, you should make it a practice to find a place where a new acquisition can be isolated and observed before putting it next to your other longtime greenhouse residents. This period of quarantine can be as short as a few days, or as long as a month. Two weeks should be plenty of time to allow any of the ordinary pest or disease problems to show up. During that time, check the new plants often. Look carefully at the foliage and the soil for signs of insects or damage. Look under the leaves as well as on the top surfaces.

Don't hesitate to return an insect- or disease-infested plant to the florist or garden center where you purchased it. It's a good idea to save receipts until you are sure the plants are healthy. Another thing I can't stress too strongly is don't be reluctant to throw out any plant that becomes hopelessly sick. A single diseased plant can ruin all your stock. It's better to lose one plant than a whole season of growing pleasure.

The spring and fall of the year are the two times when there is usually the greatest turnover in greenhouse stock. At these two times, you should make it one of your routine chores to spray thoroughly with a general fungicide/insecticide.

When you spray, use a good-quality sprayer that you keep exclusively for insect- and disease-control purposes. Follow the directions on the container carefully and precisely. Add some old-fashioned Fels Naptha in solution or dishwashing detergent to the spraying mixture. This will help the control agent stick to your plants. Bugs don't like the taste of soap any more than you do! Clean the sprayer thoroughly before and after use.

If your greenhouse is attached, close the doors and windows that lead to your home before spraying. Open doors and ventilators that lead to the outside. This will provide good air circulation and keep chemicals from collecting in one area. "Overkill" can be harmful to plants. If any plants, such as ferns, are sensitive to chemicals contained in your spraying mixture, remove them from the greenhouse until their chance of being harmfully affected is past. At least once a year you should take all the plants out of your greenhouse, clean it up, and fumigate.

Pick a nice, comfortable day in the spring or fall when it's neither too hot nor too cold. Make certain that your plants are sheltered from wind and sunburn. Hose down the walls, clean the benches, storage areas, and floors. Next, use a general insecticide/fungicide spray or fumigating bomb before bringing your plants back inside. Again, follow the directions on the container.

Control chemicals come in sprays, powders, and fumigating bombs. After use, lock them up where no one but you can get at them. Many books and pamphlets will warn you to keep dangerous chemicals out of the reach of children, but it's been my experience that most accidents with control chemicals involve the people who use them most. Be extremely careful. Keep antidotes or first aid instructions in the same cabinet as your poisons.

I've always said that plants should be treated like people. Maybe someday, someone will come out with health insurance for plants. Until that time, you should take steps to familiarize yourself with the USDA's list of approved insecticide and fungicide compounds. Most of these compounds are designed to control one or more specific pests or diseases. They are usually available in sprays, dusts, or bombs. Some of the more effective insecticides and fungicides come in standard mixtures for general prevention and control purposes. Here is a timesaving chart that will help you select the proper controls for individual pest and disease problems in your greenhouse.

AN OUNCE OF PREVENTION
TASTES LIKE HELL

PEST- AND DISEASE-CONTROL CHART
(Use all chemical compounds carefully and as directed)

To Control	Which Attack	Use
PESTS		
Ants	Ants carry aphids to most green plants	Diazinon
Aphids	Aphids suck the sap from plants and carry virus diseases; they like bud tips and undersides of leaves, leaving them sticky	Diazinon, Melathion, Nicotine Sulphate, Pyrethrum, Rotenone
Beetles	Most plants (adults eat leaves, larvae eat roots)	Carbaryl (Sevin), Diazinon, Malathion
Borers	Most hard-stemmed house plants, like schefflera and dumb cane	Carbaryl, Lindane
Capsid bugs	Chrysanthemums, Fuschias, and other composite flowers	BHC, Malathion
Caterpillars	The leaves of most plants	Carbaryl, Diazinon, Malathion, Oil Spray, Trithion, Pyrethrum
Centipedes	Spring bulbs, tuberous plants	Diazinon and snuff
Cutworms	Seedlings and other young plants; they chew stems at the surface	Carbaryl, Diazinon (Don't spray Diazinon on foliage)
Cyclamen mites	New growth of Cyclamen plants; they are nearly invisible	Sodium Selenate to soil Dicofol; destroy badly infected plants
Earwigs	Chrysanthemums and other plants	BHC, Diazinon
Eelworms	Chrysanthemums, tomatoes, cucumbers, bulbs, and leafy plants. Also African violets, begonias	Sterilize soil for these greenhouse plants and seedlings. Get rid of affected bulbs
Foliar nematodes	They leave ugly brown spots on leaves of plants as evidence of their presence	Be careful not to water foliage when spots appear. Get rid of badly infected leaves and plants
Leafhoppers	Suck the undersides of leaves of such plants as chrysanthemums, geraniums, dahlias, and other softwood varieties. They also carry virus diseases	Carbaryl, Diazinon, Malathion, Methoxychlor, Nicotine Sulphate
Leaf miner	These maggots make "mines" or white tunnels in leaves of chrysanthemums, cinerarias, and other plants	Diazinon, Malathion, Meta Systox-R
Mealybugs	These suck plant juices, leave excretions that attract fungus disease	For infestations on ferns use warm soapy water. Other plants, use Malathion, Diazinon

PEST- AND DISEASE-CONTROL CHART (*Cont.*)
(Use all chemical compounds carefully and as directed)

To Control	*Which Attack*	*Use*
Mites (red spider mites)	They attack underside of leaves of such plants as azaleas, carnations, and other woody plants, and make mottled spots to indicate their presence	Add humidity to greenhouse atmosphere. Diazinon, Dicofol, Malathion, Oil Spray. Several applications will be needed
Scale insects	Evergreens, shrubs. They are sap-suckers about 1/8″ long	Dormant Spray with Carbaryl, Diazinon, Melathion, Oil Spray. Fels Naptha soap and water scrubbings is also a good routine practice
Slugs and snails	Foliage near surface of soil. They are chewers. Leave silvery trails behind	Metaldehyde. Also pie tin of beer will trap them
Springtails	Seedlings of most plants, bulbs, and orchids	Diazinon. Apply to soil
Thrips	Feed on inside buds, and scar foliage. They leave silvery coating on foliage, deformed flowers	Carbaryl, Diazinon, Malathion, Rotenone. Weekly until eliminated
Vine Weevil	Adults eat vines of grapes. Also attack Primulas and other ornamentals. Larvae eat roots and tubers	BHC
Whitefly	Sucking insects that attack geraniums, tomatoes. Foliage turns yellow or silvery. They secrete honey dew that attracts mould	Malathion, Rotenone
Woodlice	Seedlings and young plants at night	Diazinon. Directly to soil
DISEASES		
Black spot (leaf spot)	Leaves and all plant surfaces. Small black spots turn to blotches on plants like chrysanthemums, delphiniums, and others. Plants die if not attended to immediately	Benlate, Captan, Ferban, Maneb, Folpet. Cover all plant surfaces
Botrytis blight (gray mould)	Leaves, flowers, and bulbs. This fungus is small colored blotches on chrysanthemums, daisies, peonies, tuberous begonias, tulips, etc.	Phaltan Zineb, Thiram
Powdery mildew	Upper and lower surfaces of leaves. A mild disease, but unsightly	Acti-Dione PM. Dinocap, Sulfur
Damping off	Young seedlings at the soil surface, rotting them through and causing them to fall over and die	Sterilized soil, Captan, Thiram, Zineb
Rust	Undersides of leaves. On carnations and other plants, especially snapdragons	Thiram, Maneb, Zineb. Don't water foliage. Destroy badly infected plants

To Control	Which Attack	Use
Rot (blossom-end rot)	Tomatoes. Leaves black spot on fruit opposite stem	Pick off infected fruit. Water more often. Avoid overcrowding
(stem or root rot)	Many plants on stems and roots at soil level or just below soil surface	No effective control or cure. Destroy infected plants
Mosaic	Most late spring and summer bulbs including tulips, cannas, crocuses, dahlias, and tuberous begonias. This virus disease stunts the plants and disfigures leaves and flowers. Often carried by aphids	Destroy infected plants. Destroy aphid carrier as described above
Other viruses	Wide range of microorganisms that are systemic diseases that stunt plant growth, disfigure flowers and foliage. Eventually these diseases kill your plants	No known cures. Destroy insect carriers as described above

It's a sound idea to keep a greenhouse record book in which you make regular notations each time you spray, dust, or fumigate. Mark down each time you notice a pest or disease problem and note the chemical controls you use to try to eliminate it. Good recordkeeping will help increase your knowledge of what controls are most effective and also help you establish a regular spring and fall pest- and disease-prevention program.

Fighting Bugs and Disease Grandma's Way

Most insecticides and control chemicals are by-products of the process of refining crude oil. As petroleum becomes more and more scarce, these chemicals are bound to go up in price. When this happens, you might want to take a page from the organic gardeners who have been using the same nonchemical controls as our grandparents used years ago. Some of these old-time remedies are just as effective now as they were in Grandma's day.

Regular soap and water showers help protect your plants from insects and work as a surfactant to allow moisture to collect on the foliage. Remember, bugs don't like the taste of soap. I use old-fashioned Fels Naptha soap or dishwashing detergent in a solution of 10 parts water to 1 part soap. A soft, gentle spray of this will also wash away dust and dirt that is a playground for pests.

Every once in a while, use skimmed milk instead of soap, in the same proportions. Milk seems to ward off disease-carrying bacteria. Use vinegar water to water your acid-loving plants like azaleas. Vinegar water is also good for making your cut flowers last longer.

To fight spider mites, try one-half cup of buttermilk and 4 cups of unprocessed wheat flour, which you can purchase in a health food store. Mix the two ingredients thoroughly and add them to 5 gallons of water. Spray on your plant foliage. This will kill the mites and their eggs.

Garlic or yellow-flowering nasturtiums can also be diluted with water to make effective natural insect-repellent sprays.

Finally, it never hurts to take on an ally or two in the long and continuing war against pests and disease. Organic gardeners who have tried it will tell you that a toad, a few lady bugs, or a praying mantis here or there inside your greenhouse will serve as a vigilant and effective line of defense against the harmful insects that can threaten your plants' health. However, if your greenhouse is attached, be prepared to explain to friends and visitors when your toad comes hopping across the living room rug!

PLANT LIST FOR GREENHOUSE GROWERS

It is true that any plant that grows out of doors will grow inside, that is if you can recreate its (a plant's) normal living condition. A greenhouse will allow you to do just about that for most plants that are available to you either through seeds, cuttings, roots, or leaves. But they may not grow as tall, dark, and handsome, or as flowery and full as they do when they are free to take advantage of Mother Nature's offerings of rich deep soil, pleasant breezes, and refreshing rains. Don't despair. I am just letting you know what you might expect so that you will not easily discourage and give up before you get the nack of greenhouse growing.

Selecting plants to grow in your greenhouse takes a little more than picking the prettiest pictures in the seed catalogues. You must take into consideration the size of your structure and your ability to control more than one temperature zone at a time.

Remember, there are basically three types of greenhouse growing:

Cool house

The night temperatures are held between 45° and 50°

Warm house

Here we push the night temperature up to 55° or 60°

Hothouse

Now you are getting up to the 60° to 70° mark and a heck of a heat bill

The coolhouse is the choice of all annual flowers and vegetable seeds. Azaleas, Cayrellias, Fuchsias, acacias, geraniums, and oleanders.

Most of your bulb stock, perennials, such as bleeding hearts and lillies of the valley, also prefer it. English ivies and grape round out the coolhouse gang.

The warmhouse will grow begonias, African violets, Gloxinias, Impatiens, ferns, Hoyas, calla lilies, and Coleus. Cactus and the succulents will feel at home as well. Be very careful not to start your annuals and vegetables too soon, especially if you must run a warmhouse, or they will grow too fast, soft, and tall, not to mention the probability of damping off and dying.

The hothouse is the place to put darn near all of your tropical foliage plants and the tender, thin-leaved plants. No matter what I or any of my collegues recommend, you will only learn by trial and error. Start small and slow—you will soon gain confidence and experience.

For prices of structures and all equipment and accessories you will need, send $2.00 to:

Lord & Burnham
Division of Burnham Corporation
CSB 3181, Department #9900
Melville, NY 11747

Lord and Burnham is also a forerunner and giant supplier of greenhouse-type rooms for home, restaurant, and industrial-building use as living areas for both plants and people. If you are considering an addition to your home, office, or business, and you would like to include a little bit of nature in your decor, why not consider a greenhouse-type room?

13

You're in Trouble!

SPOTTING PROBLEMS

I can recall as a youngster always being told, "Don't go looking for trouble, because you probably will find it."

Well, let me give you a word of advice, one gardener to another, "Go looking for trouble anytime you visit your plants, and hope you find it if it is there."

I am always lifting leaves, inspecting stems, poking around the soil in pots, eyeballing the flowers and color of foliage. I am troubleshooting. The earlier you find a problem, insect, or disease, the easier it is to control it.

Most plant problems are easy to spot and identify. Here is what to look for and what it means when you spot it:

Buds Drop

This can be a heartbreaker when you and the plants have worked so hard. It can mean:

1. Feeding during the bud's forming.
2. Underwatering.
3. Insufficient light.
4. Aphids.

Early Flower Drop

This condition can be blamed on:
1. Not enough light.
2. Dry, warm air.
3. Not enough water.
4. Temperature is too high.

Green Mossy Slime on Pots

Slime may result from:
1. Plants too close together.
2. Poor drainage.
3. Too much humidity.

Leaf Curl

Curl followed by leaf fall means:
1. Not enough heat.
2. Cold draft.
3. Overwatering.
4. Leaf rollers (if leaf rolls down).

Leaf Drop

This can occur for several reasons if:
1. A new plant is purchased from a greenhouse and brought home to a strange environment, different temperature, humidity, and light.
2. Broad rise or fall in the temperature.
3. Allowing the soil to dry out and come away from the edges of the pot.
4. Moving a plant from one room to another.
5. Overwatering and letting the plant sit in the excess.
6. Cold drafts.

7. Not enough light (leaves dry up).
8. Too hot (dry drafts).
9. Underwatering.

Leaf Wilt

This is caused by the opposite extremes:
1. Soil is too dry.
2. Soil is soggy wet.
3. Air is too dry (no circulation).
4. Insect damage to roots.
5. Root bound.
6. Way too hot.

Leaves Turn Brown on Edges and Tip

I am not trying to confuse you when I give you all the reasons for these occurrences. I am trying to show you all of the different problems plants can have, and since they cannot talk and answer your questions, you must consider everything:
1. Lack of humidity (air too dry).
2. Overfertilizing.
3. Insufficient light.
4. Too hot.
5. Too much sun (direct).

Leaves with Blisters and Tissue-Thin Leaves

You should definitely look for:
1. Leaf miners.

Leaves with Chewed Edges and Holes

These signs can only mean:
1. Insects.

Leaves with Marks, Spots, Dents, Dry Patches

Usually such damage indicates:
1. Too much direct sun.
2. The spray can has been held too close.
3. Disease.
4. Water too cold on leaves.
5. Overwatered with too cold water.

No Flowers

There are several possible causes:
1. You are overfeeding.
2. Not enough light.
3. Poor air circulation.
4. Aphids and thrips.
5. Improper light.

Pale Leaves

This can tell us that the plant:
1. Needs less light.
2. Is polluted from dust and oil.
3. Has spider mites.
4. Needs warm air and wet soil.
5. Is underfed (too long between meals).

Emergency—Plant Trauma Reaction

When you find a problem, take immediate action. Don't wait!
1. Feel soil or check with moisture meter.
2. Remove plant from its current pot, and repot in a clean, damp, new clay pot of the same size.

3. Always check for insects and disease, even if the symptoms are obvious it is something else. These two problems attack weak, injured, or sick plants.

4. Wash all foliage with a warm, soapy, weak tea solution with 10 drops per quart of Listerine mouthwash.

5. If insects are apparent, add 1 tbs. of tobacco juice per quart.

6. Spray foliage for insects or diseases after the above step.

7. In all cases but those involving over watering, pour the combined solution of Steps 4 and 5 through the soil.

8. Do not feed until you have done Step 7 and waited 20 minutes.

9. A week later, spray foliage with warm tea, soapy water and 10 drops per quart of household ammonia.

Plant Is Crowded at Top of Pot

Check for the following condition:
1. Root bound.

Plant Just Folds Up and Quits

When this happens, you should be ashamed. This means total neglect:

1. Dry soil for long period.
2. Dark room.
3. Cold or warm drafts.
4. Hot, dry air.
5. No circulation.
6. Dirty foliage.
7. Hot sun.
8. Too close to a window in winter.
9. Overwatering.
10. Gas fumes.

Rips, Tears, and Holes in Leaves

This can be blamed on:
1. Dry, noncirculating air.
2. Animal damage.
3. Plant foliage is in a breezy area and is hitting something.

Stem Rots

I'd bet this happened for the following reason:
1. Overwatering in winter months.

White Powdered Salt or Crust on Soil and Pot

Check for:
1. Overfeeding.
2. Hard water.

Yellow Leaves

There is a definite indication that:
1. Plant needs food.
2. Hard water is used.
3. Softener water is used.
4. If vines are green, it needs iron.
5. Overwatering.
6. Too much lime in soil.
7. Needs magnesium (small leaves yellow).

Any or all of these conditions will end a plant's life.

14

Not-So-Top-Secret Tricks and Tips

BETTER, CHEAPER PLANT CARE

I am always being asked if I don't have a little trick or shortcut for this or that indoor or outdoor job. People will always want to save time, effort, and money, and they will always be looking for safer, quicker, and easier ways to get the not-so-fun jobs done, and gardening is no exception.

The following suggestions are not magic or secrets. They are, in most cases, common sense, something that someone ahead of us did an easier, cheaper, safer, and quicker way.

Buying Plants

Insect Exposers Carry a clean white index card with you when you go to buy plants. Hold the card under the foliage and shake firmly. Now look at your card for insect movement. Most of the professionals carry a small pen light and magnifying glass for the purpose of close inspection. Disease and some insects are difficult to see. Always turn the leaves over.

Containers

Washing New Pots Always wash a planter or pot before you plant into it or set a plant into it. You do not know if someone tried it on a plant they were contemplating buying. If it had insects or disease, they could have hopped off and hid in a nook or cranny

Washing Solution For plastic, glass, ceramic, or metal, 1 oz. of liquid dish soap, 1 oz. of mouthwash, and ½ oz. of bleach per gallon of warm water will do. For clay pots, add 1 oz. of chewing tobacco juice water to the above.

Waxing Pots' Edges Use a candle to wax the top of clay pots.

Gassing Pots When pots are clean and not dripping, place them into a plastic bag with ½ a pest strip. Tie the bag shut for 24 hours.

Pots in Automatic Washer All but wooden planters can be washed in the automatic washer if they are placed on the top shelf. When dry, gas them.

Cleaning Wood, Wicker, and Woven Baskets Gas them for 48 hours in a sealed plastic bag with a full pest strip.

Sponge Waterer Half soak a sponge and then squeeze in a hanging basket.

Lighting

Fixture Go to garage sales and look for fluorescent fixtures. Bring them home, clean, wash, scrape, and spray the tops with heat-resistant stove paint, and the inside of the reflector with heat-resistant glossy white. Also, look for anything with a flexible neck to put grow lights into.

Watering

Vacation Waterer If you have a good number of plants, set several full or half bricks in dishpans, bathtubs, or sinks.

Fill the container with warm soapy water right up to the top of the brick. Now set the pots on top of the bricks. The plant will draw water from the brick.

Feeding

Vitamins for Plants The dissolving of a One-a-Day vitamin tablet in a quart of water and a 1 oz. feeding to each plant gives it a boost.

Fast Food Ten drops of household ammonia in one quart of water sprayed onto the leaves of non-hairy-leaf plants is instant energy.

Pick-Me-Up A pinch of saltpeter and 10 drops of liquid soap in a quart of water fed to the big plants at 1 oz. per plant will let them know you care.

Temperature

Warming the Air If you have a room that has a great deal of glass and it gets too cold at night, set an electric space heater on a timer with multiple settings to go on for an hour at 3-hour intervals. If you have a fan working up high on a bookshelf, you will keep the heat down, make it last longer, and cost less.

Heat Tents A single sheet of newspaper covering a plant in a room that gets very cold at night will make a 7° to 10° difference in the temperature. I make and save paper hats from 3 sheets of paper.

Humidity

Homemade Humidifier Place a large piece of Oasis—the material the florist uses to put cut flowers into (because it holds many times its own weight in water)—in a cake pan and sit it in front of a hot-air register or on top of one. Make sure that you continue to fill the cake tin with water.

Fan Humidifier Hang a washcloth in front of a fan with one end of the washcloth anchored in a pan of water. The fan will move the moist air around.

Air Circulation

Fan Out We use ordinary floor, window, or oscillating fans in the greenhouse to move air. You can, and should, do the same thing. By moving any air and keeping the foliage moving, you give your plant an even break. Overhead fans look great and help your entire personal environment.

Insect Control

Traps Yellow plastic stir sticks, the top half lightly coated with cooking oil, bottom half inserted into the soil, will attract insects that will stick to the oil. The yellow plastic tops for opened coffee cans can be coated and hung over plants to trap for identification.

Marigolds Stop Insects Dry out the flowers of marigolds and then pulverize. Now mix into potting soil (the regular garden type) to discourage insects.

Pencil Shavings These also can be added to soil to discourage insects.

Cigarette Filters Remove the paper from around a used cigarette filter and place the filter on top of the soil before watering and feeding the plant with warm soapy water and food. The mixture will spread through the soil. Remove the filters.

Disease Control

Soap The insecticidal soaps are good. However, I have had very good luck with the use of the mild, liquid dish soaps at: 10 drops per quart, 1 oz. per gallon, or 1 cup per 10 gallons. Clean plants are happy and healthy.

Mouthwash Grandma Puttnam used Listerine, soap, chewing tobacco, and never had a sick plant.

Boric Acid and Warm Carbonated Water and Tea When these are combined at a rate of ¼ tsp. boric acid, 10 drops liquid soap, to 1 quart of warm, carbonated tea and fed to plants that have been treated with Truban, it certainly seems to pick them up.

Soil

Baked Dirt To sterilize soil, I wrap a potato in foil and set it on top of a pan of garden soil and bake in the oven until the potato is tender.

Swimming Pool Powder Mix 1 oz. of swimming pool powder to each quart of sterilized garden soil to make insects sorry they dug in at your house.

Ashes and Soot If cutworms are apparent, add 3 cups of wood ashes to a bushel of soil.

Cut Flowers

Fresher Longer To keep cut flowers fresher longer, make a fresh cut on the stem under water (lukewarm) when you get them into the house. Add 1 oz. of clear corn syrup and a pinch of boric acid to a quart of water and set the flowers into it.

Potpourri

Nylon Stockings Cut into small strips to tie plants with instead of wire or plastic twist-ties. Nylon is strong, flexible, and soft. Nylon also attracts static electricity, which helps to charge the nitrogen in the atmosphere.

Chicken Wire Make cylinders of chicken wire and pack full of sphagnum moss for climbing plants to cling on and for the same static attraction as nylons.

Unburnt Paper-Match Heads Soaking these in a gallon of water makes a good base for plant food.

Chewing Tobacco Mix 4 fingers of chewing tobacco tied into the toe of a nylon stocking in a quart of hot, hot water to make tobacco juice. (I prefer to chew it. Ilene does not.) Use a little of this tobacco juice when mixing other insecticides. It intensifies the action and reaction.

Yellow Golf Tees I spray these with a material called Tangle Trap and keep them tied up in my flower pots for bug traps.

Fish Tank Water Don't you dare throw that anywhere but on your plants' soil (add soap).

Worm Castings I never pass up a small mound of worm casting soil. I collect it and mix it into my regular soil. It's super!

Eggshells I use eggshells in my water filter and I pulverize the others and fill a nylon sachet and let it sit in my good-water water (the water waiting to have food, tea, and soap added).

Camphor Rope Pieces of clothes line dipped into camphor and placed just inside of doors will keep mice out.

Dried Pumpkin Seeds I use these as bait for mousetraps around the greenhouse. Beats cheese!

15

The Something-Special Plant Groups

GIFT PLANTS, HANGING BASKETS, TERRARIUMS, CACTI, ORCHIDS, ETC.

You can go to the bookstore and buy a book solely on the care and cultivation on any one of the special plants in this chapter. So what I have attempted to do here is give you a good, fast, easy guide to their likes and dislikes and their elementary care and needs.

Hanging Baskets—Indoor

Rediscovered charm of the hanging garden gives a lively flare to home decor, and the means for growing trailing plants that are not easy to display in any other way. With today's baskets or heavy clay pots, care is reduced to a minimum. Anytime the mood strikes is the right time for making up an indoor hanging basket.

Step 1 Choose a container with at least a 4-inch diameter on up. Scale it to the plant selected, and go slightly oversize, as future shifting to a larger container is tricky. Larger sizes are correspondingly heavier when filled with growing medium. Provide a sturdy wall bracket and screw or bolt it in place where the basket will be free swinging at about eye level.

The hanging device may be of your own macrame design, an ornamental metal chain, or simple unadorned wires. Do include a swivel beneath the hook, so the basket can be given a quarter turn each day to neatly balance the plant on all sides as it develops.

Step 2 The growing medium, Hyponex Professional Planting Mix. For reducing weight, a mixture of peat and perlite will do. This must have liquid plant food added at intervals. For cacti and succulents, a grittier mix is needed. Make certain of perfect drainage. A solid-bottomed container should have a standard pot pan inside, with a one-inch layer of clear perlite underneath. Screened charcoal is advisable in the bottom of the pot and/or mixed through the growing medium.

Step 3 Choice of plant. See list, "House Plants for Hanging Baskets." Since the indoor hanging basket is most ideally used for cascading or trailing plants, reserve the bush types for the window sill. Use only one plant in each basket (or 2 or 3 of the same kind in larger baskets, but never crowd). Such plants should grow in place for years and become perfect specimens as time goes by.

Step 4 Maintaining the indoor basket. When planted, the original pot plant soil should be one-half inch below the basket rim and filled only, not over, with new planting mix.

Observe a regular feeding schedule, which varies among different plants. Daily watering may be needed. The necessary height at which the basket is suspended brings it into warmer air levels and forces rapid transpiration. Foliage-tip burn may result when humidity is too low; we suggest midday misting, and a cloak of clear, light plastic at night or when the room is not in use. If the basket becomes overly dry, take it down and set it to soak in the tub or sink. Natural soft water, at room temperature, is always best.

Never permit drafty conditions around the plant. Give the basket a quarter turn each day. Control the light to keep plants just out of reach of full sun, but not in a dark corner for most types. Groom basket plants as needed by pinching off spent blooms and leaves, and overly vigorous shoots. Watch for insects.

HIGH FLYERS

Innovative Arrangements

Variety is limited only by the imagination! Try several baskets in a group, each at a different height, each with a different plant. For the kitchen, small tandem or tiered baskets are useful for growing herbs at the window. These can drain down through the center of each, finally into the sink. Small wall planters are used in place of pictures, often in pairs. Again, the best effect is with just one plant in each—in most cases use only the shade-tolerant types.

A Real Charmer

The fern ball. Moss-lined baskets are very adaptable to fern culture indoors. Small ferns or selaginella can be tucked into the moss sides, even in the bottom, for a complete effect. Keep humidity on the high side, or reserve for a special plant room with a tile or vinyl floor so that daily misting will be no problem. Ferns and begonias make perfect companions.

HOUSE PLANTS FOR HANGING BASKETS

Bright Light: For drench, let-dry conditions

Euphorbia—Crown of Thorns
Hoya—Wax Plant
Lampranthus—Ice Plant
Lantana Oxalis—Shamrock
Pelargonium—Ivy Geranium
Saxifraga—Strawberry Begonia
Sedum Morganianum—Burro's Tail or Donkey's Tail
Senecio—Parlor or German Ivy
Setcresea purpurea—Purple Heart
Stapelia—Starfish or Carrion Flower

Bright Light: For moist conditions

Gynura—Velvet or Purple Passion
Hedera helix—English Ivy
Impatiens—Busy Lizzie
Passiflora—Passion Flower
Stephanotis—Bridal Flower or Madagascar Jasmine
Thunbergia Coleus—Black-Eyed Susan

Filtered Light: Drench, let-dry conditions

Ceropegia—String of Hearts or Rosary Vine
Cissus—Kangaroo Vine
Cissus—Grape Ivy
Scindapsus—Pothos
Tillandsia—Spanish Moss
Tradescantia—Wandering Jew
Tripogandra—Bridal Veil
Vriesea—Painted Feather

Filtered Light: For moist conditions

Aechmea (Billbergia)—Vase Plant, Urn
Asparagus—Plumosa, Asparagus Fern
Asparagus Sprengeri—Sprengeri
Begonia species
   Bromeliaceae—Bromeliads
Callisia elegans—Wandering Jew or Inch Plant
Chlorophytum—Spider or Ribbon Plant
Columnea
   Episcia—Flame Violet
Fuchsia
   Guzmania
   Maranta—Prayer Plant
Nephrolepis—Sword Fern or Boston Fern
Philodendron cordatum———
Philodendron panduraeforme———
Platycerium—Staghorn Fern
Plentranthus oert.—Swedish Ivy or Candle Plant
Rhipsalis species—Mistletoe Cactus
Schlumbergera—Christmas Cactus
Syngonium
   Tolmiea—Piggyback Plant or Mother of Thousands
Zebrina pendula—Wandering Jew
Zygocactus–Thanksgiving Cactus

Free Drainage vs. Closed Containers

All plants need oxygen in their root areas. Drainage holes at the bottom of a planter keep moisture from clogging the free circulation of oxygen. If your planter does not have drainage holes, then a generous use of broken crockery plus horticultural charcoal will provide drainage. The charcoal is very important, as it also deodorizes the soil.

Forcing Bulbs for Indoors

Variety is the spice of life, and a variety of different flowering plants will always brighten our growing lives. Bulbs, crocus, tulips, hyacinths, and daffodils will fill the bill, and the bulbs can be used over and over.

Bulb forcing is for anyone, adult or child, and can be done in either apartment or home. It takes about 10 to 12 weeks from the time you plant until you see the bright smiling faces of these beauties.

Clean clay pots are an absolute must for this project. A potting mix of one-third each of sand, soil, and peat moss is ideal. Plant your bulbs a half inch apart, with only one-half of the bulb covered with the mix. Firm the mix around the bulbs so they don't pop out. Water really well and let drain. Now, find a cool, dark location, 40°–45° constant, and leave pots for 6 weeks. Then, move to a medium-light location, keep damp for 5 days, and then move to a bright window sill or bright location where the temperature should be in the 65°–70° area. Now, just be patient. Your reward will be well worth the wait.

Avocado Tree Brooklyn

If I were to guess what question about growing a plant I am asked most, I would have to say: "How do you grow an avocado tree?"

There are two ways to grow an avocado: in water to start, or right into the soil. If I had my druthers, I would druther you go into soil. A 4-inch clay pot and any commercial planter mix will do. First, remove the thick brownish hide that covers the large seed and wash well. After soaking a clay pot, plant the seed in it with 1 inch of the pointed end above the soil. Water with a solution of one teaspoon of Epsom salts per quart of water and put in a dark place for one week; then, move to a bright location. When the stem is 6–8 inches tall, cut in half for branching. Feed regularly

WE WERE BORN TO BE SHOW-OFFS

with any flowering-plant food at the 10% formula. This plant should raise your roof.

Care of Holiday and Gift Plants

From Thanksgiving to Mother's Day comes a parade of breathtaking beauties. How we long to make them last, to bloom for us again and again. For some of these beauties this can well be; for others not.

Specifics for various varieties are given below, but temperatures on the cool side always prolong flowering. Flowering plants are expected to be used for decoration in living rooms. Keep these show periods as short as possible, then plants should be returned to a cool place. Always punch through the decorative foil wrap to open the drain hole in the bottom, and water with soft water or rainwater at room temperature.

Amaryllis

Correctly, this is Hippeastrum. Each stem will flower over 3 weeks, without leaves at this time. It looks best if set among foliage plants. From this time on, keep it growing rapidly with plenty of water and feeding, in 70° day and minimum 50° night temperatures, with 5 hours sun. Does not mind low humidity. Force into dormancy in late August. These should last for years, but need repotting every 2 years. Repot just after flowering. Potting soil requires cattle manure.

Azalea

Much like the Gardenia in requirements. Flowers will last a month at 68°, needs 3 hours of sun a day, and constant moisture (soft or rainwater only). These shrublets can be induced to flower a second year by keeping them growing in top condition; still more years can be had, if there is room for a bigger shrub. Repot every other year, using peaty, acid soil only. In summer, keep out-of-doors, with semishade for afternoons. Plunge pots to the rims, keep feeding and watering until frost time, then take inside to a very cool, bright room.

Calceolaria

Keep these at 60° or less, with fairly high humidity. Cineraria and Calceolaria take full sun, with water enough to keep evenly moist, but not wet.

Christmas Begonia

This delightful fibrous-rooted hybrid is a mass of blooms and buds on presentation, and should last several months with due consideration for the shock of moving it from one environment to another. Do not let the soil dry out. Keep on the cool side of 70°, with 3 hours of sun a day. After flowering, root leaf cutting for bloom again next season.

Christmas Cactus

I'd be shirking my growing duty if I didn't discuss one of the most popular holiday plants. She has a different name for every holiday, but she begins her show at Christmas. The Christmas cactus is a cascading leafed, thornless flowering cactus. Next to terrariums, it is one of the easiest plants to care for. Her blooming season should last way into late winter.

Water the Christmas Cactus when the soil is dry until she is done blooming. Then, let her run a little more to the dry side while she rests. When new growth begins, keep the soil damp. In June, place the Christmas cactus outside in a shaded area until September and feed with any organic liquid plant food. If your Christmas cactus misses the Christmas season, it's name changes to fit Valentine's Day—it's now a Sweetheart.

Chrysanthemum

With many tight buds to start, this should last well for 3 weeks at 50° to 60°. Sun for 5 hours a day means this does best on a cool sunporch. Give daily watering. Discard after flowering.

Cineraria

A riot of colors for all too short a time.

Cyclamen

Superb foliage for winter decoration, and blooms for a month if filled with buds. Keep it cool, 50° to 68°, or flowers will not hold up. Humidity must be fairly high, and it needs sun for 2 hours a day. This is grown from seed, which forms a corm at the soil surface. If the soil at all covers the corm, water only from the bottom. After blooming, plants can be

PRETTY PRICKLY

grown for for another 6 to 8 weeks, with dormancy following. In July it can be watered and started into growth again.

Easter Lily
Keep the plant at not more than 68°, as flowers last only a few days. For this time, sun is not important. But for fun, return them to a sunny place and keep growing until warm weather; then, plant in the open border. Usually we find them blooming again in midautumn; after that, forget about them.

Gardenia
This has a high humidity requirement. Its lack leads to immediate bud and leaf drop in the home. It must have 72° to 78° by day, not less than 60° at night. Strongly acid soil (pH 4.5) is essential, with Sequestrene given every six weeks during the growing season. Needs plenty of light. This is a small shrub that should last for years, and bloom every winter. Use acid plant fertilizer. Repot, using peat moss.

Jerusalem Cherry, Christmas Cherry
Annual bushlets. Two hours sun a day at 70° maximum, to color unripe berries. Gas fumes are hard on this plant. Discard when the show is over.

Poinsettia
New strains last beyond Easter, with only modest care. They keep at around 60°, with humid atmosphere. At higher temperatures, mist the foliage each day. No need for direct sun while bracts are at their brightest. We strongly advise discarding the plant when bracts drop, though green thumbs may wish to experiment.

Primrose
Primrose needs only 2 hours of sun a day, and can be kept quite moist, very cool. Primrose may cause dermatitis in some people, so wear gloves in handling. All in this group are annuals; discard after flowering.

African Violet Fever

Forty years this fever has raged, and millions have been its victims. All ages are susceptible—resist it not, for this delightfully contagious plant gives endless pleasure wherever it is found, singly in a kitchen or by the basementful! Varieties of this magical beauty run into the thousands, with more hundreds coming each year, in colors ranging from white through pink and deep rose, pale blue to dark sultry purples, missing only the yellows. Size is on the increase, with glorious doubles in wide favor, contrasting margin colors, frills, and fringes.

Once grown to flowering size, the African violet may bloom without pause for years; normally, it takes a brief rest along about winter. Seldom more than 8 inches high, pot and all, these plants are convenient for endless arrangements on the spur of the moment.

General Care

Light Eight hours of strong light each day, several in direct sun. In winter, a south window is ideal; later a sheer curtain should screen it, or move the plant back or to an east window. North light may reduce bloom. Violets do well under fluorescent growing lights.

Temperature Seventy to 75 degrees around the clock, *not* cooler at night. In conserving fuels, the plants can be grown in an old aquarium, or glass case, or plastic tents with bottom heat supplied by low-wattage heating cables at night. Drops to below 60° F (16° C) can cause flowering to let up.

Humidity Boost humidity, especially in winter, by using enclosures, or by setting the plants in pans of pebbles with water not quite touching the pots. African violets like fresh changes of air daily, not stuffy smoke-filled rooms.

Watering Water only when soil feels dry to the touch. Watch closely in small pots and those made of clay. Most growers prefer watering from the saucer. Use water at room temperature or slightly higher, rain or untreated water if available. Drain excess after 20 minutes; never allow soil to remain soggy. Avoid wetting leaves (except as noted below).

Feeding A well potted plant can go 6 months without feeding. From then on give liquid fertilizer once a month, not too high in nitrogen; we suggest those specially prepared for African violets. We recommend Plant Marvel.

Training Flowering remains better when plants are limited to one central stem. Side shoots can be nipped with the point of a sharp knife shortly after they appear, or allow these shoots to develop with several leaves and remove them for rooting as for leaf cuttings (below). Cut out faded flowers and yellowing foliage. The hairy leaves are great dust collectors; either whisk off the dust with a soft camel's hair brush, or dip plant upside down into tepid water, slosh gently, then dry in a warm place out of the sun.

Insects and Diseases Few insects annoy African violets, but a monthly preventive spraying with a house plant aerosol such as House Plant Spray is beneficial. Cyclamen mite causes new leaves to thicken and become distorted, so burn infested plants. Mosaic virus is seen as irregular pale spots and blotches. Isolate any plants showing this, or burn them, as there is no known cure.

The greatest crisis in African violet culture is to find suddenly that leaves are going limp but still remaining green. Watering does not help. Then the plant separates from its roots at the soil line, a circumstance caused by crown rot. This usually results from being kept too wet, or from using materials that were not sterile. Remove larger noninfected leaves for restarting. If the stem is long enough, trim it back beyond any sign of decay, treat with Rootone, and reroot as for leaf cuttings.

Starting New Plants Seeds are available for the adventurous. The thrill of hybridizing one's own selections will produce fresh seeds and lead to new surprises—and who knows? Perhaps a new variety of value.

For increasing choice varieties, the leaf-cutting method is simplest. Select firm, mature leaves and trim stems to two inches with a sharp knife or razor blade. An old practice is to root leaves in water; however, the following is preferred today. Use a moist, sterile medium of sand/peat mix or vermiculite 2 inches deep in a clear plastic box with a tight-fitting cover, or individual 2-inch pots with clear pint-size freezer bags to cover and fold under.

Always dip the cut end in rooting hormone (Rootone) and insert deep enough in the medium so the leaf is held upright, with slight compaction. Roots form in about 2 weeks, and in 3 months the new plantlet appears. When the new leaves are the size of a dime, it is time for first potting.

Prepared African violet potting soil is sterilized, light, and porous fluffy; later on one may try mixing his own for experiment. Sterilize pots, beginning small with 2½-inch clay or plastic, always with drain hole.

Lift cutting gently, shake off some of the medium without breaking rootlets, plant so as to bring potting mix firmly to one-half inch below the rim. Liquid feed, then cover with the small plastic bag for a week or two of recovery. As the new plant grows larger, cover the pot rim with a strip of metal foil (particularly for clay pots, where leaves press down upon the rim and will decay at contact). After a year, shift to next larger size pot. Finally, a 4-inch pot may be used. Transplant when out of bloom, near the end of the rest period. Try growing Arican violets hydroponically in water or vermiculite, with once-a-week feedings.

Give yourself a treat now and again. Buy a new variety of African violet. Visit the annual shows of the African Violet Society and Saintpaulians, thrilling events defying one to leave without adding to his collection. Increase the best plants for gifts to shut-ins and the elderly, and spare a few for ready sale at a charity bazaar.

Cacti and Succulents Make Fascinating Indoor Gardens

An all new gardening adventure awaits in these fascinating little jewels. Although cacti and succulents come in all sizes up to tree forms, the species best adapted to window culture are termed "miniatures." Such cacti hail from warmer regions of our own desert Southwest, Mexico, and tropical and higher elevations of South America. Unusual succulents are native to the fantasy plant-land of southern Africa. Since the plants are protected by law in the Southwest, Mexico, and South Africa, our stocks are seed grown by nursery specialists. Home gardeners can also enjoy this added experience.

Misconceptions of cultural requirements still prevail, accounting for losses and disappointments that could be prevented. Close attention must be given to proper potting soils. Long winter rest periods are essential, with very limited, if any, watering. Nights must be cool and winters colder to induce full flowering.

The Southwest and Mexico

Culture Varies with Origin Numerous and sometimes rare forms from this region are best for starters, as they reflect our first notions of what a cactus likes.

Full Sun Strong, full sun in summer, the natural growing period. With a long summer's sun bath, plants store reserve energy sufficient to hold them over a cloudy winter—they may even be kept in a poorly lighted attic at 45°, if window space is not available, or they will enjoy a south window with heat conservation at night.

For the summer growing period, maintain cacti in a south window, or better still, move them outside to a sunny spot. Place on a table or other surface off the ground, and shade with newspaper for decreasing lengths of time from 3 hours, noon on, to prevent sunburn. Remove covers entirely after 3 weeks. Return indoors by mid-September.

Soil Very porous, low in organic matter, and no peat. Trust in a sterile, prepared potting soil formulated for cactus.

Watering Twice a week to soak during summer's rapid growth. Make sure excess drains away quickly. From fall to late winter, water lightly every 2 or 3 months, enough to keep surfaces from wrinkling too deeply (some wrinkling is normal). Increase moisture slowly as growth signs appear; decrease as growth matures.

Fertilizer Weak liquid (such as fish) with summer waterings only.

Starter Plants

Astrophytum Bishop's cap, star, or sea-urchin cactus; Mexico; 41° minimum easy; ball-shaped; small yellow flowers.

Echinocactus Barrel cactus; Mexico; 41° minimum; ball-shaped; slow growing; seldom flowers in cultivation.

Mammillaria   Central and South America; 41° minimum; barrel-type and spined, in many species; give extra strong light; nice specimen; tiny flowers.

Peyote   Dumpling cactus; Arizona; cute, squat ball; controversial but easy.

South America

Greatly varying origins here require individual study. Plains and higher altitude plants usually grow within the protecting shade of bushes and do not like a hot midday sun; therefore, light shading is essential to them. Soils contain more humus, from slightly upward for the plains types to total organic for tree dwellers (epiphytes) such as Schlumbergia —one of which we know as Christmas cactus. These latter

will endure no direct sun, as they developed high up on tropical tree branches.

All must have a season's rest, though being from the southern hemisphere, the period may occur in our summer when the plants normally would have had winter. One fascinating species pulls itself down into the soil for the rest period. Several species are tuberous rooted.

This group is distinguished for its exquisite flowering. To promote blooms, a cold dormancy is required, down to within 10 degrees above the minimums given.

Starter Plants

Chamaecereus	Peanut cactus; Argentina; 35° minimum; easy; fingerlike stems lie flat on soil; flowers bright red, 1-inch diameter; cold period is a must.
Echinopsis	Argentina; 35° minimum; round; much hybridized; 3-inch flowers, white to pink, salmon, orange, or yellow; most are fragrant. Easter lily cactus.
Gymnocalycium	Northern South America; 41° minimum; the red or yellow ball, much grafted onto short, green species. Spider, chin, plaid, and moon cacti.
Lobivia	Cob cactus; Peru; 35° minimum; easy; round; small 2- or 3-year plants bloom in pink, red, purple, white, yellow, or orange; flowers, 4 inches across in rapid succession; roots tuberous, requiring a larger pot.
Notocactus	Ball cactus; Central South America; 41° minimum; ball-shaped, some covered with white spines; easy from seed.
Parodia	Tom Thumb; Central South America; 41° minimum; ball-shaped, spiny, P. Sanguiniflora has dark red flowers in summer.
Rebutia	Crown cactus; 41° minimum; ball-shaped; all flower profusely in reds or pinks, spring.
Schlumbergera	Christmas cactus; prefers filtered sun; flowering depends on maintaining short (11-hour) exposure to light.

South Africa

The leafy succulents, some mimicking the pebbles of their habitat, some with ingenious foliage, survive where annual rainfall is nil for years on end. Most of these endure near-freezing temperatures in their "winter" of July and August; a few have not been able to adjust to our reverse seasons.

More than previously, watering must be restricted with utmost caution to the actual growing season, as will be indicated by the plants themselves. Strict observance of cold requirements offsets any need for water otherwise. It should be pointed out, however, that plants from regions where rainfall is scant do receive sustaining moisture from heavy dews on cold nights, taken up through widespreading and very shallow root systems. Low humidity in homes, plus pot culture, will not provide conditions equal to this, but misting helps.

Aloe	41° minimum; the variegated form when very small is suited to the miniature garden, but soon requires single-specimen treatment. Medicinal reputation.
Crassula	Jade plant; 45° minimum; best in young sizes only, for attractive foliages.
Faucaria	Tiger's jaws; 41° minimum; keep dry in spring and summer.
Fenestraria	Window plant; 35° minimum; give plenty of sun, little water at any time.
Haworthia	41° minimum; rosettes of fleshly leaves, some marked with white; not for full sun.
Lithops	Living stones; 41° minimum; grows mostly buried in hot sand; two very fleshly leaves; daisylike flowers.
Stapelia	Starflower; 41° minimum; use only smaller species, as S. variegata; some shade; very unusual. All take soil as for Mexican cacti.

Pots and Containers For the miniature garden, 2- to 3-inch-deep bonsai bowls or trays, 10 or more inches wide, are ideal. Feather rock can be sculpted with pockets for naturalistic planting. As plants increase in size, move into individual pots, barely larger in size than the diameter of the plant. Under such treatment, repot with fresh soil every 2 years, even though a larger pot is not needed. Make absolutely certain all containers have *drainage holes* in the bottom; add a quarter inch or more of crushed pot or brick shards.

Planting The miniature cactus garden 10 inches in diameter can hold 4 or 5 tiny plants, one of which should be a taller type. Group the tall one with one or two lower ones and two or three colorful stones in varied size just off center and toward the back of the bowl. Set other plants nearer the edge, one on either side, the shortest or tiniest near the front. Colored or natural coarse sand or fine gravel is spread over the soil surface to complete.

Suggestion: If there are 4 or 5 cacti, also use one of the succulents for added interest.

The garden must have full south light or equivalent growing lamps, or give it the best light available and when plants fail, replace with new.

Note: Shading needed for some species. Also, do not mix plants requiring different rest periods.

All cacti are transplanted in early spring, with fresh soil, and at 2-year intervals. The same size pot may be reused several times. When roots are few, plants are often top-heavy, so tie them down with string over the top and under the pot until reestablished.

It is often said, "You either hate 'em or love 'em." For the cactophile there is the Cactus and Succulent Society of America, Inc., which offers conventions, shows, seed exchanges, and special publications. Permanent living exhibits to see on vacations are found from coast to coast, indoors at the Brooklyn Botanic Garden (1,000 species), the New York Botanical Garden, Bronx (1,600 species), the University of Michigan (90 species), and the Missouri Botanical Garden, St. Louis (1,200 species). Outdoor exhibits are found at Desert Botanical Garden, Phoenix (2,500 species), the University of California Botanic Garden, Berkeley (also indoors) (4,000 species), and the Huntington Gardens, San Marino, California (1,100 species in a grand garden setting).

Grafted Cacti

Grafted cacti, mounted on long, slender stalks, have been hybridized to develop their brilliant coloring. They receive sustenance from their host plant. Follow culture directions of South Americans. Remove basal suckers.

Terrariums with House Plants

Readily finding plants to fill a glass terrarium jar may dictate whether one uses wild plants or cultivated house plants.

Tropical kinds are available from foliage plant departments at all seasons. Wild plants, including partridgeberry, are gathered for sale only in the autumn.

Clear glass terrarium jars or bowls for house plants range from 6 inches in diameter to much larger. Covers are not essential here, as humidity rises to nearly 100% under cover, too high to keep plants in good health. However, some watering must be done once or twice each week. Desert land plants can be used successfully, and with less moisture: they grow slowly and last far longer.

Soil Mix

Prepared, sterile potting soil from a garden shop is available at all times, as are coarse sand and granulated charcoal.

Step 1 Line the bottom and lower third of the container with thin sheets of moss (live if possible) with the green side to the glass. Funnel sand onto bottom to one-half inch depth, sprinkle thickly with charcoal, and continue filling with potting soil mix to one-quarter the depth of the container. This should not be less than 2½ inches when lightly compacted. Plan enough to mound to the center when planted.

Step 2 Select very small, young plants for the miniature garden. Most all will outgrow the quarters too soon, as is, and will have to be shifted to normal pots in a year or so. Stage the plants with the shortest in front, the tallest in rear or just rear of center. Use only a few. Three well chosen for variety, size, and balance, can do far more than six poorer examples. An interesting small piece of driftwood can also be used, or include a sea shell, colorful stone, or figurine.

Step 3 Remove plants from pots and fork away part of the old soil mix. Using a pointed plant label, open a hole in the new soil bed to set the plantlet. Parts of the soil surface not covered by sprawling plants can take more moss, in addition to that folded over from the sides.

Step 4 A miniature figure or other feature as enumerated in Step 2 is placed, partially hidden by foliage, to complete the picture. Dust inside of glass with a soft brush, moisten the soil, and set the completed terrarium in a bright place just beyond the reach of direct sunshine. Try not to over-water, as there is no drainage hole in most containers.

Kinds of Plants to Use

Avoid hairy foliages, such as velvet plant, if the container must be covered. Always keep arid (desert) soil plants uncovered. Some suggestions follow:

Low Plants Baby's tears; Saxifraga.

Tall Plants Acuba; Aglaonema; Dieffenbachia; Fatshedera; Podocarpus; Polyscias.

Wet-soil Plants Baby's tears; Dionaea (Venus Flytrap); Drosera (sundews); Sarracenia (pitcher plant).

Intermediates Calatheas, Marantas; Dracaenas; ferns; Pilea; wax begonias

Arid-soil Plants Bromeliads, Aloes; Cacti, Crasaula, Tender Sedums, Sempervivums, other succulents; Cryptanthus; Echeveria; Fenestraria; Gasterias, Harvorthias; Kalonchoe, Euphorbias; living stones; Peperomia; Sansevieria.

Orchid Care

Orchid plants are amazingly sturdy plants, and many of the tropical varieties can be grown and bloomed successfully in your home. Choosing the suitable variety for home or greenhouse growing is most important. There are "warm" growing varieties like Phalaenopsis, many Paphiopedilum, Oncidium, and Epidendrum. For greenhouses, or cooler growing rooms, Cattleyas, many Paphiopedilum, Laelia, and most orchid genera are ideal. For cool growing areas of 50° to 70° F, Cymbidium, Miltonias, and Odontoglossum are the ideal plants.

Creating a Growing Climate

Following simple care requirements and creating a growing climate will ensure growing success. Temperature, humidity, light, and water are part of this climate.

Temperatures Temperatures should range between 65° and 85° F for "warm" growing orchids; 60° and 80° F for "intermediate" growing types; and 50° and 75° F for "cool" growing varieties. Night temperatures should go to the lower given range whenever possible, while sunny daytime temperatures may go to the higher given range and above. Plants will tolerate higher or lower temperatures, but may suffer.

Humidity Humidity should be maintained between 30% and 60%. This may be done by placing plants on trays with gravel, by room humidification, by misting plants in the morning, and by keeping plants in close proximity with each other and away from heating outlets. During the spring and summer growing seasons, plants prefer higher humidity, while they will tolerate lower readings during the "dormant" season in winter. Lower temperatures in homes result in higher humidity and a better climate for plants generally.

Light Light is very decisive in growing and blooming your orchid plants. They must be protected from bright sun from March through September or October. If too much light is given, a plant may suffer leaf damage and dwarfed growth. If too much shade is provided, plants will grow large foliage without blooms. Dark green foliage indicates too much shade, while light green or yellow foliage indicates incorrect light or too much sun.

Air Air in general is suitable for orchid growing, except under extreme conditions when adjustments may need to be made. Very humid stuffy growing areas should be ventilated to exchange some air, or a fan should be used to circulate air in basement growing rooms or very crowded greenhouses. Polluted city air will cause bud drop on Phalaenopsis orchids, and shorten bloom life on all orchids. There is no cure.

Watering Plants should be watered thoroughly when the potting medium is dry. The frequency may be at 4- to 7-day intervals, depending on pot size, growing medium, and humidity. Soft-leaved plants without pseudobulbs should not be permitted to dry out severely, and may be grown in plastic pots. Plants with pseudobulbs and hard foliage should be permitted to dry out at the root system between each watering. Water with low mineral content or rainwater is best for plants. Do not use softened water. Dehumidifier water, melted snow, or water from ponds or creeks is generally more suitable than high-mineral well water.

Feeding Feeding your orchid plants will result in larger plant size and better blooms. High-nitrogen formulas, such as 30-10-10 and 5-1-1, are ideal for orchids potted in fir-bark mixes. Frequent light solutions of feeding at 7- to 14-day intervals are better than monthly stronger feeding. Fish emulsion food given during the spring/summer growing season will give excellent results.

Repotting Repotting should be done every 1 to 2 years by replacing the old decayed fir-bark medium. Large plants may be divided. The best repotting time is spring or summer.

Insect control Insect control is only required when an infestation occurs. Most available insecticides may be used on orchids if they are suitable for use on house plants or roses. Just follow the directions on the package.

Specific care information can be found in many orchid books available through orchid societies and your orchid supplier.

Begonias, Begonias, Begonias

Begonias and ferns—what a delightful company to stir one's thoughts to faraway tropics and perpetual summer! Both these plant groups do enjoy much the same cultural conditions: modest warmth from 68° to 78°, a humid atmosphere, soil high in organic matter with constant moisture, and perfect drainage. Happily, all do best in light shade, though winter sun is helpful, as are growing lights. Experts agree the best fertilizer is fish emulsion, used every 3 or 4 weeks, and bone meal may be used in the potting soil. The more than 10,000 species of begonias fall into three cultural groups:

Fibrous-Rooted Begonias
Darlings of the shaded garden, these are so much improved as to make many varieties equally happy in full sun, where foliage becomes pleasingly bronzed. All are continuous

flowering, indoors or out. Their colors range from deep red to rose, pink, salmon, and white, all with yellow centers.

Our modern hybrids are started from seeds sown in January and February for the summer bedding trade. These do not come well from cuttings, but old plants can be divided at the crown. At the end of summer, well before frost, choice plants in the garden can be lifted and potted for winter bloom indoors. Never attempt to save the tops; cut back to 2 inches from the soil, shake out soil from roots, cut these back some too, and fit into 6- or 8-inch pots with rich soil mix. Place in a south window, liquid feed, and within a few weeks they will be renewed and vigorous, and begin flowering for the winter.

Try the handsome butterfly hybrids with their large, nearly 3-inch-wide flowers, or the new and splendid full doubles.

Rieger Hybrids Patented plants only, available most of the year in early stage of bloom. When fully grown, the Riegers are positively breathtaking, 2-foot mounds smothered under a burden of bloom. They require less humidity and stronger light. A constant watch must be kept for mildew, which can destroy a good plant within days. Control with Acti-Dione.

Rex Begonias

Strictly for the house. These are foliage plants with flowers of only minor interest, usually in winter. The large-leaved sorts exhibit a fascinating array of color patterns in silver, red, maroon, rose, cream, and iridescent tones. The "cigar store" or "beefsteak" Begonia is a rex type, together with its curious spiral-leaved forms. Among the cute miniature rex begonias are those known as "tiger kittens."

All like constant 70° temperature, no direct sun, and room to sprawl. Growth is by heavy stems that creep slowly over the soil, therefore requiring broad pots. Division is easy. Most go dormant in winter, and may or may not hold their leaves. Water lightly at this season and avoid fertilizers.

Tuberous Begonias

A flashy clan, now hybridized with up to 6-inch-wide roses, camellias, carnations, and orchids, with ruffles, picotees, or fringes. Growing from a "bulb" or tuber, foliage and flowering are seasonal, with a dormant or rest period. Tubers appear on the market in early February.

For longest performance, secure tubers early and plant at once in flats or singly in four-inch pots containing African-violet–type potting soil, rich and fluffy. Press the tuber gently into the mix, concave or hollow side up, and cover one-half inch with a more porous mix. Place in a south window or under lights, with temperature at 70°. Keep moist, but not wet. Blooms from strong bulbs will appear in only 6 to 8 weeks, possibly by the last days of winter.

Tuberous begonias are used chiefly for outdoor color. For this, start them only 6 weeks before last frost date, either indoors or in cold frames. Nicely started plants are available in May and June. All are splendid for pot or planter culture on the shaded patio, or they may be planted directly in the ground on the north side of the house or protected east. A background of dark-green yews shows the flowers off well. Be prepared to stake and tie top-heavy plants. Liquid feed at 2-week intervals.

Growth and bloom may cease in September, or be hit with frost. It is not worthwhile to dig them up for home decoration, as their season is over. Tubers may be saved and reused for 15 or more years.

Cascade or Hanging-Basket Begonias Tuberous also. May be started early, using several in a basket. Treat as above.

Multifloral Begonias Bush miniature of the large tuberous. Most useful for beds and edgings in the shaded garden.

Ferns in the Home

Philosophers and plant lovers have long agreed, ferns bring one to the very summit of appreciation for growing things, far surpassing flowers of a day. Ferns present their grace and beauty without end, year in and year out. Their varieties seem endless, too. They are not difficult; moisture, light, and tender loving care will do it.

All ferns for the home are evergreen species native to warm climates. There is no real dormant period, though some may rest for a month or two in winter. Most will do with much less light than other house plants; here the problem north window can serve well, if open to the sky. Others prefer filtered shade, or can take the sun in winter. The house temperature may vary between 40° and 70°, but ferns do best with only brief lows to around 50°, and no higher than 75° in summer.

Moisture and Humidity Always keep the soil moist, not wet. Unlike for other house plants, the soil surface must never become dry, even for short periods. Overwatering is most dangerous in the cool of winter. Above 75°, ferns in active growth may take watering every day; this is also true of small pots and sandy, fibrous soil. Use rainwater, if possible, and at room temperature.

Humidity is best at around 70%, which is more difficult to meet at higher temperatures. Low humidity causes leaves to wilt, turn brown, and die, especially young fronds. Lack of water in soil will cause this also.

Some growers suggest a good shower once a week, with misting every other day or so. Blechnum fern does not like water clinging to fronds more than briefly. Setting pots in a tray of moist gravel, as well as growing several ferns close together or mixed with other plant types, such as Begonia, is very helpful. Soil in pots can be kept moist with a topping of spagnum moss. Here too, plastic pots are often best, with proper porous soil mixes.

Epiphytic and Terrestrial Ferns

The most challenging group, few in number, grows on tree trunks and rocks. The chief representative is the staghorn fern. It is now grown in special pots as for orchids, or in wire baskets. Under high humidity it will establish itself upon slabs of cork bark or redwood. For pots and baskets, the "soil" mix consists of ground fir bark (one-half part), leaf mold or peat (one-quarter), and clean sharp sand with composted cattle manure (one-quarter). Root systems are first tightly packed in sphagnum moss. Daily mist spraying is required.

Terrestrial ferns are the larger group, requiring a loose, porous, moisture-retentive potting mix with a pH of 6.5. Prepared potting mixes are convenient for small-quantity potting. Or a mix can be made of thirds each of sandy loam, peat moss or leaf mold, and coarse, sharp sand to which is added a sprinkling of cow manure. Allow this to age for a week before using. Do not pack soil too tightly. Make absolutely certain that drainage is rapid by using large pot shards in the pot bottom and top these with osmunda fiber or sphagnum.

Fertilizing Do lightly and often at least every two weeks if using liquid plant food; slow release pellets are the modern way. Newly potted ferns are not fertilized until new growth gets well under way. Divide and transplant in the spring, when possible, using only one pot size (1 inch) larger. Six-inch pots are about as large as ever needed before splitting apart or dividing is done, after which replant to smaller pots.

Insects Scale, whitefly, mealybug, and aphids are the most common pests. Worst affected fronds should be cut and burned. Spray, using a fine mist; Malathion at half strength works best, at above 70°. Never use an oil-based spray on ferns.

Sori These contain the spores, or "seeds," and occur in dots on the undersides of leaves. Sometimes they are confused with insects.

Other Ferns to Try

With many species decidedly easy, the faithful Boston fern should get the beginner off to a good start. There are some 100 different "Bostons," but the typical plant is for use on a pedestal where the long fronds may arch to the floor. These fronds are in continuous growth. If tips are bumped and bruised, they die, yet the frond itself remains green indefinitely. Runners form, like stiff strings, and may be cut off. Boston fern will take winter sun, but once doing well in a place should not be shifted about.

Decorative little ferns like Pteris, or brakes work well in lighted planters, or in the kitchen and bathroom.

Pellaea, the button fern, prefers higher humidity. They make a charming table centerpiece.

The most dramatic of all is bird's-nest fern, with entire leaves up to 4 feet long. This becomes a handsome floor plant, but it requires more sun, higher average temperature, and more daily moisture than other ferns.

Gloxinias, Streptocarpus, Achimenes, and Their Kin

With African violets at the peak of popularity among flowering house plants, we find others in its family vying for attention. Gloxinia (properly Sinningia) has reached a close second, and Achimenes, or "nut orchids," are enjoying a revival as very compelling pot or basket plants. Streptocarpus, the Cape primrose hybrids and species, as well as Smithianthas, Kohlerias, and the trailers Episcia (or flame violets), Columnea, and Eschynanthus all demand our notice.

Culture is generally as for African violets, with potting soil, moisture, and temperature the same also. South windows are ideal in winter light, shading at other times. Growing lights are very highly recommended.

Gloxinias

Recent hybrids developed in this country are no less than dramatic for color effects, with profuse flowers in huge flaring trumpets of velvety reds, pinks, purples in single and double, frills, fluted edges, and contrasting colors. Florist gift plants are irresistible.

Gloxinias develop rapidly from tubers or bulbs, which are offered in February and March. For best results, select the larger 1½ to 2 inch size. Some may already show tiny shoots. Plant at once in 5-inch plastic pots, with perfect drainage. Use African violet potting soil with one tablespoon of bone meal added per pot; firm to 1½ inches from the top. Place tuber in the center, growing-shoot side up (note stem scars, if there are no shoots), and continue filling with soil to allow only top of tuber to show. Set in pan of tepid water, only until surface is moist. Keep temperature at 65° nights, 70° to 75° days.

When growth develops two flowers, remove all but the most vigorous shoot; others can be cut back to two bottom leaves, and rooted as for violets. After 6 weeks, flower buds should appear; begin feeding biweekly with liquid fertilizer, like fish emulsion, until the flowering period is over. Avoid higher temperatures, as flowering will stop prematurely.

As the rest period nears, bud formation ceases; reduce

watering gradually, and allow leaves to yellow. Tubers may remain in the pot with very light watering until new growth appears again. For many tubers, space can be saved by storing in vermiculite, at 55°. Repot whenever new shoots appear, no matter what the time of year.

Gloxinias grow easily from seed, in sterile conditions. Forced under lights, some may show buds in a mere 6 to 8 weeks. Any change in light intensity, temperature, moisture, or humidity will cause unopened buds to blast. Overwatering soon kills the plant. Mealybug and thrips are rare, but Ortho's aerosol insecticide controls them.

Achimenes

Delightfully old-fashioned. A fine color range makes these popular basket or pot plants for porch and patio living. Like light summer shade best. The small jointed tubercles are available in February and March for starting immediately. Use African violet soil with bone meal added. Set tubercles 3 inches apart in pot or basket, covering not more than one-half inch. Use all broken pieces, as most will grow. Provide biweekly feedings all summer, and keep just moist for highest rewards. Store during dormancy in vermiculite.

Smithiantha

Temple bells. New and exciting hybrids, also from Cornell, make this American plant a winner for pot culture through summer and fall. The rhizomes rest in winter, and may be stored in vermiculite at 65° to 70°, then restarted in March.

Streptocarpus Hybrids

The Cornell hybrids rank highest among these show quality plants, having large 3-inch trumpets in many colors. All are produced from seed. If planted in midsummer, they should flower by Christmas. Culture is considered easier than for African violets, with somewhat less light needed and night temperature in the upper 50s.

Winter is the normal rest period. At that time, divisions of crowns can be made; a single crown is best for flowering, as in violets and Gloxinias. Leaf cuttings are possible, using only the basal portion. Always dip in rooting hormone.

Streptocarpus Saxorum

Streptocarpus saxorum, or Dauphin violet, flowers almost continuously. Faded blooms should be snipped off to keep the plant attractive. Use several stem cuttings in a 4-inch pot for best effect, and liquid feed regularly. Full winter sun or less does nicely for this very obliging pot plant.

16

Tough Questions to Find Answers to

PRACTICAL ADVICE, QUICK SOLUTIONS

In 1959, I answered my first question about gardening on a radio show in Detroit, Michigan, called "Ask Your Neighbor," starring Bob Alison on WWJ. Twenty-six years later, I've made thousands of radio and television appearances, written dozens of books and articles, and millions of letters have passed before me, and I am still answering the same questions all over the world. Yes, it's true, I have answered these questions at the ends of a couple of previous books. As a matter of fact, I once wrote a book of just questions and answers on both indoor and outdoor gardening. So why should I take the time to include the same thing here? That's kind of obvious. You don't have one of those books handy, but you do have the problem: chemicals change, techniques improve, and I have a few new funny lines. As I begin to write down and answer your questions, I have no idea how many we will end up with, but I do know one thing for sure, you folks never seem to run out.

Selecting Plants

Q. *What are the best tree-form plants for a home with high ceilings?*

A. Tough ones. In most of your homes, you don't have good humdity or air circulation, so you had better improve both and then look at: schefflera, corn plant, Norfolk Island pine, dragon tree, lady palm, weeping fig, or Dracaena Reflexa Pleomele. And, by all means, stay alert.

Q. *Which are the best foliage plants for office waiting rooms?*

A. Ones with gas masks on! The smoke is unbearable. I am prone to the Aglaonema family (silver queen, golden snow, silver king evergreen, and silver evergreen). I also suggest you decorate with a no-smoking sign.

Q. *Are there really hardy hanging plants for entryways?*

A. What's waiting for them in the entryway? I am assuming that a cold draft is the reward. The ivy family likes it cool, 40° to 60°, medium light, and to be sprayed with a coat of Wet-Pruf, a coating that holds in moisture.

Q. *Why do most restaurants only use pothos, grape ivy, and Philodendron ivy in hanging baskets? Aren't there other selections?*

A. Two of the three take a little longer to die (grape ivy and pothos). Sure, there are other selections, but you must keep a couple of things in mind: Your soup and their light source (the restaurant's). In European restaurants, you find herbs in hanging baskets, decorative pots, and room dividers. They look good, smell good, and taste good in my soup or stew. Rosemary and thymes hang around well. Mint, along with parsley and chives, keep them coming back.

Q. *Can you have too many plants in a room?*

A. You can overdo anything, but in the case of plants, the only reasons would be having more than you can take care of, too close together for their comfort, blocking each other's light source, overpowering the rest of the decor. As for your health, never.

Q. *Why do the same plants in the same pot, with the same grower tag, and the same size, cost so much more in one store than another?*

A. Greed! That's not fair of me. Overhead and volume are the answers. If they fit my plans and they are clean (no bugs visible) and healthy, I buy where I get the best price.

Q. *Is it worth having a professional florist maintain plants in offices?*

A. I am a firm believer in the Richest Man in Babylon philosophy: "If you want bricks laid properly, use a bricklayer." Professional florists have the personnel, products, tools, and knowledge to meet the needs of the plants in an interior environment with professional understanding.

Q. *Is it true that a room with plants can calm a person down?*

A. You bet it is! Try it. One of my pet projects is totally plant oriented. It is Hardrock Horticulture Center, a two-year college degree program in landscape, nursery, and greenhouse management. It is administered by Jackson Community College of Jackson, Michigan, and is the only one of its kind in this country. It's behind the walls of the Michigan State Prison at Jackson, Michigan, and greenhouse and outdoor gardening are the vehicles for one of the most spectacularly productive prison educations anywhere. If we can calm these folks down to achieve 2.8, 3.5, and 3.95 grade point averages, then their friends, the plants, can calm anyone down.

Q. *Why don't you see too many flowering plants in home decor?*

A. Because they go through a bloom cycle and then must rest and start over. Unless you have a greenhouse or know what you are doing, you run out of patience before they bloom again.

Q. *What are the thick, droopy, spike-leaved plants that have colors in the centers, not flowers? You see them in photos of expensive homes in magazines.*

A. Bromeliads. It is said, "If you can't grow Bromeliads, you can't grow anything." This is almost true. These plants will do well in normal room temperatures and humidity as well as medium light.

Identifying Plants

Q. *Why do they confuse us with botanical names and common names? And to top that off, one plant may have more than one common name. Why?*

A. The botanical name of a plant is a worldwide, recognized name, no matter what common name it may get tagged with. If you see a picture of a plant you admire, or the plant itself, jot down the Latin name, as well as the common name, and no matter where you go in the world, or what language you speak or write, you can communicate botanically. Why so many common names for the same plant? Because of guys like me who write books and give their own descriptive name for a particular plant. Sansevieria is commonly known as the snake plant and mother-in-law's tongue, but back a few years ago I wrote that I call it the barbershop begonia because that's where I always see it. Now some books refer to it as that. I also gave the schefflera the common moniker of shopping center palm. It stuck. Sorry.

Q. *How come the care tags on plants make it seem so easy?*

A. Because it is. If you create the normal living conditions the plant needs, and then remember to feed, water, and wash it. It's easy!

Decorating with Plants

Q. *Where can you get real help when it comes to interior decorating, using all of the proper elements—style, color, plants, water, sound, and lighting?*

A. Your psychiatrist. I went to my Ethan Allen furniture store and bought a catalogue so that I could identify furniture style. I went to the library and read up on color psychology. I talked to a psychologist about sound, an interior designer about decor, a professional landscaper about plant care, and Robert Vincent Sims about environmental compatibility of plants. Then I wrote this book. You have it in your hands. Do purchase or collect several home furnishing catalogues featuring the style of furniture you prefer.

Q. *I know this may sound stupid, but I have a very limited budget and I already have some artificial plants that were given to me. Can I use them together with live plants in good taste?*

A. You're darn tootin' you can! I have seen real plants used in conjunction with paintings of the same, porcelain flowers and paintings of the same, and have seen a very famous orchid grower use artificial foliage as supports and to cover up the ugliness of the orchid stems. The key word here is *good taste*.

Q. *How long will the flowers on pot mums hold if they are sprayed with floral spray?*

A. As long as they would if you hadn't sprayed them, provided you properly care for them.

Q. *Can you rent plants for short periods of time, for a party?*

A. Sure you can. When you rent plants (big ones mostly), you will pay a pretty good price, so be prepared. And don't bother to ask for flowering plants. Those they seldom rent at a price you would be willing to pay.

Plant Containers

Q. *Which are the best pots to plant or transplant into?*

A. The right size—to begin with. You only go one size larger at a time. You start new plants in small pots first, and then work up. I always use a compressed peat pot, filled with my selected planting media, to plant or transplant my plants into sort of as a sock. I then only use clay pots.

Q. *Can you wash clay pots in an automatic dishwasher?*

A. If your wife will let you! Mine does, my Ma didn't. If you wash plastic, place it on the top shelf.

Q. *Should you creosote the inside of wood in planters and window boxes?*

A. Not if you want to plant live plants in them. Use tree-wound paint, if you just have to paint. Plastic liners are available.

Q. *How do you get the excess water out of big planters?*

A. First you must remember to place three raised pieces in the bottom to support the pot the plant is growing in. Now attach a piece of plastic hose to a turkey baster and suck the water out. Or, use a foot syphon and hose.

Indoor Lighting for House Plants

Q. *Can you really grow plants under lights without special shelves and lights?*

A. Yes and no. Yes, you can grow plants indoors under lights without special shelves. No, you can't do it without special lights. Hell, I have plants on the floor, tables, ladders, hanging all around, but no special shelves. I do cluster the girls in the bridge club (my African violets) in trays under the regular lamps on the end tables, and I have a flood light or two—all with different types of grow lights to supplement the regular lights—aimed around the room where plants are and I have better than 50 healthy, happy, plants in my family room.

Q. *What happens when you grow plants under colored lights? I mean real red, blue, yellow, green, orange?*

A. Some fun and funny things. I have children place plants into boxes set on their sides, ventilated and covered with different color cellophanes. Blue will produce darker foilage, red will grow crooked, green—skinny. Try it, especially the blue.

Watering House Plants

Q. *Do you really use all of the different kinds of water you say on television and radio?*

A. Would I lie to you? Certainly I use them for my plants. Tap water is my last resort. You can always find a natural source of water if you look around. If I must use tap water, I bring it to a boil and add a 2 oz. shot of vodka per gallon and 1 oz. of household ammonia before using it on my plants.

Q. *I know cold water hurts leaves, but how about roots?*

A. How do you react to cold feet? Plants are also shocked, and it can kill them if it is cold enough. Room temperature or just a little warmer, with liquid soap and weak tea added, helps plants.

Q. *Why do they say only to water in the daylight hours?*

A. Because we always have food in the water system in the greenhouse, and we don't feed plants at night. Wet or damp foliage tend to stimulate fungus diseases as well.

Feeding House Plants

Q. *What's this malarkey about not feeding plants at night?*

A. A great way to spend a restless night is to go to sleep on a full stomach. Well, plants are like people. When their entire metabolic system is not in operation, they can't ingest and digest their food. Plants need both light and carbon dioxide to change the sugars and starches into chlorophyll when the lights go out. So does digestion. Plants and people should sleep all night because that is when they both grow.

Q. *What do aspirins do for plants?*

A. Give them a headache and a stomachache.

Q. *Do plants really eat through their leaves?*

A. It's called osmosis, by which plants "eat" the natural nitrogen, which constitutes 78% of the atmostphere. It can also take the esters of gas from household ammonia plus liquid soap. Ten drops of each in a weak solution of warm tea sprayed on the foilage of nonhairy leaves.

Heating House Plants

Q. *Can I build a shallow frame of wood and line it with plastic, insert a soil-heating cable, fill with stones and water, and then place my plants on the rocks? Will this heat and humidify them* right?

A. Wrong! First, it is unsafe, for you, your carpet, and the plants. Yes, I have seen it done with plastic, metal, and slabs of cement. Don't. If you could safely do it, you would be inviting root rot, stem rot, and crown rot, for starters. Then comes mold and mildew, not to mention a couple of others. Last, you still haven't heated the room air, so the foilage can still suffer.

Humidity and House Plants

Q. *I have a warm water vaporizer that I used when my children were small. Can I use this for my house plants?*

A. If they have a cold. I have heard pro and con. If your heating system is working well, and you have it set for a specific temperature, the warm steam is supposed to increase the temperature. My only objection to a hot vaporizer is the chance of knocking it over and injuring a person.

Q. *I have heard that you can add _____ to a warm or cold vaporizer and destroy insects at the same time you humidify. Is this true?*

A. Yep! And along with the bugs, you kill the cat, dog, birds, fish in the aquarium, and there is a pretty good chance you could join them. I left the blank space so you wouldn't accidentally try it. Don't you ever, ever, ever add anything to your environment as a convenience or shortcut.

Air Circulation and House Plants

Q. *Is it necessary to move any air around for good circulation?*

A. Does dusting with a dry feather duster get rid of dust? No, to both your question and mine. They both just move the problem around. Good air circulation means to inject a source of clean fresh air into the environment and eject the stale, stagnant, dust-, smoke-, and cooking oil-laden air out. The best way is to open a window or vent at both ends of a room or home. A fan does the trick.

Q. *How do you make a humidifier if you have a regular fan?*

A. I make a frame out of coat hangers in the form of a wire square and then set a glass cake pan through the square and fill it with water. Next, I place a piece of cloth over the top of the wire frame so that both ends are in the water. The cloth will soak up the water and the fan blowing on it will moisten the air nearby.

Insect Controls and House Plants

Q. *What insects does boric acid kill?*

A. Cockroaches. You can also use swimming pool powder (diatomaceous earth) for the same purpose. I mix the powdered earth at a rate of 2 tablespoons per quart of potting soil to aggravate all soil insects—and it does.

Q. *Do pest strips really work for plant insect control?*

A. I use them, constantly, on new arrivals that are left on my porch, car seat, office stoop, or in the radio and television studio, with great results.

Q. *How effective are the systemic pest sticks?*

A. I use them, as an added insurance, after I have treated my plants in my normal manner.

Disease Control of House Plants

Q. *Is soapy water a control for all plant diseases?*

A. Of course not, but it sure makes the diseases uncomfortable. The use of warm soapy water along with a mild bacteriastat, such as a pinch of boric acid per quart or a capful of Listerine mouthwash, seems to stop the momentum of the disease so that the prescribed fungicide can do its job.

Starting New and Restarting House Plants

Q. *Why are they telling us not to use regular potting soils anymore?*

A. They aren't. What they are saying is that the new professional mixes on the market—like Hyponex's Professional Plant Mix—are cleaner and safer (no insects or diseases) to start plants in. You still use potting soil on mature plants, or you mix half and half of each. Good clean, fresh, compost mixed with rich, well-drained loam in still a treat for the planter and the planted.

Growing Plants in a Greenhouse

Q. *Is it really advisable for everyone to have a home green-house?*

A. Absolutely not. A greenhouse is a big responsiblity in capital outlay, upkeep, and plants' comfort and care. You sure better know what you are getting into before you invest. Please read the chapter entitled "The Glasshouse Gang" in this book before you go greenhouse shopping.

Index

Golden Bird's-nest Sanservieria *(Sanservieria trifasciata Hahnii),* 40, 66, 89, 103, 115, 126, 142

Golden diffenbachia, *see* Dumb cane

Golden pothos *(Scindopsus aureus),* 41, 66, 89, 103, 115, 126, 142

Golden trumpet *(Allamonds catharteca),* 41, 66, 91, 103, 115, 126, 142

Gold vein bloodleaf *(Iresine lindenii formosa),* 41, 91, 103

Golf tees, yellow, 218

"Grandma Putt's Homemade Plant Food," 112–13

Grandma Putt's Pot Soak, 154

Grapefruit trees, *see* Citrus trees

Grape ivy *(Cissus rhombifolia),* 41, 66, 89, 103, 115, 126, 142

Greek revival furniture, 61

Greenhouse Distributors, 168

Greenhouses, 165–206, 254
  attached, 166
  benches for, 178
  clock radio for, 181
  curved-wall, 166
  disease and plant control, 198–204
  doors for, 169
  drainage of, 168
  drip systems for, 108, 184
  floors for, 169
  fountain for, 168
  freestanding, 166
  in greenhouses, 182–84
  heat and temperature of, 171–74, 207–08
  humidity and staging of, 177–78
  lean-to, 166
  lighting for, 169–70
  location of, 167
  open or even-span, 166
  plant list for, 204
  pots, flats, seed trays, and bulb pans, 184
  propagation, 191–98

  shading for, 167
  soil-heating cables, 181
  soil mixtures and feeding, 185–92
  storage in, 179–80
  straightline-wall, 166
  tools, gadgets, and greenhouse equipment, 180–81
  ventilation of, 174–77
  water sources and watering, 182–84

H

Hagenburger's ivy *(Hedra canariensis variegata),* 42, 66, 91, 103, 115

Hahn's self branching ivy *(Hedra helix),* 42, 66, 91, 103, 115, 126, 143

Hanging containers, 78, 219–22, 247

Hardrock Horticultural Center, 248

Hastatum philodendron *(Hastatum Philodendron),* 42, 66, 89, 103, 115, 126, 143

Hawaiian Ti *(Cordyline terminalis),* 42, 66, 89, 103, 115, 195

Health, your, and selection of plants, 14

Heart-leaf philodendron *(Oxycardium),* 42–43, 66, 89, 103, 115, 126, 143

Heat, *see* Temperature

Heating devices, 107, 122–23, 215, 252
  for greenhouses, 172–74

Height, your, and selection of plants, 16

Heleniums, 197

Hepplewhite furniture, 61

Hibiscus, 66, 91, 103, 115

High ceilings, tree-form plants for home with, 246–47

Holiday and gift plant care, 224–26

Holly fern *(Mahonia lomarifolia),* 43, 66, 88, 103, 115

Humidifier, 122, 215, 252–53

Humidity, 120–21
  favored by common houseplants, 125–30
  in greenhouses, 177–78

STAYING HEALTHY

(0452)

☐ **JERRY BAKER'S FAST, EASY VEGETABLE GARDEN.** Whether you're a seasoned gardener or a beginner, whether you've got a big patch to fill or just a few boxes on your windowsill, whether you believe in going organic or are willing to give nature a chemical boost, Jerry Baker, America's Master Gardener, can help you. (256704—$8.95)

☐ **NATURAL COOKING: THE** *PREVENTION*® **WAY edited by Charles Gerras.** A guide to good cooking and good eating that offers more than 800 health-filled recipes from *Prevention*® magazine. It shows how meals, rich in nutritional value, can be prepared without sugar, salt, or deep-fat frying.

(252601—$5.95)

☐ **DELICIOUSLY LOW The Gourmet Guide to Low-Sodium, Low-Fat, Low-Cholesterol, Low-Sugar Cooking by Harriet Roth.** Delight your taste-buds and protect your health at the same time—with this unique collection of spectacular recipes from a former director of the Pritkin Longevity Center Cooking School. "Exciting food with a minimum of fat and sugar . . ."—Simone Beck, *author of Mastering the Art of French Cooking* (256178—$7.95)

☐ **WHOLE FOODS FOR THE WHOLE FAMILY: The La Leche League**® **International Cookbook. Edited by Roberta Bishop Johnson.** Here is a wondrous variety of over 900 time-saving, kitchen-tested recipes created by the women of La Leche League®, the worldwide organization devoted to healthful, joyful family-raising. Broad in scope, thorough in detail, this nutrition-conscious cookbook is a treasury of flavorful, authentic recipes and menus, complete with protein and calorie counts, serving suggestions, and friendly tips on how to make each meal a family favorite. (255031—$10.95)

Prices slighly higher in Canada.

To order please use coupon on next page.

FOR THE GAME PLAYER

(0452)

All prices higher in Canada.

To order, use the convenient coupon on the next page.